Twenty First Century **Unrest in West Asia**

Socio-economic and Political Scenario

Twenty First Century

Unrest in West Asia

Socio-economic and Political Scenario

Edited by

K.M. Sajad Ibrahim

Head, Department of Political Science,
University of Kerala, Thiruvananthapuram

New Century Publications
New Delhi, India

NEW CENTURY PUBLICATIONS
4800 / 24, Bharat Ram Road,
Ansari Road, Daryaganj,
New Delhi - 110 002 (India)

Tel.: 011-2324 7798, 4358 7398, 4101 7798
E-mail: info@newcenturypublications.com • indiatax@vsnl.com
www.newcenturypublications.com

Editorial office:
LG – 7, Aakarshan Bhawan,
4754-57/23, Ansari Road, Daryaganj,
New Delhi – 110 002

Tel.: 011-4356 0919

First Published: **2019**

ISBN: **978-81-7708-478-8**

Published by New Century Publications and printed at Milan Enterprises, New Delhi.

Designs: Patch Creative Unit, New Delhi.

PRINTED IN INDIA

About the Book

In the twenty-first century, West Asia is moving in different directions—politically, culturally and economically—with far-reaching consequences for global peace and security. On the one side, political change through Arab Spring uprooted many authoritarian regimes and brought democratic elements in West Asian polity while on the other side instability and uncertainty continue to challenge many countries like Syria, Iraq, Egypt and Lebanon.

Religious fundamentalism assumed new twist with the rise of forces like ISS that triggered a wave of violence in many West Asian countries and other parts of the world. Insecurity has resulted in millions of refugees in West Asia to seek migration to Europe and other parts of the world. The global powers, which spoiled the peace and prosperity of the region through colonialism and imperialism, show least interest in the present West Asia imbroglio.

Most of the turmoil in West Asia is linked with its history and culture. It is not possible to address the deep-seated problems involved in the social transformation in these countries through overthrow of old regimes. These countries need more political and economic stability with popular participation. However, mistrust and uncertainties are threatening peace and security in the region.

This book contains 13 articles by leading West Asian scholars on different dimensions of the geo-political scenario of the region.

About the Editor

K.M. Sajad Ibrahim is currently Head, Department of Political Science, University of Kerala, Thiruvananthapuram. He was the Director, UGC-Nehru Studies Centre, University of Kerala during 2011-18. In recognition of the friendship, co-operation and dedication to exemplary civic service, he was conferred Honorary Citizenship by the Mayor of the City of Harrisburg, Pennsylvania, USA in July 2008. He is the recipient of Dr. Ramaswamy Mudaliar Gold Medal (1990) of the University of Kerala. He also won Professor Nandan Menon Prize from the University of Kerala in 1990.

He has authored four books, viz. *Palestinian Distress: The Ambiguity of Former Soviet Policy* (2007); *Globalisation, Fundamentalism and Terrorism: Issues in South India* (edited, 2012); *South Asia: Post-Nehruvian Dynamics of Diplomacy* (edited, 2013) and *Democracy and Development in India: Nehru and Beyond* (edited, 2016).

He has also contributed about 35 research articles in various national and international journals including *Economic and Political Weekly*, *India Quarterly* and chapters in edited books. His areas of research include West Asian politics, Indian democracy, Indian Muslims, comparative politics and international relations.

Contents

Contributors

Fabian K.P. is an Indian Diplomat who served in the Indian Foreign Service (IFS) between 1964 and 2000.

Paulami Sanyal is doctoral candidate at Centre for West Asian Studies, School of International Studies, Jawaharlal Nehru University (JNU), New Delhi.

Poonam Khatana is doctoral candidate at Centre for West Asian Studies, School of International Studies, Jawaharlal Nehru University (JNU), New Delhi.

Nayneet Samuel is research scholar, Department of West Asian Studies, Aligarh Muslim University (AMU), Aligarh, Uttar Pradesh.

Lirar Pulikkalakath is Assistant Professor, School of International Studies, M.G. University, Kottayam, Kerala.

Divya Malhotra is doctoral candidate at Centre for West Asian Studies, School of International Studies, Jawaharlal Nehru University (JNU), New Delhi.

P.R. Kumaraswamy is Professor at Centre for West Asian Studies, School of International Studies, Jawaharlal Nehru University (JNU), New Delhi.

Manjeri Singh is doctoral candidate at Centre for West Asian Studies, School of International Studies, Jawaharlal Nehru University (JNU), New Delhi.

Minakshi Sardar is doctoral candidate at Centre for West Asian Studies, School of International Studies, Jawaharlal Nehru University (JNU), New Delhi.

Syed Jaleel Hussain is Assistant Professor, Nelson Mandela Centre for Peace and Conflict Resolution, Jamia Millia Islamia (JMI), New Delhi.

A.K. Pasha is Director, Gulf Studies Program, Centre for West Asian Studies, School of International Studies, Jawaharlal Nehru University (JNU), New Delhi.

Jatin Kumar is Research Assistant at Institute for Defence Studies and Analyses (IDSA), New Delhi.

Bansidhar Pradhan is Professor, Centre for West Asian Studies, School of International Studies, Jawaharlal Nehru University (JNU), New Delhi.

K.M. Sajad Ibrahim is Head, Department of Political Science, University of Kerala, Thiruvananthapuram, Kerala.

Introduction
By the editor

West Asia is one of the most important regions in the world mainly for its rich oil deposits and the geopolitical location in the world. This is an area which is strategically situated at the junction of the three continents of Asia, Europe and Africa. As such, it commands the approaches of these continents. This centrally-located region extends from Atlantic coast of North Africa to the Western edges of Central Asia and lies between the southern littoral of the Mediterranean and the north-western shores of the Indian Ocean. Because of its tri-continental location and its central position in the world island, the region has historically been crossroad of the world.

In the twenty first century, West Asia is moving in different directions—politically, culturally and economically—which lead to far-reaching consequences for global peace and security. On the one side, political change through Arab Spring uprooted many authoritarian regimes and brought democratic elements in West Asian polity. On the other side, instability and uncertainty continue to challenge many West Asian countries like Syria, Iraq, Egypt, Lebanon etc.

Unstable states and insecurity led to the flood of millions of refugees in West Asia, and their attempts to migrate to Europe and other parts of the world brought much opposition from the global society. Finally, the global powers, which spoiled the peace and prosperity of the region through colonialism and imperialism, show least interest in the present West Asian imbroglio. Most of the political and social turmoils in West Asia have relations with their history and traditional culture. It is not possible to address the deep-seated problems involved in the social transformation in these countries by overthrowing old regimes. These countries need more political and economic stability with popular participation.

However, mistrust and uncertainties led to the emergence of

new forces and movements which threatened peace and security in the region. The Palestine question still remains as the core issue in West Asian politics as millions of Palestinians in West Bank and Gaza live in most precarious conditions. Violence unleashed by Israel towards the Palestinians and the silence maintained by the US and the West transformed West Asia as the most volatile region in the world. Ethnic, sectarian and political violence continue in many parts of the region, especially in Iraq, Syria, Lebanon, Egypt, Iran, Libya etc. The issues in West Asia affect global security and peace in a variety of ways. The global community has been deeply concerned with the fragile conditions of the region in recent years.

The Arab Spring, the pro-democracy uprisings in West Asia, was the first important event in West Asia in the twenty first century for realizing democracy. It started with Tunisia, where the dictator Zine El Abidine Ben Ali fled the country, which transformed the country into a democratic one. The Tunisian movement was not confined to its borders, rather it went beyond, thereby first affecting Egypt. The situation it Egypt was not different from Tunisia, where the people were living without any rights under the authoritarian regime of Hosni Mubarak. As such, circumstances were favourable to set the fire of democratic movement in Egypt, which led to the removal of the regime of Hosni Mubarak who was president for 28 years.

In Libya, the Arab Movement was not easy as in Tunisia and Egypt. Hence, the US and Western military intervention killed the Libyan dictator and the most ruthless ruler in the region, Muammar Gaddafi. Finally, the movement also affected other countries like Syria, Yemen and Bahrain. Although the Arab Spring could not bring democracy, except in Tunisia, but its impact heavily influenced the overall political situation in most of the countries. One notable change was the role played by women and youth during the movement.

This book presents 13 articles by leading West Asian studies scholars' on different dimensions of the twenty first century West Asian scenario.

Fabian K.P. in his article, *The Arab Spring That Was and Wasn't* examines the major undercurrents in the Arab Spring and its after effects in West Asia. The Western powers led by the US had double standards in dealing with the Arab uprising. They did not intervene in Tunisia and Egypt. But their intervention in Libya and Syria had been disastrous. According to Fabian, excessive force used by the authoritarian regimes to suppress the popular demand led to the popular uprising. Its character and nature were different from state-to-state. The Arab uprising also made its impact on the overall character of West Asia.

Paulami Sanyal in her article, *Egyptian Blogs during the Popular Protests from 2011 to 2013* depicts the role of blogs during the popular uprising in Egypt.

Egyptian blogs analyzed domestic and international political and economic situations and held problem-solving discussions. A different positive aspect of blogs was their multi-perspective nature. Being an open forum for discussion, blogs generated both support bases and critical narratives of any argument. As such, blogging was able to create a unique as well as an alternative practice of reporting thereby producing a system of journalism where politically active or interested citizens remained involved.

Poonam Khatana's paper, *Democratization and the Role of Women in the Arab Uprisings* highlights the challenges and the contribution of women in politics and the policies of the countries, especially during and after the Arab uprising period. During the movement, the women underwent a lot of pain of being imprisoned or severely tortured for their activities. She narrates the role of several women leaders in the struggle.

Navneet Samuel in his paper, *Arab Feminism and its Socio-Political Impact on Arab Society* explores the status of women in the Arab world. Arab women are largely portrayed by many as being oppressed, weak, and passive. According to the author, the present situation of Arab women is far better than some major developing countries in terms of education, living conditions, employment and social rights.

Lirar Pulikkalakath in his paper, *Options and Obstacles to*

Solve the Refugee Crisis in West Asia makes an attempt to focus this issue with his own analysis. His article seeks to analyse the problems and possibilities of solving the regional refugee crisis by discussing repatriation, rehabilitation and resettlement as major solutions. Millions of refugees, asylum seekers and internally displaced people in West Asia are contributing to the global displacement crisis.

Divya Malhotra in her paper, *Oil as a Tool of Diplomacy in Iraqi Kurdistan* narrates strategies of Iraq Kurdish Regional Government to use oil for independence and secession. She focuses on how Kurdish leaders have been trying to use oil as a tool to part ways with Baghdad and establish independent diplomatic ties with the neighbourhood.

P.R. Kumaraswamy and Manjeri Singh in their article, *Water Scarcity in Jordan: Demand and Supply Side Factors* illustrate the water scarcity in Jordan. They explore how to address the issue of water scarcity in a relatively backward Arab country like Jordan. The growing scarcity of water has driven the Jordanian Government to develop a water demand management strategy to maximize water use efficiency and minimize wastage. At present, the growing water scarcity in Jordan is managed through a combination of supply and demand-driven approaches. However, the present strategies for management of water would be insufficient to secure water for future.

Minakshi Sardar in her article, *Hostage-Prisoners Swap: Israel's Experience* elaborates the strategies of Israel to address the issue of hostages. A study of Israel's experience with hostage taking, suggests that hostage taking has been used as a common tactic to release prisoners from Israeli jails. Israel has strongly supported the use of military and has strictly followed the policy of not surrendering to the hostage takers. The focus of the article is to find the relevance of such negotiations for Israel in hostage scenario and the rationale behind such decision-making.

Syed Jaleel Hussain in his article, *Saudi-Iran Rivalry and its Effects on West-Asian Stability* narrates the undercurrents of Sunni-Shia encounter which adversely affects the security in

West Asia. Iran needs to provide a degree of reassurance to Arab countries about regional security and its positive role in it.

A.K. Pasha's article, *Major Issues in the New Cold War in the West Asian and North African Region* documents major issues in the West Asian region during the contemporary period. The US has been an active participant in all major events in West Asia. From the first Gulf War until the present Syrian crisis, the role of Washington has been crucial. Islamic Republic of Iran is viewed with threat by most of the Sunni dominated Arab world. Iranian nuclear issue led to the imposition of economic sanctions against it by the US-led Western world. In fact, most of the American policies in West Asia are dictated by Israel. Many important issues are highlighted in his article like lack of democracy in the GCC states, terrorist activities by the IS in the name of Islamic State, Iran-Saudi rivalry, Syrian crisis etc.

Jatin Kumar in his article, *Al-Qaeda and Franchise Terrorism* presents the grave threat from Al-Qaeda. He predicts the re-emergence of Al-Qaeda as a powerful terror outfit. A decade long fight against terrorism has made it clear that military option will not solve this problem alone. There is need to find other ways as well to deal with this danger.

Bansidhar Pradhan in his article, *Israel's Continuing Zionist Project: The Main Obstacle to Palestinian Statehood* exposes the continuing Zionist project by Israel as the major roadblock to Palestinian statehood. According to him, the ultimate objective of the Zionist project is Greater Israel which undermines the very roots of Palestinian self-determination and statehood. The recent declaration of Israel as the Jewish state by Knesset is viewed as a step in the direction of realizing the ambitious project of Zionist to uproot all Palestinians living inside their state.

K.M. Sajad Ibrahim's article, *Hamas-Fatah Contradictions and Their Impact on the Palestinian Movements* discusses the contradictory approach of Hamas and Al-Fatah as the most important weakness of the Palestinian movements for an independent statehood. Both the movements have been employing different lines of thinking and strategies which adversely affect the Palestinians' dream for statehood. Despite some recent progress on reconciliation, it is rather unlikely that Fatah and Hamas will unify of their own accord any time soon as neither side has anything to offer the other that is greater than the power each currently holds.

Hence, the twenty first century West Asia is vulnerable with several issues. Terrorist organisations like Islamic State, Syrian crisis, Palestinians ordeal unattended by the world community, Israeli atrocities against Palestinians inside and outside Israel, refugee issues of Palestinians, Kurds, and Syrians, economic sanctions against Iran, Sunni-Shia confrontation led by Saudi Arabia and Iran, denial of rights by unpopular authoritarian regimes, degraded status of women, US and Russian active intervention, fall in oil prices and the economic crisis, etc. are going to decide the future of West Asia.

Acknowledgements

I place on record my deep appreciation and gratefulness to all the scholars who have contributed to this volume. Their valuable papers would surely add to the existing body of literature on West Asia and its geopolitics.

I am indebted to Mr. Ameer Ahamed, Chairman and Group Managing Director, Manappat Group of Companies and Mr. M.S. Faizal Khan, Pro-Chancellor, Noorul Islam University for their co-operation and support in bringing out this book. I also thank my colleagues Mr. Shaji Varkey and Mr. Joseph Antony for their help and moral support.

Thanks are also due to Indian Council of Social Science Research (ICSSR), New Delhi and University of Kerala for all types of help for the present endeavour.

K.M. Sajad Ibrahim

1

The Arab Spring That Was and Wasn't

Fabian K.P.

The title calls for an etymological excavation. The description "Arab Spring" of what happened in the Arab world in early 2011 in general, but more specifically, in Tunisia, Egypt, Syria, Yemen, and Libya is no longer in fashion and rightly so. There is talk of 'Arab Winter' and even of 'Arab Nightmare', expressions not far off the mark to describe the ongoing horrendous carnage with no foreseeable end. As estimated by UN, the human cost includes 2.3 million dead or injured, while the economic cost is US$ 614 billion, with Syria alone bearing a loss of US$ 259.6 billion (Barrington, 2016). The total number of the displaced is more than 14.389 million as estimated by the UAE based Arab Strategy Forum. [1]

However, the fact remains that when President Ben Ali fell on January 14, 2011, to be followed by the rising of the people of Egypt who ceased to fear the might of the autocratic state and curtly demanded Mubarak to leave office, leaving him no option but to leave, many Arabs and their friends and well-wishers the world over could have recalled the immortal lines of William Wordsworth, 21, about the French Revolution penned in 1791:

Oh! pleasant exercise of hope and joy!
For mighty were the auxiliars which then stood
Upon our side, we who were strong in love!
Bliss was it in that dawn to be alive,
But to be young was very heaven!

The fact is that there was an Arab Spring, however brief it was, and it still lingers on in Tunisia where democracy is growing strong roots confounding the dogmatists who declare with overweening certitude that democracy and Islam are by their very nature incompatible. It is arguable that but for certain factors such as the enduring vitality and Machiavellian craftiness of the Deep State in Egypt, hasty and ill-judged foreign military interventions in Libya, Syria, and Yemen, and the incompetence, selfishness, and immaturity of the elite, the countries in question could have and would have marched towards a democratic destination, however tortuous and obstacle-ridden the path might have been. The Tunisians did not coin the expression 'Arab Spring'.

Historically, it was coined by the conservative writer Charles Krauthammer, famous or notorious as one may choose, for the coinage of 'Unipolar Moment' to describe the international order cum disorder following the collapse of the Soviet Union (Krauthammer, 1990). However, Krauthammer used the expression "Arab Spring" not in the context of the 2011 Revolutions. He was writing in 2005 about the possible move by Arabs towards democracy following the end of Saddam Hussein's dictatorship in Iraq after the disastrous invasion by President George Bush in 2003. Krauthammer was exaggerating as there was no real movement towards democracy. In his article titled "Arab Spring of 2005", he hinted that President Bush could have taken the credit for that '2005 Arab Spring'. [2]

Obviously, some American pundits truly believe that the international system resembles the solar system with US as the sun around which others revolve in their pre-determined orbits defined by gravity exerted by the sole super power. The same US-centric thought is discernible in Mark Lynch who wrote a piece under the title "Obama's Arab Spring" for the conservative magazine *Foreign Policy.* He wrote on January 6, 2011 after the death of Tarek Bouazizi, a fruit vendor without a shop, selling from a cart on the street. [3] There were simultaneous protests demanding democratic rights in Tunisia and elsewhere in the Arab world:

"If these protests continue to spread, both inside of countries and across to other Arab countries, then we could talk about this being Obama's 'Arab Spring', only with the extra intensity associated with climate change. Arab regimes will do everything they can to prevent that from happening. At most, everybody is carefully watching everyone else to see what's going to happen, with news travelling across borders and within countries through an ever growing role for social media layered on top of (not replacing) satellite television and existing networks. I'm not hugely optimistic that we will see real change, given the power of these authoritarian regimes and their record of resilience. But still...interesting times" (Lynch, 2011).

It is ironic that Lynch should call it "Obama's Arab Spring" considering that US has been monumentally ineffectual in Syria and to a lesser degree elsewhere too in exerting any influence. Mark Lynch was not sure that the protests will bring down the regimes protested. Nor was he certain what advice to give to Obama. "I don't expect these protests to bring down any regimes, but who knows? It's an unpredictable moment. Many of these regimes are led by aging, fading leaders such as Hosni Mubarak and Zine el-Abedine Ben Ali who could pass from the scene in a heartbeat—literally. Nor do I particularly know what to recommend that the Obama administration do. The traditional calls to "promote democracy" are largely irrelevant to this situation, except in the longer-term. What we are now seeing is the fruit of the failure to promote meaningful reform in the past, but that doesn't mean that doing so now would meet the challenge". Lynch's sense of dilemma about US policy foreshadowed Obama's own dilemma over the years starting from 2011.

On January 25, 2011, as the revolutionary virus spread from Tunisia to Egypt, Mohammad ElBaradei in an interview to *Der Spiegel* adopted the term 'Arab Spring':

"Perhaps we are currently experiencing the first signs of an "Arab Spring" (e.g. similar to the so-called Prague Spring of political liberalization in Czechoslovakia in 1968). Our neighbours are watching Egypt, which has always played a pioneering role. I hope that my country will be one of the first in which freedom and democracy blossom. We Egyptians should also be able to achieve what the Tunisians have done (Keating, 2011).

On February 19, 2011, *The Times (London)* wrote that the Arab Spring was the 2011 equivalent of the 1989 Revolution marking the liberation of Eastern Europe (Toumi, 2011). By March 2011, the 'Arab Spring' was accepted in the non-Arab world as the right term. However, Arab scholars had a different view. Rami G. Khouri, a prominent scholar based in Beirut, wrote in *Daily Star* of August 17, 2011 under the caption: "Drop the Orientalist term 'Arab Spring'. Khouri objected that the term implied a certain passivity as the spring dawns without any effort on the part of the people and because of the likely association with the failed Prague Spring of 1968 and similar springs in Europe. He preferred 'Revolutions' or thwart in Arabic (Khouri, 2011). Tunisians preferred to call it the Dignity Revolution (Thawrat el-Karama), a term that is appropriate.

Obviously, the question arises: Why and how did the term 'Arab Spring' gain such wide currency for a while? The short answer is: Decolonization of the mind in the non-West part of the world (ROW) takes longer than political decolonization. The world of media and scholarship is still dominated, especially in the realm of the social sciences, by the West, and the ROW is not fully aware of the consequences of the unfinished decolonization process. If one is not aware that one is unfree, there is no chance of becoming free. Despite the objections raised above, we shall continue to use the expression 'Arab Spring' for the sake of convenience without accepting the 'Orientalist' baggage as the expression describes well how it all began. What is most striking about the Arab Spring is that there was no Lenin or Khomeini to lead it. It was a spontaneous revolt of the oppressed, who for once got rid of their fear of the secret police and the rest of the all-pervasive and intrusive *Mukhabarat* system prevalent in the Arab countries and stood up for their rights.

Equally striking, the Arab Spring took the West, and therefore the ROW, by surprise. The West was comfortable with the dictators, and pundits such as Francis Fukuyama, Bernard Lewis, and Samuel Huntington had advanced with certitude the thesis that Islam and democracy were incompatible and therefore Arabs were destined to be ruled by autocrats. In the case of Tunisia, the French Foreign Minister Michele Alliot-Marie told the Foreign Affairs Committee of the National Assembly, "Be honest, all of us, politicians, diplomats, researchers and journalists, were surprised by the Jasmine Revolution" (BBC, 2011 A). This admission of hers is rather puzzling since there were 22,000 French citizens and 1,200 French companies in Tunisia and 700,000 Tunisians in France (Dlugoleski, 2011). It is doubtful whether the 722,000 individuals in question would have agreed with her and even if they had agreed it is difficult to say how she would have known that they had agreed.

Incidentally, Alliot-Marie was factually incorrect when she claimed that French diplomats did not know that Ben Ali was to lose power. She should have known that she was misquoting them. As a matter of fact, Yves Aubin de La Messuziere, France's Ambassador in Tunisia from 2002 to 2005, had reported to his government that Ben Ali's regime would be overthrown one day. French Embassy used to report the harsh measures adopted by Ben Ali against dissidents and the French diplomats were shocked when President Sarkozy on a visit to Tunis in 2008 complimented Ben Ali for promoting civil liberties (RFI, 2011). There is another reason for Foreign Minister Alliot-Marie's surprise. She was very close to a businessman who was close to Ben Ali and she had spent vacations with that businessman at his expense (BBC, 2011 B). Even the BBC with its long years of coverage of Egypt in its report on January 17, 2011 did not expect Mubarak to fall after Ben Ali fell (BBC, 2011 C). The BBC was confident that Mubarak will outwit his foes as he had done in the past many a time.

Students of revolutions distinguish between what triggers a revolution and its underlying causes. The assassination of Archduke Franz Ferdinand on June 26, 1914 by Serbian patriot Gavrilo Princip, 19, was the trigger, but not the cause of World War 1. The trigger in the case of Tunisia was the attempted self-immolation and subsequent death of Tarek Bouazizi. But, the reasons or rather the causes of the Dignity Revolution are not unfathomable. Above all, Tunisians wanted to get rid of the Ben Ali regime to recover their lost dignity. The regime was corrupt to the core and to get anything done from the government it was necessary to bribe or beg even when no favour was sought. Tarek was humiliated by petty officials and his defiant act of self-immolation struck a chord among his compatriots who saw in him a brave fighter for the dignity they all had lost.

The crony capitalism under Ben Ali who was praised by the West for his liberalization enabled the family of Ben Ali's wife, Laila Trabelsi, to 'pillage' the wealth of the state. Her brother Belhassen bought government land at absurdly low prices and sold it making huge profits. Tunisia promoted tertiary education successfully, but the young who entered the labour market found it difficult to get jobs. The press freedom shrank rapidly under Ben Ali whose son-in-law Fahed Sakhr al-Matri bought a publishing house that printed four newspapers (April 2009) (Andrew-Gee, 2011).

In short, even though the official France was taken in by surprise, diligent observers could have seen that the Ben Ali system could not last for too long. There was an accumulated stock of gun powder in the room and Tarek only lighted a match triggering an explosion of people's anger. However, a number of scholars in the Arab world honestly believe that behind the Arab Spring was a conspiracy by the West, in particular by the CIA and the State Department of US. It is difficult to agree to such a thesis unless more evidence is produced. But the fact that it is taken seriously makes it necessary to say more about it. The thesis has many variations, but Ahmed Bensada, a French Canadian born in Algeria, has in his book *Arabesque Americaine* (Bensaada, 2011) has argued the thesis in detail. We give below some of his arguments:

1. Following institutions based in US trained and influenced the young people to revolt against the rulers:

- National Endowment for Democracy.
- National Democratic Institute for International Affairs.
- Centre for Non-violent Action and Strategies.
- US Agency for International Development.
- Open Society Institute of George Soros.

2. The Tor *Project* developed by Google, US Naval Research Laboratory, and State Department linked Human Rights Watch enables anonymous navigation in countries that resort to internet censorship. Many young Arabs were trained in such navigation.
3. Gael Ghonim, a Google employee based in UAE started a Facebook "We are all Khalid Said" in memory of Khalid Said brutally killed by the secret police, a Facebook that mobilized the January 25 anti-Mubarak protests.

That the US institutions in question did give IT training and otherwise influenced the thinking of some young Arabs is beyond question. But, the evidence provided does not support the conclusion that the CIA and others planned or instigated the 2011 Revolutions. The Russian Revolution of 1917 might not have occurred in the manner it did if Germany had not arranged for Lenin to reach Russia secretly in a 'sealed trunk'. Germany calculated that if Lenin seized power he might sign a ceasefire and withdraw from war which Lenin did. But, it will be wrong to say that Germany engineered the Bolshevik Revolution. We can only say that Germany facilitated it. Similarly, the CIA and its friends might have facilitated the Arab Spring, but it is inadmissible to say that they designed and arranged for it. History is not susceptible to such engineering.

Tunisia as we have said is a happy exception. The main architect of the success of Tunisia by promoting a democratic framework is Rached Ghannouchi (born 1941), the best leader that the post-2011 Arab world in turmoil has produced. He took the lead, inspired by the 1979 Iranian Revolution and the Muslim Brotherhood in Egypt, to found the Islamic Tendency Movement in 1981; it became Ennahda (Renaissance) in 1989. He came back to Tunisia from a 20-year exile in January 2011; his party won the first ever free election ever held in Tunisia in 2011 and led a coalition government.

In response to calls for the resignation of the government for its failure to ensure security, it agreed to resign to be replaced by a government of technocrats after finalizing and getting approved a constitution; the constitution that was approved easily the best in the Arab world.

Ennahda lost the 2014 elections, but agreed to be a junior partner to Nidaa Tounes, an unstable collection of Ben Ali's high officials, the corporate sector, the trade union, and civil society; even after the Nidaa Tounes broke up in January 2016 Ennahda has not claimed its right to lead the government though it is the single largest party; and what is of utmost importance is that Ennahda in May 2016 decided to cut all connections with religion and become a political party, indeed a long journey for the Islamic Tendency Movement that drew inspiration from the 1979 Khomeini Revolution in Iran and the Muslim Brotherhood in Egypt. The Nobel Peace Prize for 2015 was awarded to the National Dialogue Quartet consisting of trade union, lawyers, human rights activists, and industrialists. A more discerning judgment on the part of the Nobel Committee would have included Ghannouchi too.

As of now, Tunisia is still passing through severe economic difficulties; GDP grew by 0.8 percent in 2015; debt service requires US$ 3 billion a year and the government will find it difficult to find the amount of US$ 450 million a month required for paying salaries. The West should give more assistance as the rich GCC is not keen to promote a democracy in the Arab world.

Democracy will find it difficult to grow firm roots in Tunisia if the economy, especially the job situation, does not improve soon. Youth unemployment is running at 40 percent. [4] About 6,000 Tunisians have joined the Islamic State, too large a number for a country of 11 million. [5]

Before leaving Tunisia, it is useful to reflect on the role of the adventitious in history. On January 14, 2011, Ben Ali had no plans to relinquish power. He went to the airport to see off his wife to Jeddah. She was sent out as she was extremely unpopular, the houses of her family had been attacked and looted, and it was judged that she was not safe in Tunis. It was Ali Seriati, the chief of presidential security, who persuaded Ben Ali to accompany his wife to Jeddah so that he can come back after a few days when the situation would be calmer.

That he had no intention of leaving Tunisia is clear from the fact that Ben Ali had not taken his passport or clothes with him. The main argument used by Seriati was that it was not safe for Ben Ali to go back to his office or residence from the airport. That assessment was based on some wrong assumptions and wrong information as became clear later. However, even if Ben Ali had not left for Jeddah on the January 14, he could not have continued in office for long unless he was prepared to disown his wife and take back the illegally acquired wealth from her and his family.

Our next logical stop is Egypt. The key question is why Egypt could not replicate Tunisia's success? The short answer is that the Egyptian Revolution of 2011 was an incomplete one and Egypt has a Deep State unlike Tunisia. [6] Contrary to the popular notion of Mubarak's leaving office on February 11 transferring power to the SCAF (Supreme Council of the Armed Forces) what happened was different: The SCAF signalled on February 10 that it was going to take charge; on the 11th morning it announced that it had taken charge; and hours later Vice President Suleiman announced that Mubarak had left asking SCAF to take over.

In other words, Mubarak left office partly because of the

thunderous demand from the Tahrir Square, but mainly because the SCAF had disowned him and announced its taking over the charge of Egypt. Hardly anyone in Tahrir Square or elsewhere in Egypt paused to think that under the constitution the president should have been succeeded by the speaker of the lower house of the parliament. By not firing at the demonstrators, the army had earned the goodwill of the people who naively believed the army when it promised to lead Egypt into a democratic destination.

The post-Mubarak developments in Egypt are reasonably well known, but the media have not brought out a coherent account of what happened, especially of Morsi's rise and fall. We need to start with the Deep State in Egypt. Even as Mubarak fell, the Deep State led by the SCAF decided to retain control, if possible with a democratic façade, and if necessary without it.

We shall attempt a brief account of the post-2011 Revolution in three parts:

1. The SCAF was in no hurry to conduct an election that will generate a civilian government to which power will have to be transferred. It wanted to hold on to power as long as possible. It surveyed the political scene and figured out that the Muslim Brotherhood (MB), founded by Hasan al-Banna in 1928, was the strongest force. Similarly, the MB did a survey and spotted the SCAF as the strongest force. The two decided to form a tacit alliance to advance their respective their immediate agenda though their visions for Egypt differed radically. The SCAF will legitimize the MB so that it can form a political party and contest elections. The MB with its street power will protect the SCAF from others, mainly secular parties, wanting an immediate transition to a civilian government. The MB will respect the pre-eminence of the SCAF in decision-making on major issues and let it retain virtual autonomy as well as its huge financial empire. [7]

2. The alliance worked well for a while. The SCAF was not expecting the MB to do as well as it did in the general elections of 2011-2012. The MB-led coalition got 37.5 percent

of votes and 44.9 percent of seats. The Deep State led by the SCAF had made sure that the Parliament will have no powers as the SCAF-nominated Prime Minister was not answerable to it. When it became clear that the MB candidate Morsi will get elected as President, the Deep State got the Lower House of the Parliament dissolved on a rather flimsy technical ground and made constitutional changes rendering the Presidency toothless. Morsi tried to recover the powers due to his office but with limited success; the police and the bureaucracy decided to disobey him; and the economic situation got worse. Shortages of petrol were artificially generated.

3. The Deep State funded a group of young people who formed an association in April 2013 by name Tamarod (rebel in Arabic) and with the active cooperation of the police it collected signatures calling for Morsi's resignation. It claimed that it had collected 22 million signatures, a claim that was never verified independently. All the non-MB political parties joined in as a huge disinformation campaign was mounted to project Morsi as a Pharaoh who wanted to transform Egypt into an Islamic State under Sharia. As anti-Morsi demonstrations spread, the SCAF gave an ultimatum to Morsi to arrive at a negotiated settlement with the opposition knowing fully well that it (the opposition) was refusing to talk to him. As Morsi was completing one year in office on June 30, 2013, huge demonstrations were arranged and once again a disinformation campaign exaggerated the number of demonstrators. The SCAF gave another ultimatum to settle matters in 48 hours and on July 3, the Army kidnapped Morsi and took him to an undisclosed destination.

The above is an abridged narration of what happened and why it happened. After bringing down Morsi, General El Sisi, the chief of SCAF decided to 'exterminate' the MB. On August 14, 2013, a large group of pro-Morsi were holding sit-ins in two places and the security forces repeated a Jallianwala Bagh type of cold, calculated massacre killing hundreds. The disinformation campaign was so successful that many Egyptians applauded the carnage. The Egyptian Deep State did much better than the British Government in India when it tried to fool the Indian public that the carnage at Jallianwala Bagh was justified.

The MB was declared a 'terrorist organization' and banned; its offices and assets were confiscated. Absurd charges were levelled against Morsi. It was alleged that he was trying to sell the Suez Canal to Qatar. The intention was to put an end to the MB as a political force so that it will not be able to contest elections. General El Sisi, by then promoted as Field Marshal, though he has never fought a war, was elected with 97 percent of the votes as President in June 2015. Sisi had to blackmail a political leader (Hamdeen Sabahi) to stand, as otherwise the uncontested election would have looked dubious.

Currently, Egypt remains as far away from democracy as it was under Mubarak, and even farther according to some observers. The regime does not permit dissent and the media have been intimidated into subordination. According to one estimate, the number of Egyptians under detention, with or without charges, runs into 60,000. In short, Egypt has been ruled by a man in uniform since 1952 (Naguib, Nasser, Sadat, Mubarak, Sisi). There was a brief aberration when Morsi became President in 2012. In any case, he had no powers but the aberration was rapidly corrected.

Our next stop is Libya, rich in oil, but lamentably deprived of institutions because Muammar Mohammed Abu Minyar Gaddafi (1942-2011) who grabbed power through a military coup in 1969 destroyed all of them. He was inspired by Nasser to stage the coup. What is most striking about Libya is that the West that was taken in by surprise in Tunisia, and remained silent for a while before asking Mubarak to leave when it was clear that he had to go, intervened in Libya with surprising alacrity. The main intention was to control and exploit Libya's vast oil wealth. Libya has reserves of 48.36 billion barrels of oil, as compared to 36.52 of US and 37.07 of Nigeria.

Protests in Libya began in the middle of February 2011. Gaddafi resorted to repression, but the revolt spread. UK Foreign Secretary Hague spread the false report that Gaddafi was on his way to Venezuela, and on the February 26, the UN Security Council unanimously passed Resolution 1970, referring the Libyan government to the Prosecutor of International Criminal Court of Justice. An arms embargo was established; and the assets of the government were frozen. France, UK, US, and Germany moved the resolution under Chapter 7 making it binding on all member-states. The day after the passing of Resolution 1970, a National Transitional Council was formed in Benghazi. The US Navy positioned ships near the Libyan coast and froze US$ 30 billion of assets belonging to Libya.

As the rebels gained military advantage, the Arab League called for establishing a no-fly zone and recognized the National Transitional Council as the government of Libya. On March 18, the West got adopted a new resolution, No. 1973 on Libya establishing a no-fly zone, demanding an immediate ceasefire, and authorizing "all necessary means to protect civilians and civilian protected areas". Russia, China, Brazil, Germany, and India abstained. None of those who abstained, especially, the first two, figured out the true intentions of the West to bomb Gaddafi's forces and to effect a regime change by stretching the words "all necessary means". The initial coalition that started bombing within two days of the adoption of the resolution attracted more powers and finally the NATO took charge of the operations. The coalition included Belgium, Bulgaria, Canada, Denmark, France, Greece, Italy, Jordan, NATO, Netherlands, Norway, Qatar, Romania, Spain, Sweden, Turkey, UAE, UK and US, in all 18 plus NATO.

Obviously, Gaddafi stood no chance against such a coalition. By August, Gaddafi lost control of the capital and on October 20, 2011 he was killed. By October 31, NATO announced the end of its military operations. After the killing of Gaddafi, the NATO concluded that its mission was accomplished. If the West thought, and it seems to have thought so, that with Gaddafi's death there will be peace and normality in Libya and all that was required was holding of an election to let the people decide who should govern them, that was deplorably irresponsible and culpably naïve. We have pointed out earlier that Gaddafi had destroyed all institutions one by one. Obviously, once the government of Gaddafi collapsed, there will be anarchy. President Obama has blamed UK and France, or more specifically, Prime Minister Cameron and President Sarkozy, for neglecting to work out a plan for the post-Gaddafi Libya. However, it is difficult to be convinced that any Western plan would have worked out.

Regime change is an act fraught with unintended consequences as anyone who has followed recent events in Iraq and Afghanistan should know. But, sadly it is possible for decision makers in government to ignore the obvious and create situations where people suffer. It is not possible to give a coherent account of post-Gaddafi Libya because there is not much coherence in the situation, with two or even three governments at a time, no proper national army, and any number of militias clashing with each other. The UN efforts to promote a government of unity have not delivered the intended results so far and the prospects are bleak as of now. The West has acted most irresponsibly propelled by their greed to avail of Libya's oil wealth.

We now move to Syria. Basher al Assad succeeded his father Hafez in 2000. Hafez al Assad who captured power through a coup d'état, once again inspired by Nasser, was President from 1970 till his death in 2000. He did not believe in democracy and it was a one-person rule. When Basher came into office, there was a hope that he would dismantle the autocratic structure and replace it with democracy. However, this did not happen though Basher made hesitant moves in that direction. Mass protests began on January 26, 2011 asking for reforms and if Basher had responded in the right way, perhaps, the course of history might have been different. Basher responded with violence and the protests spread. External powers eager to get involved stepped in to pump in money and arms to the rebels.

The involvement of external powers has made a settlement between Basher and his foes difficult. In any case, the foes were not united as they were supported by different external powers. In July 2011, US Secretary of State Hillary Clinton announced that Assad had "lost legitimacy". That statement from US, was obediently echoed by London, Paris, and Berlin. It is bad diplomacy to make such a statement and not to follow it up with a supportive action. The West tried to repeat 'Libya' by proposing resolutions at UN Security Council paving the way for military intervention by NATO. That was rather naïve on the part of the West as by then Moscow had realized its mistake in not vetoing Resolution 1973 referred to earlier. The West and its allies did give some arms, but not the type of arms necessary for winning a war against the Syrian army. Iran started giving military support to Assad within months of the outbreak of the civil war. As Assad's forces were losing rapidly, Iran and Hezbollah sent fighters and Russian weapons and Assad has regained some territory and has overall the military edge. But, it is most unlikely that he would recover his rule over the whole of Syria.

The rebels are of different kinds: those supported by the West, misleadingly referred to as 'moderates'; the more extreme ones such as ISIL (Islamic State of Iraq and Levant); Al Nusra (a variant of Al-Qaeda); and the Kurds. Qatar and Saudi Arabia are believed to have extended support officially or otherwise to both ISIL and Al Nusra for a while. As the support from the West was rather weak, many 'moderates' have built up close connections with Al Nusra, better armed and more resourceful than any of them. Since September 2015, Russia started an air campaign ostensibly to destroy ISIL, but directed against all foes of Assad.

Repeated efforts by UN appointed mediators, Kofi Annan (February to August 2012), Lakhdar Brahimi (August 2012 to

May 2014) and conferences in Geneva and Vienna co-sponsored by US and Russia have failed to arrange for a ceasefire as a prelude to political transition. Currently, UN mediator Staffan de Mistura appointed in 2014 is working hard to make the warring parties to agree to a political transition process, but so far without any success. Repeated Kerry-Lavrov negotiations have produced no results so far.

The solution to the crisis is made difficult by a few factors:

1. President Assad is not willing to sit down with his foes who insist that he should immediately step down. Saudi Arabia insists on Assad's removal from power though it knows that it and other foes of Assad do not have the clout, military or political, to throw him out of power.
2. The US and Russia are pursuing incompatible goals in Syria though they have succeeded in agreeing to joint communiques issued from Geneva or Vienna, communiques which concealed their differences by clever use of words. US does not mind if Syria is divided into many statelets whereas Russia though it recognizes the practical impossibility of installing Assad as President of the whole of Syria, is prepared to see him holding securely only a part of Syria including the Mediterranean coast where Russia has a naval base in Tartus.
3. The external powers supporting the anti-Assad rebels are only pumping in money and arms. They do not have to take casualties. Their interest in reaching an agreement on a ceasefire is not strong.
4. The leaders of the armed groups have hardly any incentive to agree to a ceasefire. If there is a ceasefire, their external support base will shrink or disappear.

In short, if there is no convergence of interest in seeking peace, it becomes unavoidable to continue fighting till either one or more of the warring parties are exhausted. The grave yard is peaceful. None of the external powers engaged in seeking a negotiated solution does care much about the carnage and destruction of Syria.

Our next stop is Yemen. President Ali Abdullah Saleh, in power since 1978 in North Yemen and since 1990 in the reunited Yemen, making him the Arab dictator longest in office, reluctantly conceded to leave office in February 2012. According to a panel of UN experts, Saleh accumulated anywhere between $ 32 billion to 60 billion stacked in at least 20 countries (United Nations, 2015). When Saleh's deputy Abdrabbuh Mansour won the presidential elections, and succeeded Saleh in February 2012, it looked as though Yemen was going to move towards democracy in a peaceful way, especially so after a ten-month long National Dialogue produced a document to serve as the basis for writing a new constitution. But, there was a lurking danger. The Houthis, a Shia group that has carried on war with the government for years when Saleh was in power refused to accept the new constitution proposed by Hadi as well as the formation of a federation of six regions as they felt that they were being short changed.

The Houthis started a revolt, found support from Saleh who retained influence over sections of the army and the bureaucracy, and in September they captured Saana and made Hadi virtually a prisoner. Hadi fled to the south and later to Saudi Arabia when Aden fell to Houthis. The Saudis formed a coalition (UAE, Bahrain, Kuwait, Qatar, Jordan, Morocco, Senegal and Sudan) and launched *Operation Decisive Storm* (ODS) in March 2015. Egypt was in the coalition for a while. The US, UK, France, Turkey, and Canada lent logistical support. The death toll crossed the 10,000 mark by October 2016 (Hatem, 2016).

However, ODS has proved to be far from decisive and there is a virtual stalemate. Repeated efforts by UN to arrange for a ceasefire and negotiations for a political settlement have not borne fruits so far. As of now, there is no reason to believe that the Saudis will score a decisive victory in the near future. Al-Qaeda and IS (Islamic State) hold sizable parts of Yemen. Hospitals are short of medicine and Saudi Arabia has violated international law with impunity by bombing repeatedly hospitals run by *Doctors without Borders*. It is painfully clear that Riyadh made a grave mistake in starting a war it is incapable of winning.

Next stop is Bahrain. We have noticed that in general monarchies in Jordan, Morocco, Qatar, Oman, and Kuwait could address the political pressures brought on them by the Arab Spring that felled four dictators in a span of one year. Bahrain is an exception in the sense that the turbulence posed the strongest threat to the Sunni monarchy in Bahrain with a Shia majority. [8] But, it is wrong to assert that it is only the Shias who are seeking change and to look at the political situation through the lens of Shia-Sunni contestation. Demonstrations, peaceful to start with, but turning violent mostly as a response to the violence on the part of the security forces started in the middle of February 2011. Saudi Arabia watched with concern and as the Bahraini security forces were not able to suppress the agitation, took the lead to send troops to suppress the revolt.

In June 2011, Bahrain established the *Bahrain Independent Commission of Inquiry* (BICI) with eminent internationally known persons, led by Cherif Bassiouni, who led the UN investigation into war crimes in Bosnia and Libya. The 513-page report of the Commission repays reading. [9] The highlights are:

1. The Government and the Opposition are responsible for escalation.
2. No evidence was presented to the Commission of Iran's giving material assistance, by way of money or arms, to the Opposition.
3. The GCC intervened militarily on March 14, 2011 by sending a force of 5,000 from Saudi Arabia, UAE, and Qatar; Kuwait sent ships and Oman did not participate in the intervention.
4. While allegations of violations against human rights by the GCC force remains unsubstantiated, there is evidence that the Bahraini Security forces used force more than

demanded by proportionality and necessity.

5. There were instances of Sunni-Shia clash, and the first instance was on March 3. The Commission does not go into the question whether there was a deliberate attempt on the part of the Government or anyone else to instigate such clashes.

Though the Commission was criticized by human rights activists for refraining from blaming the Governments where necessary, the fact remains that Bahrain did appoint an international commission in sharp contrast to Egypt where much worse atrocities were committed by security forces. We need to say a word about the Islamic State (IS). It is a mistake to see the IS with its capital at Raqqa in Syria as a by-product of the Arab Spring. The seeds of the IS were sown in Afghanistan where US funded and otherwise assisted the Mujahedeen (those who carry out jihad) to fight the Soviets who fell into a trap prepared by US whose Special Forces had been operating in Afghanistan for months before the Soviet troops came in. When Soviet troops entered Afghanistan in December 1979, Zbigniew Brzezinski, National Security Advisor to President Carter congratulated him for giving 'Vietnam' to the Soviet Union. In an interview in January 1998, Brzezinski claimed that he and Jimmy Carter "started the Mujahedeen" (Cockburn, 1998).

Therefore, Carter and Brzezinski can claim partial paternity for IS. Similarly, George Bush by invading and occupying Iraq prepared the ground for the rise of IS. US threw into prison Iraqis and others suspected of insurgency. US helped the rise of IS in two ways:

1. The prisoners were tortured in flagrant violation of international law and thus hatred for US spread. The torture included: "Breaking chemical lights and pouring the phosphoric liquid on detainees; pouring cold water on naked detainees; beating detainees with a broom handle and a chair; threatening male detainees with rape; allowing a military police guard to stitch the wound of a detainee

who was injured after being slammed against the wall in his cell; sodomizing a detainee with a chemical light and perhaps a broom stick, and using military working dogs to frighten and intimidate detainees with threats of attack, and in one instance actually biting a detainee". [10]

2. Some of the prisoners held by US emerged later as top IS leaders. They were permitted to engage with other prisoners and to convert them into their way of thinking. US prisons in Iraq were 'jihadi universities for IS". Thus, President George Bush can legitimately claim some credit for the birth and growth of IS.

President Obama also can claim similar credit. In 2012, US intelligence told Obama that by 2014 Salafis might hold territory and establish a state in Syria/Iraq. Obama did not see IS as a threat to US and ridiculed them as a "j v (junior university) team". In January 2014, the Iraqi town of Falluja fell to IS. In June 2014, Mosul fell. Obama could have used air force against the advancing IS fighters before they captured Mosul. In August 2014, the Yazidi city of Sanjir was captured and the Yazidis were killed in large numbers. The IS made inroads into Christian villages and killed many. Obama looked on doing nothing. It was only when IS threatened Erbil where there are many US companies and nationals that Obama felt the need to bomb IS. The military campaign against IS in Mosul began on October 17, 2016 by an Iraqi force of about 50,000. US Special Forces are assisting the Iraqi Army, without engaging in battle, we are told. It is difficult to foresee when Mosul will fall. But, it is painfully clear that the historic city of Mosul will be destroyed and hundreds or thousands will be killed before Iraq recaptures Mosul.

It is useful to recall how and why Mosul fell to IS in June 2014. Iraqi Army is corrupt and Mosul had only 10,000 troops in position though on paper there were 25,000. Mosul with a population of 2 million is predominantly Sunni and the army consisting of a majority Shia soldiers was unpopular. The Shia officers had no interest in risking their lives to defend the

Sunni population which hated them. The IS fighters were about 2,000 and the Iraqi army ran away without fighting, leaving their uniforms and weapons. The branch of the Central Bank in Mosul had over US$ 429 million in its coffers (Moore, 2014).

We conclude that the progenitors of IS include Jimmy Carter, George Bush, and Barack Obama. We mentioned the role of the adventitious in the context of Ben Ali's departure to Saudi Arabia. The election of Donald J. Trump can be considered an adventitious factor. He might engage with President Putin, hitherto demonized by the West, and the two might agree to a ceasefire in Syria with Assad holding on to the part of Syria under him. If the senseless carnage in Syria stops, that will be a great blessing.

To conclude:

1. The Arab Spring was inevitable and could have been foreseen. The rulers could have responded positively to the demands for reforms, but they chose to use force, often excessive force, and such use of force caused the protests to spread.
2. Foreign powers did not intervene in Tunisia and Egypt. Their intervention in Libya and Syria has been disastrous.
3. Saudi Arabia made a mistake in starting a war in Yemen it cannot win.
4. US under Obama had not covered itself with glory by pursuing an erratic policy in Syria.
5. Russia has emerged as the strongest player in Syria.
6. Syria is unlikely to regain its territorial integrity.
7. While IS might lose territory sooner or later, its ability to carry out terrorist strikes might increase for a while.

Perhaps, Shakespeare can help us understand what happened and what might follow:

"O, how this spring of love resembleth
The uncertain glory of an April day
Which now shows all the beauty of the sun
And by and by a cloud takes all away". [11]

The clouds prevent the sunshine from reaching us. But, the sun is there and the clouds will disperse sooner or later, perhaps, sooner rather than later.

Endnotes

1. This estimate is on the low side as it does not seem to have taken into account the cost of reconstruction. A more comprehensive study by the Arab Strategy Forum puts the cost at US$ 833 billion, available at: http://www.emirates247.com/business/cost-of-arab-spring-estimated-at-833bn-2015-12-15-1.614104.
2. "The Arab Spring 2005" (2005), available at: http://www.seattletimes.com/opinion/the-arab-spring-of-2005.
3. The name of the fruit vendor has been mistaken by the media and scholars who call him Mohammed. Abdelaziz Belkhodja and Tarak Cheikhrouhou in their well-researched book, "14 Janvier: L'ENQUETE" have pointed out the error; www.14janvier2011.com.
4. OECD Report, "Youth Unemployment in Tunisia is a True Social Tragedy", available at: http://www.tunisia-live.net/2015/03/12/oecd-report-youth-unemployment-in-tunisia-a-true-social-tragedy.
5. How Tunisia became a top source of recruitment for ISIS, *Wall Street Journal*, February 25, 2016, available at: http://www.wsj.com/articles/how-tunisia-became-a-top-source-of-isis-recruits-1456396203.
6. The term 'Deep State' was originally used in the context of Turkey in the 1990s, "derindevlet" in Turkish. It is a coalition of unelected wielders of power, preferring to remain in the background, but willing to come into the open if need be. The Deep State in Egypt is led by the SCAF, with the higher judiciary, the police/intelligence/security set up, the higher bureaucracy, the corporate barons, and the media barons as the components.
7. Nobody outside the top echelons of the Army knows the size of the financial empire as it is not subject to audit. Safa Joudeh, a Cairo based journalist has estimated or guessed that it is about 40 percent of Egypt's GDP, available at: http://www.atlanticcouncil.org/blogs/menasource/egypt-s-military-protecting-its-sprawling-economic-empire.

8. There is no official or reliable information on the break up between Shias and Sunnis. The last official census in 1941 estimated that Shias and Sunnis accounted for 52 percent and 48 percent respectively. It is believed that the current ratio is 60 to 70 percent for Shias and 30 to 40 percent for Sunnis, as quoted by BICI at files.bici.org.bh.
9. For details see http://www.bici.org.bh/BICIreportEN.pdf.
10. Hersh, Seymour M. (2004), "Torture at Abu Ghraib", available at: http://www.newyorker.com/magazine/2004/05/10/torture-at-abu-ghraib.
11. William Shakespeare, *Two Gentlemen of Verona* (1, iii, 84-87).

References

Andrew-Gee, Eric (2011), "Making Sense of Tunisia", available at: https://newrepublic.com/article/ 81611/making-sense-tunisia.

Barrington, Lisa (2016), "Arab Spring Has Cost Region 6 percent of GDP UN Agency", *Reuters*, November 10, available at: http://news.trust.org/item/20161110171822-zlu4b/?source=reTheWire.

BBC (2011B), "French Foreign Minister Alliot-Marie Quits over Tunisia", available at: http://www.bbc.co.uk/news/world-europe-12591452.

BBC (2011C), "No Sign Egypt Will Take the Tunisian Road", available at: http://www.bbc.com/news/world-middle-east-12202937.

BBC (2011A), "Tunisian Crisis Took France by Surprise–Minister", available at: http://www.bbc.co.uk/news/world-europe-12214746.

Bensaada, Ahmed (2011), "Arabesque American", available at: http://www.ahmedbensaada.com/index.php?option=com_content&view=article&id=136:smoking-gun-us-government-role-in-arab-spring&catid=37:societe&Itemid=75.

Cockburn, Jeffrey (1998), "How Jimmy Carter and I Started the Mujahideen", available at: http://www.counterpunch.org/1998/01/15/how-jimmy-carter-and-i-started-the-mujahideen.

Dlugoleski, Deirdre (2011), "The French Response to Tunisia", available at: http://tyglobalist.org/onlinecontent/blogs/the-french-response-to-tunisia.

Hatem, Mohammed (2016), "Saudi Conflict with Iran Takes Its Biggest Toll in Yemen", available at: http://www.bloomberg.com/news/articles/2016-10-24/a-14-hour-trip-in-yemen-shows-toll-of-saudi-proxy-war-with-iran.

Hersh, Seymour M. (2004), "Torture at Abu Ghraib", available at: http://www.newyorker.com/magazine/2004/05/10/torture-at-abu-ghraib.

Keating, Joshua (2011), "Who First Used the Term Arab Spring?", available at: http://foreignpolicy.com/2011/11/04/who-first-used-the-term-arab-spring.

Khouri, Rami G. (2011), "Drop the Orientalist Term Arab Spring", available at: http://www.dailystar.com.lb/Opinion/Columnist/2011/Aug-17/146410-drop-the-orientalist-term-arab-spring.ashx.

Krauthammer, Charles (1990), "The Unipolar Moment", available at: https://www.foreignaffairs.com/articles/1991-02-01/unipolar-moment.

Lynch, Marc (2011), "Obama's Arab Spring", available at: http://foreignpolicy.com/2011/01/06/obamas-arab-spring.

Moore, Jack (2014), "Mosul Seized: Jihadis Loot $ 429m from City's Central Bank to Make Isis World's Richest Terror Force", available at: http://www.ibtimes.co.uk/mosul-seized-jihadis-loot-429m-citys-central-bank-make-isis-worlds-richest-terror-force-1452190.

RFI (2011), "France Knew of Ben Ali Regime's Failings, Says Ex-Ambassador", available at: http://en.rfi.fr/africa/20110126-france-knew-ben-ali-regimes-failings-says-former-diplomat.

Toumi, Habib (2011), "Who coined Arab Spring?", available at: http://gulfnews.com/news/gulf/who-coined-arab-spring-1.952310.

United Nations (2015), "Security Council, Letter dated February 20, 2015 from the Panel of Experts", available at: http://www.un.org/ga/search/view_doc.asp?symbol=S/2015/125.

2

Egyptian Blogs during the Popular Protests from 2011 to 2013

Paulami Sanyal

Introduction

It is impossible for a media institution to exist independently of the social and political structure (Rugh, 1979). This dependence only increases in the context of an authoritarian system. Media's ability to act as a watchdog of issues and disseminate reports on them is further compromised in this context because its role tends to get reduced to serving the purpose of the government alone. Such predisposition is evident in the West Asian media or more specifically, in Egypt, which is the focus of this paper.

The internet has become the newest addition in the field of media through its successful role in the distribution of information. Egyptian protests were characterized by the use of social media like Twitter, YouTube, text messaging and Facebook. Indeed, Facebook helped in instantly spreading any information among thousands and with the faster dissemination of news, helped in organizing the protesters. Similarly, Twitter, by allowing users to discuss on a specific subject through the hashtag, helped in the building up of conversation among a larger number of population. Nevertheless, there is no denying the fact that blogs provided a venue where citizens were able to not only stage protests but also to document underlying causes that led to the eruption of the protests in the first place.

Aim of this paper would be to focus on those areas where blogs came unique to the cause of the Egyptian uprising. The concept of citizen's journalism is significant here because, away from the government influenced television, radio or print media, blogs build a dialogue forum with active participation from the viewers. Thus, the information flow continues with the help of common media consumers making blog a part of citizen's journalism process. This paper will briefly give an account of the concept and then discuss what qualifies Egyptian blogs to be part of the process.

Weblogs and Citizen's Journalism

Weblogs, according to Torill Mortensen and Jill Walker (2002), are frequently updated websites, usually personal, often coming with viewers' comments and different website link. They contain time-stamped posts organized in reverse chronology. Personal blog-texts tend to be informal, brief and direct. By allowing users to comment on a post, blogs create a debate arena where a conversation is built up with piece by piece information or opinion and readers can follow it up actively. It is also noteworthy here that except from a few live shows in televisions or radios or letters to the editors in newspapers or journals, a debate arena is almost absent from the traditional audio-visual and print media (Blood, 2002; Domingo and Heinonen, 2008).

Blogs enjoy a certain amount of openness in terms of its content, accessibility, and availability. The content of blog depends on the creator entirely, that is, whether a certain post is worthy of being published for others to read is only for the blogger to decide (Mortensen and Walker, 2002). Besides, blog posts are created without editors' interference thus making them free of any supervision (Faris, 2013). In the words of Aaron Barlow, blogs are 'not hierarchical but connective power coming from the aggregate and not through planning or the decisions of elite' (Barlow, 2007: 155). Unless being restricted by the owner, accessibility of internet is the only condition to open a blog or comment on an existing one.

To understand bloggers' functioning as citizens' journalists, a brief idea on the very term is required. The term citizens' journalism denotes a system where people without professional training can join in journalistic practices with the help of modern technology (Glaser, 2006). The process does not claim its emergence in the twenty-first century; in fact as Dan Gilmour (2004) has pointed out, pamphleteers like Thomas Paine or the anonymous authors of the Federalist papers at the backdrop of American revolution too can be considered as a part of it. After the emergence of the internet, there was a leap in the process through the inclusion of personal web pages, Indymedia and then blogs (Anderson, 2006).

As Axel Bruns quoted from JoBardoel and MarkDeuz (2001), citizen's journalism adds an annotational and orientational aspect to the world of journalism where, instead of disseminating new information as a watchdog, the citizen's journalists would offer information about information. In a rather 'guide dog' role, they would perform 'gate watching' by observing continuously the output gates of key institutions and news outlets, later collating and publishing the stories (Bruns, 2010: 2). Editorial oversight in this process remains limited. Moreover, users or receivers of the published news are equal participants in the news producing system through their response or commentary. Such post-publication filtering would induce discussion and debate, making citizen's journalism process more of a discursive phenomenon rather than the mere distribution of facts. Characteristically the process is decentralized, participatory, community-based, multi-perspective and always unfinished.

Axel Bruns (2010) used a term '*produsage*' to explain the system of citizen's journalism. In an attempt to analyze the new method of news content production, he argues, 'In collaborative content creation environments it is becoming difficult if not impossible to tell mere users from producers...We are entering an environment where users are always already also producers of content, or indeed have become hybrid *produsers*' (Bruns, 2010: 9). News *produsage* can be characterized with several aspects: open participation, any contributions evaluated by other participants; the manufactured news becoming an unfinished artefact and continuing process; news also becoming a common property and the whole system works like an ad hoc meritocracy (Bruns, 2010; Jurrat, 2011).

Blogs, even though started as a form of personal diaries, thus gradually built their expertise in the field of journalism. The difference between the blogs and the traditional modes of journalism (audiovisual or print) arises in the context of objectivity. Since bloggers are mostly volunteers, they tend to be inclined towards certain subjective ideas and propagate them through their posts. However, bloggers employ certain professional journalist-like qualities as well; such as credibility, accuracy, investigation and reporting-methods. Furthermore, blogs use similar mechanism i.e. eye-witness accounts, quotes, images, videos and the bloggers reputation to prove the validity of any news (Radsch, 2013). The most important function that all the well-connected and influential bloggers have in common is that they are experts in the 'art of linking', which is to point people to other sources of information on the web, thus allowing the existing raw materials to build a new information flow (Rosen, 2005). While maintaining the flow of information, blogs are also able to fill in the news gap; build up on existing information and even sometimes contradict the official statements (Jurrat, 2011).

On the basis of these characteristics discussed above, the Egyptian blogosphere too was able to create a new zone of information which attracted Egyptians both within and outside the country as well as foreign nationals. The next section will focus on the role these blogs played in the Egyptian uprising that began in 2011.

Egyptian Blogs

Egypt was introduced to internet in 1993 and blogging started to gain popularity around 1999 after Pyra labs developed a software helping people to publish online without requiring any special programming oriented knowledge. By the beginning of the twenty first century, Arabic language was available for online publishing. Even with the scarcity of personal computers, public places like cyber cafes, libraries and schools offered access to internet. In 2004, there were approximately 400 cyber cafes in Cairo alone and personal high-speed DSL connections were charged around US$ 50. By 2008, personal internet connection charges dropped to US$ 10 to 22 depending on the speed (Radsch, 2008). Table 2.1 shows the increasing internet penetration rate (percent of population introduced to internet) in Egypt from 2000.

Table 2.1: Internet Penetration in Egypt (2000-2016)

Year	Total Population	Penetration (percent)
2016*	93,383,574	33
2015	91,508,084	32.6
2014	89,579,670	31.7
2013	87,613,909	29.4
2012	85,660,902	26.4
2011	83,787,634	25.6
2010	82,040,994	21.6
2009	80,442,443	20
2008	78,976,122	18
2007	77,605,327	16
2006	76,274,285	13.7
2005	74,942,115	12.8
2004	73,596,068	11.9
2003	72,247,626	4
2002	70,908,710	2.7
2001	69,599,945	0.8
2000	68,334,905	0.6

*Estimated for July 2016.

Source: Adapted from Egypt, Internet Users, *Internet Live Stats*, http://www.internetlivestats.com/internet-users/egypt.

Initially, a limited number of bloggers existed (only 40

before 2005); writing mostly in English; primarily belonging to left liberal ideals and maintaining an anti-establishment approach. These early bloggers were able to expand blogs' ability beyond a medium for personal communication. Not only did they encourage others to create new blogs and provide technical assistance; but also paved the way of reporting local events (Radsch, 2013; Faris, 2013).

Among the most well-known English language blogs from this first generation were The *Arabist* (Issandr al-Amrani), *Rantings of a Sandmonkey* (Mahmoud Salem), the *Big Pharaoh* (Anonymous), *Baheyya* (Anonymous), and *Nermeena* (Nermeena Idris), *3arabawy* (Hossam el-Hamalawy) and some of the first blogs in Arabic were *Beyond Normal* (Ramy), *Digressing* (Mohammed), *Manalaa* (AlaaAbd el-Fattah and Manal Hassan), *Malek-x* (Malek Mustafa) and blogs of Gharbeia brothers, Amr and Ahmad. Arabic bloggers' focus was Egyptian audience whereas English bloggers attempted to draw more English speaking audiences beyond the region. Most of these early bloggers were journalists by profession (Hossam el Hamalwy, blogger of *3arabwy*); some were self-described experts in technology (Manal and Alaa, blogger of *Manalaa*; Malek Mustafa, blogger of *Malek-x*) (Radsch, 2008; Radsch 2013).

Importance of blogs is rarely discussed for the purpose of understanding Arab uprising because of the role that Facebook and Twitter played in the subsequent events. However, as scholars like Christina Riegert (2015), Mohammed el-Nawawy and Sahar Khamis (2013) or Courtney C. Radsch (2013) noted, blogs initiated the trend of sharing ideas which in turn helped in formulating collective public opinion. In the Egyptian context, that turned the blogs into a mouthpiece of anti-government discourse revealing former governments' dysfunctions and corrupt practices. Indeed, a look at the famous blogs of the past decade will reveal, how these blogs for the very first time introduced the idea that criticism of Egypt' formerly red-lined areas is possible.

During Kefaya, a protest movement against President

Mubarak's fifth term, bloggers' practice of analyzing and disseminating information made them a part of the broader resistance. Several individuals later to be known as leading activists in 2011 established their public personas, contacts and reputation through blogs. In the pre-2011 decade, bloggers started to document and criticize human rights abuses practiced by Egyptian government. For example, a mass sexual assault of downtown Cairo on October 23, 2006 was reported for the first time by a blogger Malek Mustafa (blogger of *Malek x*) or the case of solmization of a micro bus driver by the Egyptian police in the same year was first reported by Wael Abbas in December 2006 (blogger of *Misrdigital*) (Socialist Worker, 2006; Faris, 2013). [1]

On the eve of 2011 protests and afterwards, Egyptian bloggers turned activists were joined by a fresh batch of social media users, actively critising government and organising protests. Nevertheless, the importance of the blogosphere remained fundamental to the Egyptian cause. Performing as a guidedog, Egyptian bloggers gave detailed account of day by day events both inside Tahrir Square and in any other protest areas during and after the 2011 protests. Political news analysis, household affairs, personal troubles due to insufficient security measures, local news etc. all came under the purview of bloggers' reports. Most of these reporting did not rise up to covering an entirely new incident. For example, when *3arabawy* reported about labourers' protest throughout the year 2012, this incident was also covered by national (Al Wafd newspaper, ON TV and so on) and international (The Guardian) print and audio visual media, sometimes hyperlinked into the blog posts itself. However, bloggers' detailed discussion with additional little tidbits helped in building up on the existing information. For example, in the context discussed above, Hossam El Hamalawy (blogger of *3arabawy*), coupled his reports with analysis on the critics of these workers' strike, giving the discussion a new perspective (El Hamalawy, 2012).

Analyzing the events is one aspect of blogs that sets it

apart from other forms of internet-generated media. While photo sharing or video sharing mediums such as Flicker or YouTube represent verification of a certain report and Twitter or Facebook contains features to promote a cause among a large number of people, critical discussion encircling a particular issue is mostly found in blogosphere. Egyptian blogs analyzed domestic and international political and economic situations and held problem-solving discussions. *Rantings of sandmonkey* tried to solve the issue of security for the people who were gathering in Tahrir square. From 2011 to 2013, this blog contained a varied range of discussions from a detailed analysis of the 25th January protests to possible solutions of arranging the thousands of people gathering in Tahrir square; or from an understanding of 2012 presidential elections to reasons why Muslim Brotherhood is getting international support in 2013 after the ouster of Morsi.

Nawara Negm (blogger of *Popular Front of Sarcasm*), in her blog post on November 21, 2011, denounced that Supreme Council of Armed Forces (SCAF) committed violence and proposed a decree asking to end their rule. She proposed that the ruling authority during the transition period would be with a committee of judges as long as the new government is not elected. She also suggested that the new government should be formulated through first, a parliamentary election, followed by a presidential election and then a constitution. Different arguments like these provided a counter narrative, contributing to the shape of the debates around different issues (Al-Ani, Mark, Chung and Jones 2012).

Other than information distribution, bloggers tended to assume the traditional watchdog role of journalism as well. [2] Frequently, blog posts contained critical arguments against government policies and media houses' performances. Liberal secular blogs such as *Egyptian Chronicle,* Misrdigital or *Rantings of Sandmonkey* criticized against Muslim Brotherhood's policies or after the ouster of President Morsi, the SCAF's decision. Bloggers sometimes even criticized other online activists as well.

Egyptian Chronicle criticized complete silence of *We are all Khaled Said* Facebook page and asked the moderators to continue with the resistance and *3arabawy* criticized the moderator of *We are all Khaled Said* page, WaelGhonim, a middle class activist who would think a revolution's goal achieved after the change of the government and go back to normal activities (El Hamalawy, 2012, Egyptian Chronicle, 2013). Watchdog role also led the bloggers to go beoyng the territorial boundary and share any news they found worthwhile. Zeinobia's (blogger of *Egyptian Chronicle*) post of December 20, 2013 based on Rohingya Muslims in Myanmar, covered by one of her friend from Al Aan TV channel, was one such news. Zeinobia discussed the despicable situation that the Rohingya Muslims are forced to live in and how the community is forgotten by the rest of the world. She even blamed Aung San Suu Kyi as a hypocrite like any other politician.

A different positive aspect of blogs was their multi-perspective nature. Being an open forum for discussion, blogs generate both support bases and critical narratives of any argument. Uncensored debate base adds up to information building process thus making the news, a product persistently unfinished. This feature again maintains two aspects. First, most of the blogs contain an open comment section which is used by the readers to read and debate on a certain blog post. Readership to any blog is unlimited thus attracting people of different ideological backgrounds with their varying ideas, sometimes overtly critical of the blog post or the blogger. In the example of NawaraNegm's blog, discussed above, comments of the viewers ranged from wholehearted support for the proposal to criticism of the judges nullifying them for carrying the legacy of Mubarak regime and even to the banality of having a constitution after parliamentary and presidential election. Some even went on to give different ideas as to how an ideal people's government should be chosen.

Another aspect pertains to the presence of bloggers from different ideological backgrounds. Generally, people from liberal and secular orientation are more inclined to assume an activist's role in the blogosphere, but there are blogs belonging to Muslim brotherhood members (*Ana Ikhwan* or *I am Muslim Brotherhood* by Abdelmenem Mahmoud) or Coptic Christian (*Big Pharaoh*) as well. There have been instances where blogs belonging to a certain ideological sect becomes critical of another. But, with the blog hosting servers remaining open to anyone with an internet connection, different opinions continue to emerge.

Authenticity of the blog posts was confirmed by their shared news sources. As mentioned above, bloggers sourced their blog posts with hyperlinks containing reports of the same incident from different national or international newspapers or other blog posts. For example, Zeinobia filled some of her blog posts only with hyperlinks. In the year 2013, she had 38 blog posts that contained only news links, sometimes followed by a little paragraph of her annotations. Moreover, most of the active bloggers of this time period had past experiences as journalists in formal media institutions. Thus, they were, not just random political analysts but respected journalists, having contacts with and influence over many others of the same profession, and skilled in ways of reporting.

Hossam El Hamalawy covered issues such as protests and repression for Cairo Times in 2002 and later became Cairo Correspondent for the Los Angeles Times. He was also a frequent contributor in Bloomberg News and the BBC, and was senior or founding members of Al Badeel, Egypt Independent and Ahram Online. NawaraNegm worked for Al Shabab (Youth) magazine, Al Ahram Weekly and Nisf al Dunya. Wael Abbas worked as a journalist and a photographer for Al Dastour and as a correspondent of the West Asian region for the German News agency, DPA. The bloggers' association with traditional journalism made them reliable, therefore commanding further influence on public opinion (Naomi Sakr, 2013).

It must be understood at this point that bloggers were certainly not a homogeneous group. Bloggers belonging to different ideological fraction criticized each other. But together they were able to present a different genre of reporting where citizens actively participated rather than being the passive user of produced news. Blogs were not the perpetrators of this uprising, yet their role in this uprising could not be minimized.

Conclusion

Discussions have been made on blogs functioning as citizen's journalists, opening up a new public sphere for people, or as an alternative medium. But as it has been stated before, not so much discussion was held in the context of Arab uprising. The paper, therefore, analyses blogs for playing a critical role in Egyptian uprising. During Egyptian uprising, every day's events were informed and analyzed by the bloggers. While most of the bloggers were already reputed online journalists covering news from the grass root level for a decade at the time of 2011 uprising, the vibrant comment section meant the reader's active contribution.

Moreover, belonging to people from different backgrounds, blogs were able to report the ground news with diversified perspectives. Most of the bloggers' bi-lingual posts allowed people from a broad spectrum to connect themselves with the news of those blog posts. Thus, blogs were able to be multi-perspective, decentralized, participatory and always unfinished; fulfilling the criteria for citizen's journalism. This does not nullify or minimize the significance of social media avenues used for almost the same purpose. But undoubtedly, blogging was able to create a unique as well as an alternative practice of reporting thereby producing a system of journalism where politically active or interested citizens remained involved.

Endnotes

1. It should be noted here, that for the purpose of the paper, the focus would be on the bridge bloggers or bloggers who with an

intention to enable interpersonal communication, crossed the gaps of language, culture and nationality. Mostly these blogs were in English (Zuckerman, 2008).

2. Watchdog journalism pertains to an investigative role that journalists take to make public aware of a certain social or political issue. It is expressed via objective, factual and critical reporting (Eisenman, 1996; Jebril, 2013).

References

Al Ani, B., Mark, G., Chung, J. and Jones, J. (2012), "The Egyptian Blogosphere: A Counter-narrative of the Revolution", Proceedings of ACM 2012 conference on Computer Supported Cooperative Work; retrieved from Donald Bren School of Information and Computer Sciences, University of California, available at: https://www.ics.uci.edu/~gmark/Home_page/Research_files/CSCW2012Egypt.pdf.

Anderson, C. (2006), "Actually Existing", Citizen Journalism Projects and Typologies: Part I, message posted to http://indypendent.typepad.com/academese.

Anderson, C. (2006), "Actually Existing", Citizen Journalism Projects and Typologies: Part II, Message posted to http://indypendent.typepad.com/academese.

Barlow, A.J. (2007), "Rise of Blogosphere", Westport: Praeger Publishers.

Blood, R. (2002), "The Weblog Handbook: Practical Advice on Creating and Maintaining Your Blog", New York, NY: Perseus Publishing.

Bruns, A. (2010), "From Reader to Writer: Citizen Journalism as News Produsage", in J. Hunsinger, L. Klastrup and M. Allen (eds.), 'International Handbook of Internet Research', pp. 119-133, London, England: Springer Science+Business Media B.V.

Bruns, A. (2011), "Citizen Journalism and Everyday Life: A Case Study of Germany's *myHeimat.de*", in B. Franklin and M. Carlson (eds.), 'Journalists, Sources, and Credibility: New Perspectives', pp. 182-195, New York: Routledge.

Domingo, D. and Heinonen, A. (2008), "Weblogs and Journalism: A Typology to Explore the Blurring Boundaries", *Nordicom Review*, 29: 3-15, available at: http://www.nordicom.gu.se/en/publikationer/nordicom-review/nordicom-review-12008.

Eisenman, S. (1996), "Watchdog Journalism: Function and Future", Columbia University, New York, available at: http://www.ee.columbia.edu/~shane/words/watchdog.htm.

El Hamalawy, H. (2012), "MB Official Denounces Labour Protests", Message posted to http://arabawy.org.

El Nawawy, M. and Khamis, S. (2013), "Egyptian Revolution 2.0: Political Blogging, Civic Engagement and Citizen Journalism", New York, NY: Palgrave Macmillan.

Etling, B., Roberts, H. and Faris, R. (2014), "Blogs as an Alternative Public Sphere: The Role of Blogs, Mainstream Media, and TV in Russia's Media Ecology", retrieved from Berkman Klein Centre for Internet and Society, Harvard University, available at: https://papers.ssrn.com/sol3/papers.cfm?abstract_id=2427932.

Faris, D.M. (2010), "Revolutions without Revolutionaries? Social Media Networks and Regime Response in Egypt", available at: http://repository.upenn.edu/edissertations/116.

Faris, D.M. (2013), "Dissent and Revolution in a Digital Age: Social Media, Blogging and Activism in Egypt", London, England: I.B. Tauris.

Gilmour, D. (2004), "We the Media: Grassroots Journalism by the People, for the People", Sebastapol, California: O'Reilly Media.

Glaser, M. (2006), "Your Guide to Citizen Journalism", *Media Shift,* available at: http://mediashift.org.

Jebril, N. (2013), "Is Watchdog Journalism Satisfactory Journalism? A Cross-national Study of Public Satisfaction with Political Coverage", retrieved from Reuters Institute for the Study of Journalism, University of Oxford, available at: http://reutersinstitute.politics.ox.ac.uk/publication/watchdog-journalism-satisfactory-journalism.

Jurrat, N. (2011), "Mapping Digital Media: Citizen Journalism and the Internet", *Open Society Foundations*, 4, 6-18, available at: https://www.opensocietyfoundations.org/reports/mapping-digital-media-citizen-journalism-and-internet.

Mortensen, T. And Walker, J. (2002), "Blogging Thoughts: Personal Publication as an Online Research Tool", in Morrison, A. (ed.), 'Researching ICTs in Context (Inter Media Report 3)', Oslo: University of Oslo.

Negm, N. (2011), "Important Statement", message posted to

http://tahyyes.blogspot.in.

Poell, T. (2009), "Conceptualizing Forums and Blogs as Public Sphere", in Boomen, M. Lammes, S., Lehmann, A., Raessens, J. and Schafer, M. (eds.), 'Digital Material: Tracing New Media in Everyday Life and Technology", Amsterdam: Amsterdam University Press.

Radsch, C. (2008), "Core to Commonplace: The Evolution of Egypt's Blogosphere", *Arab Media and Society,* 6, 1-14, available at:
http://www.arabmediasociety.com/?archive=13.

Radsch, C. (2013), "Digital Dissidence and Political Change: Cyber Activism and Citizen Journalism in Egypt", doctoral dissertation), American University, available at:
http://arabtradeunion.org/sites/default/files/Digital%20Dissidence%20%26%20Political%20Change%20%20Cyberactivism%20and%20Citizen%20Journalism%20in%20Egypt.compressed.pdf.

Riegert, K. (2015), "Understanding Popular Arab Bloggers: From Public Spheres to Cultural Citizens", *International Journal of Communication*, 9, 458-477, available at:
http://ijoc.org/index.php/ijoc/index.

Sakr, N. (2013), "Transformations in Egyptian Journalism", London, England: I.B. Tauris.

Zeinobia (2013), "The Time for Kolena Khaled Said Facebook to be Active", message posted to:
http://egyptianchronicles.blogspot.in.

Zeinobia (2013), "The Completely Forgotten #Rohingya Suffering", message posted to:
http://egyptianchronicles.blogspot.in.

Zuckerman, E. (2008), "Meet the Bridge Bloggers", *Public Choice*, 134 (1/2), 47-65.

3

Democratization and the Role of Women in Arab Uprisings

Poonam Khatana

"Women may need democracy in order to flourish, but the converse is also true: democracy needs women if it is to be an inclusive, representative, and enduring system of government"

—Valentine M. Moghadam [1]

In late 2010, many countries in the Arab world witnessed the waves of widespread protests against the authoritarian regimes, prevalent in the region for last many decades. Democratization, enactment of new constitutions based on equality, liberty and fraternity, free and fair elections etc. were some of the goals of these democratic movements.

Ranging from Tunisia to Egypt, Libya, Yemen, and elsewhere in the region, people from all walks of life participated in these uprisings. Women played a key role in these movements. They have been an integral part of these uprisings marching alongside men. They were on the forefronts in demonstrations that expressed discontentment with the status quo.

In addition to protests on the streets, they used social media (Facebook, Twitter) as a means for mobilizing people. They were detained, beaten, and raped in squares and streets across the region but for protecting the future of the region, they remained in the vanguard of the struggle. Many protagonists of gender parity and women empowerment anticipated that the promotion of women's rights can be done by political transition. Moreover, they believed that the courses of reforms would surely enlarge their role in public sphere. The increasing sense of empowerment and experiences acquired in collective action were some reasons behind this anticipation. Nevertheless, these desires and expectations were sidelined post-Arab uprisings.

Women Uprising in the Arab world

In Arabic, *thawra* means revolution which is known by feminine noun. Even the words *huriya* (freedom) and *intifada* (uprising) come under feminine noun (McDonald, 2013). Women in the Arab world religiously justified the gender of these words by intensely participating in the Arab uprisings. They were at the vanguard of these movements. It is a well-known fact that marginalisation of women in the region is embedded in the social, cultural and religious beliefs which traces its roots from more than a century of suppression. Women raised their voice not only to eliminate ruthless dictators and their dictatorships, but also cultural norms which enforced segregation of women from the public domain.

In mobilising people as well as providing support systems for these movements, women played a critical role. When they were physically absent on the streets in terms of active protests, they used social media as a means to spread their word. They used Facebook and Twitter for publishing videos, creating pages for mobilization, blogging, sending messages, transmitting reports or supplying food, medical aid etc. There were some cases (like in Libya) in which women helped in smuggling arms, collecting intelligence information and providing assistance services. Initially, the aspirations of Arab women were alike to their male counterparts like justice, dignity and democracy. However, later on, they called for their rights as citizens along with challenging the patriarchal structure which limited their role in the Arab society (Tannirm and Badaan, 2013; Raddaoui, 2014).

From Tunisia to Yemen, their activism played a crucial role in order to establish democracy in the region. According to Gallup [2] survey, women made up almost one-third of the protesters in Egypt's January 25, 2011 uprising. In this process, they underwent a lot of pain of being imprisoned or severely tortured for their activities. However, among these courageous women, some female activists played an influential role for the advocacy of womens' rights by upholding the consistent momentum of struggle against the regimes. Lina ben Mhenni, Asmaa Mahfouz, Tawakkol Karman, Fathi Terbil, Danya Bashir Hobba and many more registered their names in that list of leading female activists in the Arab uprisings (Good, 2012; Tannirm and Badaan, 2013).

Leading Women Activists: A Brief Description

Since the wave of the uprising began from Tunisia to the other parts of the region, description about the activists has been written accordingly. During the regime of former Tunisian President Zine el-Abidine ben Ali, a Tunisian blogger Lina ben Mhenni, was one of the cyber activists who blogged using her real identity. However, Ben Ali regime expurgated her blog *A Tunisian Girl*. Her writings played a critical role in providing first hand information of activities occurring in Tunisia in the absence of national media due to censorship by the government. Even after the collapse of the regime, her persistent role in condemning the double standard of the Ennahda Party regarding women was quite significant. For her commendable contribution during the Tunisian uprising, [3] her name was nominated for the 2011 Nobel Peace Prize (Dhillon, 2014; Lowrance, 2016).

The Facebook video which instigated a wave of protests against Egyptian President Hosni Mubarak was posted by an Egyptian activist Asmaa Mahfouz [4] on January 18, 2011. This video was an attempt to urge Egyptians to break the fences of fear and protest against the authoritarian regime in Tahrir Square. The credit for the mass protests of January 25, 2011 went to her video which got viral widespread (Economic and Social Commission for Western Asia, 2013; Amnesty International, 2012).

She was arrested on charges of disparaging Egyptian military officers and infuriating unrest in the region. Though she was referred to a military court, but a wave of support from activists ultimately forced Supreme Council of the Armed Forces (SCAF) to withdraw charges against her. Nawara Negm is one more well-known Egyptian political activist and blogger who played a leading role in the Egyptian Uprising. She stated that "Just like there is no giving up on the call for freedom, democracy, and human rights in the Arab world, there is also no giving up when it comes to calling for women's rights, political representation, and equal participation in all walks of life" (Khamis, 2011).

The protest of hundreds of women against the detention of Fathi Terbil [5] in Benghazi marked the commencement of the uprising in Libya (Mayar, 2013). These protests which got started against the detention eventually got developed into a country-wide demonstration to end Muammar al-Qaddafi's 42-year rule due to violent suppression. Danya Bashir Hobba and Alaa Murabit became leading figures in these uprisings. By organising shipments of medical and humanitarian aid during the civil war, Hobba contributed significantly.

Similarly, Alaa Murabit by forming *The Voice of Libyan Women*, one of the first womens' associations post-uprising, exhibited her important contribution. The main objective of the organization is to cater the need of the political participation and economic empowerment of Libyan women along with elimination of all forms of gender-based violence. Inspirations from the other parts (Egypt, Libya and Tunisia) of the region motivated Yemeni women to raise their voice against the regime of President Ali Abdallah Saleh. In this whole struggle against the regime and to establish democracy, Tawakkol Karman, a journalist played a crucial role by organising student rallies. She is known as "the Mother of the Yemeni Uprising". For her contribution in Arab Uprisings, she was awarded the 2011 Noble Peace Prize (International Crisis Group, 2011).

Samar Yazbek, a renowned novelist and journalist, published her views regarding cruelties happening in the streets, prisons and hospitals under the regime of President Bashar Al-Assad in Syria. As a result, she was imprisoned and tortured by the regime. Though she fled Syria and has taken shelter in Europe, she continued her struggle against the regime by her writings and other online works. Her recent book, *A Woman in the Crossfire: Diaries of the Syrian Revolution*, discusses alarming opinions on the Syrian uprising. Razan Zaitouneh, writer and human rights lawyer is another leading Syrian activist who played a very important role by providing information on the atrocities being committed when severe restrictions were imposed on national media and foreign journalists.

She is the co-founder of the Local Coordination Committee (LCC) [6] which played a major role in the Syrian uprising (Edemariam, 2012). Even in Bahrain, women were very active to demand democracy and to end sectarian discrimination. Mariam al-Khawaja was among them. This young activist used social media for publicising human rights violations taking place during these protests. Jalilaal-Salman, teacher and Vice President of the Bahrain Teachers' Association (BTA) contributed in these pro-democracy movements by organising the teachers' strikes against the authoritarian regime. As a result, she met with the same harassment as occurred in above cases. She was arrested and tortured both in terms of verbal and physical abuse by the security forces.

Role of the Social Media

Social networks played their crucial role not only during the uprisings but also became influential devices post-uprisings for women fighting back. Women strongly used social networks such as Facebook and Twitter to mobilise women as well as to proliferate about the injustice prevailing in the region. In addition to this, promoting gender equality and raising awareness regarding challenges faced by Arab women post-uprising were also demonstrated by using this medium of social media. Some of the cases of using social networks for raising their voice against the prevailing authoritarian regimes from Lina ben Mhenni (Tunisia), Asmaa Mahfouz (Egypt) Alaa Murabit (Libya), Samar Yazbek (Syria) to Mariam al-Khawaja (Bahrain) have already been discussed.

BaheyaYaMasr, an online womens' group, founded in 2012 is one more example of it. Following the overthrow of President Mubarak in Egypt, their exclusion from decision-making process forced them to form this online group. The main objectives of this movement included full citizenship rights, equality of gender in the constitutional process along with eradication of gender-based violence. Other movements in the form of Facebook pages like *Girls Revolution* created by a young Egyptian girl Ghadeer Ahmed and *Revolution against Patriarchal Society,* formed by a young Iraqi girl RuqayaAbidalli in 2012 are other significant examples of using social media for spreading their struggle against the injustice that was taking place in the Arab societies. Since the motive behind these online movements was to unite Arab women and men across the countries, forming a collective identity and character were never confined to particular countries (Al-Rawi, 2014).

Apart from this, Diala Haidar, Yalda Younes, Farah Barqawi and Sally Zohney, four women living in different countries, were the motivational forces behind the creation of Facebook page titled *Uprising of Women in the Arab World* in October 2011. Even this campaign advocated for the equal rights of Arab women along with establishing unity across the region. This initiative was taken by seeing unfavourable prospects for gender justice after the uprisings. In addition to these two movements, other online campaign, such as the "Voice of Egyptian Women" was also launched. This was initiated in order to remember the legacy of famous Egyptian women such as Hoda Shaarawi, Doreya Shafiq and Umm Kulthum. For making ordinary people to understand that women are more than the sexual object was also one of the objectives of this campaign (Tannirm and Badaan, 2013).

Regime Changed but Challenges Exist

The participation of women in the popular uprisings can be described as the roller coaster ride. They protest and mobilize support in order to achieve rights of women to live with dignity. However, after the collapse of regimes, women were sidelined by pushing them into their private spheres. Women have made their voices heard in the Arab uprisings at many levels. However, these voices of women have lost in the post-uprisings period. Both old and new Arab regimes alike considered women participation and their raised voices a threat to the patriarchal nature of Arab society. As a result, they reacted ruthlessly. In some countries, women and young girls have become prone to the risks of trafficking, exploitation and sexual abuse. Apart from this, rape has become a major weapon for preventing women to raise their voice, which left many in traumatised condition. Many women due to all these fear of physical and sexual violence were forced to hide or flee. However, none of these brutal tactics achieved success in crushing the spirit of Arab women seeking justice.

The Arab uprisings encouraged women to challenge gender based discrimination and move assertively into politics. However, domestic factors did not allow them to pursue that. Post-uprising, religion is not the greatest challenge to women but the lack of economic and social development along with security poses a crucial challenge. At present, Arab women face three interconnected challenges namely, guaranteeing gender equality and women's rights in the new constitutions; increasing women's political participation; and mitigating the potential impact of conservative politics and political Islam on their empowerment.

After the Arab uprisings, the outlook for women's rights remains mixed and uncertain. In the World Economic Forum's 2012 Global Gender Gap report, Middle East countries ranked poorly in which UAE came at 107 out of 135 countries while the Yemen attained the last place. The paradox is that almost all Middle East countries scored more poorly than in 2011, due to low political participation for women (Care International Policy Report, 2013). According to the recent report released by UN Women, 99.3 percent of women have faced sexual harassment in Egypt, while 49 percent accepted increase in sexual harassment after January 2011.

Moreover, 83 percent reported about the insecurity felt by them in public places. Six years later, we witness that although women supported the Arab uprisings, it appears the Arab uprisings did not support women. They have been sidelined in the official decision-making roles in some countries despite witnessing their presence at the forefront in these uprisings.

According to the Inter-Parliamentary Union, in 2012, Arab States still had the lowest representation of women in Parliament, with women holding only 13.2 percent of parliamentary seats throughout the Arab region. In the Sultanates of Oman, Qatar and Saudi Arabia, there was no female representation due to the absence of elected parliaments in these countries (Soufi, 2009). It was only in 2015, when Saudi Arabia for the first time in its history allowed women to vote as well as to contest in the municipal elections (Murphy, 2015). In this historic election of Saudi Arabia, 17 female councillors got elected which is a great breakthrough in the Saudi society where women are still banned from driving and face routine discrimination (Black, 2015).

According to a report published by UN Women in 2011, there was no legislation that prevents violence against women in Tunisia, Libya, and Yemen. Egypt is the only exception in this case. Nevertheless, all these countries have ratified the Convention to Eliminate All Forms of Discrimination against Women (CEDAW) (Weiss, 2003). Therefore, instead of making new commitments, to cleanse the already existing system with transparency and effectiveness has become a major challenge.

Most transitional bodies, such as the Syrian National Council (SNC), had no women representatives. The number of women participating in drafting the new Egyptian constitution was minimal. Women and youth shared only 10 percent of the drafting committee's representation. Egypt abolished its quota for women's parliamentary seats, which reduced women's representation from 12 percent in the 2010 parliament to less than 2 percent of seats before the 2012 parliament was dissolved. It indicated a significant rollback of political rights (Inter Parliamentary Union, 2014; Esfandiari and Kendra, 2015; Baradei and Dina, 2013). This is almost contradictory to the UN mandate which called for at least 30 percent share of female parliamentarians since this much of share is necessary to make a difference in policy and political decisions (Moghadam, 2014: 138). Despite standing side-by-side with their male fellows in public squares during the protests, women were once again relegated out of the public space and subjected to the regression of many of their rights.

While many countries witnessed a regression in women's status, some managed to protect women's rights. Tunisia provided a model for other countries in the region of a successful transition. Prior to the uprising, the country already had a progressive constitution and a personal status law. Following the overthrow of President Zine El Abidine Ben Ali in 2011, Tunisia elected the National Constituent Assembly and more than 20 percent of the deputies were women. After Libya's 2012 elections, 33 women held seats in its 200 member parliament. Libyan women also held 6 out of 60 seats in the constitutional drafting committee (Doherty, 2012; Human Rights Watch, 2013).

In Yemen, during the period of constitutional drafting and before the country descended into civil war, women secured 4 out of 17 seats in the country's constitutional drafting committee (Esfandiari and Kendra, 2015). However, at present, considering Tunisia as an exception, women in other Arab countries are paying the price for raising their voice against the regime and demanding equal rights. Tawakkol Karman mentioned the cases of Yemen, Syria and Egypt where women are getting punished by counter-revolutionary forces to suppress their voices. However, these measures failed to break them and they are still fighting for their equal rights (Karman, 2016).

The waves of transition and impact of uprisings was not confined to places where it actually occurred. The impact can be seen in the overall regional landscape. Men and women from all walks of life felt empowered more than ever before to participate in protests and debate, and voice their opinion in solidarity with others hoping for change, freedom and dignity. A process of constitutional revision is an important initiative in any political transformation. The foundation of a new constitution should be based on the system of good governance and new social contract. The relationship between citizens and the state is very much shaped in accordance with the nature of constitution. Constitutional processes will be incomplete until it fulfils the aspirations of all its citizens without any gender based discrimination. In short, it should be inclusive and participatory and utilize public debate and broad-based consultations to ensure that the aspirations of all citizens are met.

Conclusion

Arab uprisings can be seen as a new window of opportunities for the mobilization of women. The involvement of women in transitional processes will contribute to the advancement of womens' rights. It will give a voice to voiceless women, to initiate legislations and reforms with regard to their gender in the society. The commitment to gender balance can only make democratic systems stable and legitimate. Women should be part of the policy and law-making for fulfilling their diverse needs and interests. In addition to the constitutional provisions, Arab countries need to develop short-term and long-term plans to empower women politically, economically and socially. There also needs to be a system of proper and meticulous follow-up of these plans, where the governments and civil societies engage in a meaningful partnership to ensure women's empowerment. If we look at the whole gamut carefully, we can very well see that women are the cornerstone to any democratic society and they are the ones who nurture and educate children.

Therefore, from the above discussions, it can be concluded that participation of women in political and economic processes is an urgent need in the Arab region during the time when transition, re-establishing and reconstitution of the governments and political processes are taking their due place. It will not be appropriate to say that changes are not there. Women are getting their share but that share is very less and does not cover the wider part. So, increasing their role in the political process whether giving them charge of policy makers or create that space of their say in decision-making process is the need of the hour.

Endnotes

1. Valentine Moghadam is a famous feminist scholar, sociologist and an activist. She has authored many books such as 'Globalizing Women: Transnational Feminist Networks' (2005); 'Identity Politics and Women: Cultural Reassertions and Feminisms in International Perspective' (1994); 'Modernizing Women: Gender and Social Change in the Middle East' (1993); 'Women, Work and Economic Reform in the Middle East and North Africa' (1998). In addition to this, she has written articles like 'Engendering Democracy: Women and the Mass Social Protests in the Middle East and North Africa' (2011).
2. Gallup, Inc. is an American research-based, global performance-management consulting company. It was founded by George Gallup in 1935. It is known for its public opinion polls conducted in several countries.
3. This is also known as Jasmine Uprising.
4. She is one of the founders of the April 6 Youth Movement. It is an Egyptian activist group established in spring 2008 to support the workers in El-Mahalla El-Kubra, an industrial town, who were planning to strike on April 6.
5. She was the lawyer who represented the cases of over 1,000 prisoners allegedly massacred by Libyan security forces in the Abu Salim Prison in 1996.
6. LCC coordinates demonstrations, documents and disseminates information on human rights abuses and links with international and independent media.

References

Al-Rawi, Ahmed (2014), "Framing the Online Women's Movements in the Arab World", *Information, Communication and Society*, 17:9, 1147-1161.

"After the Arab Uprisings: Women on Rights, Religion and Rebuilding (2012), Gallup, available at: http://www.gallup.com/poll/155306/arab-uprisings-women-rights-religion-rebuilding.aspx.

Al-Qazzaz, Ayad (1978), "Current Status of Research on Women in the Arab World", *Middle Eastern Studies*, 14(3), 372-380.

Al Rawaf, HayaSaad and Simmons Cyril (1991), "The Education of Women in Saudi Arabia", *Comparative Education*, 27(3), 287-295.

Alsuwaigh, Siham A. (1989), "Women in Transition: The Case of Saudi Arabia", *Journal of Comparative Family Studies*, 20(1), 67-78.

"Arab Spring or Arab Autumn? Women's Political Participation in the Uprisings and Beyond: Implications for International Donor Policy" (2013), *Care International Policy Report*, London, Care International.

Bahry, Louay (1982), "The New Saudi Woman: Modernizing in an Islamic Framework", *Middle East Journal*, 36(4), 502-515.

Dhillon, Aamna (2014), "Social Media and Revolution: The Importance of the Internet in Tunisia's Uprising", Independent Study Project, (ISP) Collection Paper 1938.

Dodd, Peter C. (1974), "The Effect of Religious Affiliation on Women's Role in Middle Eastern Arab Society", *Journal of Comparative Family Studies*, 5(2), 117-129.

Doumato, Eleanor Abdella (1991), "Women and the Stability of Saudi Arabia", *Middle East Report*, No. 171, 34-37.

Edemariam, Aida (2012), "Syrian Writer Samar Yazbek: A Woman Like Me Makes Life Difficult", available at: https://www.theguardian.com/books/2012/oct/13/interview-samar-yazbek-syria-revolution.

El Deeb, Bouthaina (n.d), "Study on Ways and Methods to Eliminate Sexual Harassment in Egypt: Results/Outcomes and Recommendations Summary", UN Women, available at: http://www.un.org.eg/Publications.aspx?pageID=43.

Esfandiari, Haleh and Kendra Heideman (2015), "The Role and Status of Women after the Arab Uprisings", *Strategic Sectors,*

Culture and Society, Mediterranean Year Book.
"Expansion or Contraction? Women's Rights in the MENA Region in 2015", Middle East Program, Washington DC: Woodrow Wilson International Centre for Scholars, available at: www.wilsoncenter.org/publication-series/expansionor-contraction-women%E2%80%99s-rights-themena-region-2015.
Fargues, Philippe (2005), "Women in Arab Countries: Challenging the Patriarchal System?", *Reproductive Health Matters*, 13(25), 43-48.
Garvey, Amy Jacques (1972), "The Role of Women in Liberation Struggles", *The Massachusetts Review*, 13(1-2), 109-112.
Good, Allison (2012), "The Heroines of the Arab World", available at: http://foreignpolicy.com/2012/04/23/The heroines-of-the-Arab-world.
Hussein, Aziza (1953), "The Role of Women in Social Reform in Egypt", *Middle East Journal*, 7(4), 440-450.
Ibnouf, F.O. (2012), "To Arab Women: Golden Opportunity to Stand-up for Your Rights", *Global Advanced Research Journal of History, Political Science and International Relations*, 1(5), 113-117.
Ibnouf, F.O. (2013), "Women and the Arab Spring: A Window of Opportunity or More of the Same?, available at: http://www.e-http://www.e-ir.info/2013/05/21/women-and-the-arab-spring-revolutions-is-there-a-window-of-opportunity-or-can-we-expect-more-of-the-same.
Joseph, Suad (1986), "Women and Politics in the Middle East", *Middle East Report,* 138, 3-7.
Lowrance, S. (2016), "Was the Revolution Tweeted? Social Media and the Jasmine Revolution in Tunisia", *Digest of Middle East Studies*, 25, 155-176.
Mayer, Ann Elizabeth (2013), "Building the New Libya: Lessons to Learn and to Unlearn", *Journal of International Law*, 34(2), 365-387.
McDonald, David A. (2013), "My Voice is My Weapon: Music, Nationalism, and the Poetics of Palestinian Resistance", Durham: Duke University Press.
Moaddel, Mansoor (2006), "The Saudi Public Speaks: Religion, Gender, and Politics", *International Journal of Middle East Studies*, 38(1), 79-108.

Moghadam, Valentine M. (2004), "The Gender of Democracy: The Link between Women's Rights and Democratization in the Middle East, available at: http://carnegieendowment.org/sada/?fa=21226.

Moghadam, Valentine M. (2014), "Modernising Women and Democratisation after the Arab Spring", *The Journal of North African Studies*, 19(2), 137-142.

Moghadam, Valentine M. (2011), "Engendering Democracy: Women and the Mass Social Protests in the Middle East and North Africa", available at: http://www.nidemocracy.org/en/publications/engendering-democracy-women-and-the-mass-social-protests-in-the-middle-east-and-north-africa.

Munn, M. and N. Cleminshaw (2013), "Has the Arab Spring Been Beneficial for Women?", *The Parliamentarians Network for Conflict Prevention*, available at: http://pncp.net/opinions/has-arab-spring-been-beneficial-women.

Murphy, Brian (2015), "Women in Saudi Arabia Vote for the First Time", available at: https://www.washingtonpost.com/world/saudi-women-vote-for-the-first-time/2015/12/12/9ad0b898-9ad0-11e5-aca6-1ae3be6f06d2_story.html?utm_term=.9868e9438a47.

Raddaoui, Ola (2014), "Role of Women in the Arab Spring Revolutions: A New Perspective on Islamic Feminism (Tunisia-Egypt-Yemen)", Social Justice Research Centre Grant Awards, Paper 24.

Peterson, J.E. (1989), "The Political Status of Women in the Arab Gulf States", *Middle East Journal*, 43(1), 34-50.

Saif, Shaima (2014), "The Role of Women in the Arab Uprising Across the Middle East", available at: http://uk.upf.org/leadership-conferences/645-womens-role-in-the-arab-spring.

Saleh, Saneya (1972), "Women in Islam: Their Role in Religious and Traditional Culture", *International Journal of Sociology of the Family*, 2(2), 193-201.

Sau, Ranjit (2004), "Democracy and Reform: Voices in West Asia", *Economic and Political Weekly*, 39(38), 4232-4234.

Soufi, H. (2009), "Parliamentary Democracy and the Representation of Women in Arab Countries", *Contemporary Arab Affairs*, 2(2), 252-271.

"Supporting Women in the Democratic Transition Process in Libya", The International Institute for Democracy and Electoral Assistance (IIDEA), available at: http://www.idea.int/wana/supporting-women-in-the-democratic-transition-process-in-libya.cf.

Tannirm, Dina and Vivienne Badaan (2013), "Women and Participation in the Arab Uprisings: A Struggle for Justice", Economic and Social Commission for Western Asia (ESCWA), New York.

Touba, Jacquiline Rudolph (1991), "Roles of Women in Muslim Countries", *International Journal of Sociology of the Family*, 21(1), 1-6.

Waylen, Georgina (1994), "Women and Democratization: Conceptualizing Gender Relations in Transition Politics", *World Politics*, 46(3), 327-354.

Weiss, A.M. (2003), "Interpreting Islam and Women's Rights: Implementing CEDAW in Pakistan", *International Sociology*, 18(3), 581-601.

"Women Rights and the Arab Spring Middle East/North Africa Overview and Fact Sheet" (2011), International Women's Democracy Networks, available at: http://www.iwdn.learningpartnership.org/tag/middle-east-and-north-africa.

"Women and Participation in the Arab Uprisings: A Struggle for Justice" (2013), Economic and Social Commission for Western Asia (ESWA), New York.

"Women and the Arab Spring: An Ongoing Struggle for Equal Rights", United Nations Human Rights, Office of the High Commissioner for Human rights, available at: http://www.ohchr.org/EN/ NewsEvents/Pages/WomenandtheArabspringanongoingstrugglef orequalrights.aspx#sthash.XTOldR8U.dpuf.

4

Arab Feminism and its Socio-Political Impact on Arab Society

Navneet Samuel

Introduction

Women's status in the Arab world has been a critical issue in many recent debates especially in the West. There have been many perceptions and assumptions about how women in the Arab world live and how they are treated by society, state, and their families. Arab women are largely portrayed by many as being oppressed, weak, and passive. However, Arab women have demonstrated their skills and egalitarian status in all fields of socio-political life. Women's oppression in the Arab world has been depicted and interpreted through the lens of Western feminists and audiences. Women's status in the Arab world, most of the time, has been read out of its social, political, cultural, religious, and historical context. Women are potent symbols of identity. They signify a vision of society that identifies a nation. The Arab world provides a perfect example of this. Arab women have taken active roles in the gender debate and the socio-political struggles within their societies. The results of this participation have yielded a number of different interpretations of what is meant to be a feminist. It has also created a very complex relationship between the West and Western feminism which has deep implications in contemporary gender politics.

Islamic Feminism

The term 'feminism' is a modern concept and was used in the late eighteenth century. It took many frames to suit the voices of women across globe in demanding equal status in their respective societies. Feminism as a phenomenon engaged with issues of women's right's liberation and gender equality. While this phenomenon spread rapidly on all shores, it went deep into the West Asian region. The Arab women are the most discussed on the issues of rights, liberty and gender equality. However, the feminism of the West changed into multiple names relating to its usage in a particular region or class. The Western feminism, turned into Arab feminism among the women of the Arab region as discussed but what interesting perspective it gave was the assimilation of indigenous cultures, religion and ideologies. It was further conceptualized by neo-feminism where scholars argued that Islam is compatible with feminism and gave it a religious dimension.

The Middle Eastern women who embraced feminist identities which are closely associated with Islam had turned aside from the Western modernization. The re-emergence of Hijab is an example as it signals an adherence towards Islamic morals. The Islamic codes for the way of life gave women multiple roles and duties which according to Muslim women became a part of a newly developed concept called 'Islamic Feminism'. Since the Westerners saw the Middle Eastern women as oppressed and having no rights, the idea of Western feminism took hold in the upper class women of the Middle Eastern societies. The colonial representation of Muslim women as oppressed and victimized by a backward misogynist society ignited an urge to intervene and liberate women from their heathen societies (Zine, 2002). Many women discarded the traditional norms of their religion and started adopting Western feminism in a way to proclaim their new liberation. However, at the same time, traditional women with Islamic values cultured into a phenomenon which described feminism in an Islamic way.

Scholars challenged patriarchal reading of the Quran and the Hadiths to demonstrate that it is not the texts but the interpretations that allow patriarchal traditions to persist. Feminism although appeared during the colonial period, had shadowed the previous concepts related to women and their liberation worldwide; it reflected feminisms of all ideologies coming together under it.

The Islamic feminism built its root in the late 1980s to explicate gender equality and social justice in re-reading of the sacred texts of Islam. The scholars and activists immediately recognized the balance between Islam and feminism and then termed it as a new form of feminism called 'Islam feminism'. The tradition of Islam in treating women and gender equality became the key components of Islamic feminism. The role of women during the time of Prophet Mohammad to the sayings of the Prophet pertaining to the status of women became important, especially the issue of marriage, divorce, inheritance, education and infanticide. Feminists in the Middle East have pursued institution building and reforms of legal frameworks and policies that allows women empowerment using human rights and emancipatory Islam or Islamic feminism (Moghadam, 2007).

The first modern women to take Quranic exegesis was Aisha Abd al Rahman in 1959. Her writings constituted many of the feminist themes. Scholars from Turkey and Iran used this term in their writings and it rapidly spread among the other Muslim societies. Turkish writer Nilofur Gole used the term Islamic feminism in the late 1980s which is considered to be the first exclusive use of the concept in the Islamic world. The Arabic synonym for the word feminism is called 'Nisa-ist', from the word 'nisa' meaning women and which is now widely used by contemporary Arab women writers. The Islamic feminism is a modern progressive term but the divine rights and roles of women bestowed in Islam have taken place as early as the seventh century Islam.

Hence, it is important to emphasize the difference between Arab feminism and Islamic feminism. Primarily, Arab feminism became a movement which was inspired by Western feminist discourses and largely embraced by Arab natives of Muslims as well as Christians and other societies. Although, the concept of Arab feminism differed from Western ways because Arabs have their own culture, heritage and societal issues whereas, Western feminism was largely based on women's freedom in all sectors of public and private lives.

Secondarily, Islamic feminism became a movement among the Muslim women of the Middle East and other Muslim dominated regions; it carried a backbone of religious dogmatic approach rather than being a secular movement. Islamic feminist writers focused their works on the teachings of Islam and its compatibility with equal rights for women. In some cases, as I have mentioned, Islamic feminism came into existence as an alternative for the Western feminism in the lives of adherent Muslim women. Islamic feminism advocates rights of women given in Islam as equal to the rights demanded by Western feminists of modern times. This movement rapidly spread all over the world and thus created numerous debates on the issues of Muslim women and secular women. Women activists and scholars addressed issues of violence, hijab, property rights, inheritance, divorce etc. Still, Muslim personal law advocates women rights in many countries (Badran, 2008).

Sharia and jurisprudence is a source of legislation in many Islamic countries. Scholars emphasized on the socio-religious value of Islamic feminism as a part of divine roles given to women and they should abide by the religious structures in a progressive way. Islamic nationalists stressed women's role in the development of a nation-building. Women like Zainab al Ghazali campaigned for women and nation in Islamic terms whereas Doria Shafik campaigned for women and human rights in secular terms according to Western ideological terms. Therefore, it became a parallel narrative of the Western feminism in the Muslim societies where Islamic scholars tried to solve the issues of women by theorizing indicators of emancipation in formulating possible solutions for women under the realm of religion. It can be said that the greater task of Islamic feminists is to separate religion and culture because stability of society is met with women staying in their natural and proper places (Fowcett, 2013).

Exploring Women's Movements in The Arab Lands

Since Western feminism became a radical challenge to the premise of Islam, it also progressed in developing gender roles which were unknown to the Middle Eastern societies. The division of societies based on labour gradually lessened in the West whereas in the Middle East there was a distinct social atmosphere related to a particular place, a village, a city etc. More importantly, in the class divisions of upper and lower class, became the axis of these societies where class would decide the education and skilful level of a woman or a man.

The upper class women had a different lifestyle compared to a woman of lower class. Upper class women were encouraged to get educated and do jobs as a result of their interaction with Western women. These women would provide companionships to their husbands in their business and more often hosted westerners (Whitcher, 2005). The Western concepts rapidly grew roots in the mind sets of the upper class women which culminated into the participation of women in public sphere under a mixture of traditional and secular ideologies. This new stratum of women became the force of women's movement in the Middle East. The class and gender struggles became topics of debates with drastic socio and political and economic crises that occurred from the start of the 20th century.

Two major changes that imparted women in the region were the World War I, and the dissolution of Ottoman Empire. The colonial powers of Britain and France took hold of the entire Middle East and North Africa. The early Arab nationalism had been against the Ottoman rule but after the war, these Western countries became the focus of nationalism which was directed towards achieving independence from colonialism (Keddie and Beth, 1993). The roles of gender reforms were necessary to combat the situations during freedom struggle where women were equally important with men to carry forward the national issues. The inter-War period witnessed the rise of women's organizations, primarily in Egypt, where women emphasized national liberation along with demands for gender laws reformation.

During national struggles, women learnt new experiences, visibility and respect. Majority of the women's organizations had educational and charitable aims, which further developed into creating institutions for society as a whole so that women could become in charge of what they want to adapt to or get directions for. This provided a framework for further expansion in these fields.

The new role for women was stressed on the writings and teachings of women groups to acquire modern needs to enter public spheres and strengthen their nation. The women liberation movement first started in Egypt at the height of Egypt's National Revolution against the British. Women organizations were established under the aegis of the Nationalist movement. Huda Sahrawi headed the women committee and later formed the Egyptian Feminist Union (Roded, 2008).

The first Arab Women's Conference was held in Cairo in 1930s as a result of the change of the Palestinian question into an all Arab issue and the rise of Pan Arabism. The publications of essays and poems raised new consciousness amongst women. Salons and committees for women opened up where discussion on women topics took place. Hifni Nasif's collection of essays was published in 1910, titled, 'Al-nisaiyaatt' meaning 'feminist' (Hoda, 1998). Men also supported feminist issues like Ahmad lutfy al-sayyid. Egyptians of all religions created a secular feminist movement and struggled for the secular nationalism agenda.

From Egypt, the women's movement travelled to other Arab states with resemblance to its feminist and nationalist character. In Palestine, women's movement led to the establishment of self-help groups because of economic and political factors which existed together with more political or academic-centred women organizations (Al-Ali, 2002). Jewish women, who migrated to Palestine from other places faced limitations in their actions; they made their own interpretations of nationalism as per their experiences. They mostly came from middle class and were affiliated with the "HibbotTzion Movement". They faced poverty, harsh physical labour, lack of shelter, disease, overwork and external dangers (Katz, 2003). These women, comprising 18 percent, were mostly young and saw themselves as Halutzini and called themselves as labour Zionists. They preferred socialist module of classless society to obtain equal rights.

The Israeli women become heroines of women's movements by working very hard physically on fields and domestic chores and at the same time contributing to warfare, carrying guns in one hand and in the other a hoe. They faced criticism from men, who did not want them to go out of the houses because of the social patriarchal structure and threats from becoming victims in wars. A women workers' union called as "MoetzetHapo' was established and later Women Equal Rights league worked for several years. In Palestine, despite limitations, women participated in demonstrations during the national protests against Israel. They formed 'Arab Women's Society in 1921, and wrote many articles and poetries in magazines. They became the voice of Arab women by writings columns in Al-Ahram and other magazines. Atufa al Husayni and May Ziade, became largely popular in promoting women's agendas in public and international spheres.

In Syria, Nazik al-Abid, wrote in various journals and took part in many women conferences. In Turkey, women were granted voting rights by reforms of the Tanzimat. In 1930, the first Women's Oriental Congress was held in Damascus, which called for gender equality reforms. The most important aspect of these conferences was the intermingling of Arab women and their issues which gave them an ideology of Pan Arab Feminism. The Cairo conference of 1944 by the Arab feminists formulated fifty one resolutions for the equal rights for women and even feminized the language (UNESCO, 2010).

Without doubt, the education among women progressed rapidly since illiteracy was widespread among women before the independence. A high rise in literacy among women came after such movements where girls were ahead of boys in countries like Algeria, Lebanon, Tunisia, Kuwait and Jordan. The demographical transition also started in these countries and the growth of population fell down. Women's participation in job market also rose up in these countries with some having their own businesses (Ibid.)

Rise of Arab Feminism and Feminist Writings

Since the realization of Western education, culture and technology accounted for the European strength throughout the world. It led to the modernizing of reforms among the women of the 19th century Arab world. Starting with the colonization of Algeria in 1830 by France to the downfall of Ottoman Empire, the Arab world was under the realm of Western ideas. The advancement of education became a key factor in the realization of gender equality among the Arabs. It was Muhammad Ali's educational mission and Rifa'a al Tahtawi's advocacy towards women education which became a cornerstone in making Arab women stand up for equal rights.

While arguments for reforming women's position were first stated by the Ottomans who wrote in Turkish and in Arabic by many other thinkers from Egypt, educator and Islamic modernist Mohammad Abduh was the first Arab modernist who argued that Islam is gender egalitarian and it advocates for equal treatment of women. Arab Modernism, pioneered by Abduh continued in the works of Jamal-al-din Afghani and Rashid Rida. By the late 19th century, women launched journals and articles advocating new women's roles (Keddic, 1993). The Egyptian debates on women rapidly spread among other Arab countries where voices of modern

Arab feminism began to grow deeper. Women started participating in arts, poetry, press and most importantly in the national liberation movements.

This new enlightenment in the Arab women culminated in the birth of new feminist discourses in the entire Arab world. The proliferation of these discourses was maintained by a large number of printed journals and magazines. Women talked on issues of education, marriage, work, suffrage etc. which further culminated in the formation of women's associations and committees. The study of Arab feminism revolves around the way women come up with power structures and how they behave to reshape the limits of the liberty. The most discussed writer on women was Egypt's Qasim Amin who wrote "Liberation of Women' (1899), which advocated Western ideas and ways for women, though, criticized by many clerics of that time but it very widely touched the issues of Arab women. He advocated equal rights for women in all social spheres for the development of the society. He is considered by many scholars as the 'Father of Arab feminism'. However, women were not in unity and uniformity in all the Arab world to call oneself an Arab feminist in those days.

Although, Ottoman women played crucial roles but it was the Huda Sharawi of Egypt who first formed the Egyptian Feminist union. She advocated Pan-Arab feminism which led to movements of women liberation debates in the whole Arab world. Not only did Amin write on women's issue after the modernization call of Abduh and Afghani, women also came forward for reforms in education for women. Among these women, Aisha al-Taymvriyya, daughter of an Egyptian Turkish family, is considered as the first to raise the idea of gender parity by many.

She advocated education for women which was published in 1889 but was based on conservative premise. Another woman by the name Fatima AliyeHanin, daughter of a prominent Ottoman reformist, argued against polygamy and published a book on Muslim women in 1891. Another innovation of that time was the first series of lectures by women for women. Huda Sharawi wrote in her diary about her visit to French feminist Margret Clement and invited her to give lectures in Egyptian university under the patronage of Royal Highness 'Ayn-al-Hayat', wife of crown prince (Roded, 2008).

It was the start of the lecture series where a large number of women gave talks. The feminism of Sharawi acted on the unveiling to be an important and significant act for women's liberation. She openly valorized Western ways being as civilized as their native ways. Another feminist writer of that time was Malak Hinfi Naseef (b.1886), also known as Bahithat al-Badiyar. Naseef valorized native culture, history, traditions etc. and at the same time, she opposed unveiling because she understood her society (Hankin, 1996).

Nassef was very well welcomed among Muslim women and her writings were widely published. A co-worker for Sharawi, Al Gahazali, was a major influence in Egypt, though she was in disagreement with Sharawi in many ways. She founded her own organization by the name of Muslim Women's Association. It was a huge success as more and more women joined hands. Therefore, two kinds of Arab feminism rose in spheres, the one which had Western values, ideas and ways and the other was the native and indigenous call for emancipation of women. Both had strong roots and followings which often clashed in ideological contexts of Western imitation and indigenous egalitarianism. Women were recruited to be national actors but their ability to become so was still bound by culturally accepted feminine boundaries (Whitcher, 2005).

It should be understood that the women in Arab Societies had different roles and social structures from the colonizers. From the Ottoman women to the rural class women, they had certain rights according to their culture. The Western examples of feminism drew remarkable attention in the Arab world because of the traditional breakings of bonds prevalent in their societies and how women spoke up about their issues publicly. The role of education and technology provided a platform for the Arab women to stand for their causes and triggered debates over their newly adopted liberty in the name of feminism and the traditional norms of religion which dominated their society.

Conclusion

Thus, women organizations and committees proved to accelerate women's participation in organized sectors which improved their status and living conditions. The progress in social, political and cultural fields gives testimony of women's emancipation in the Arab world, despite having political and socially unfavourable conditions. In countries like Iraq, women are still deprived and have a low status when compared to the women of Maghreb (North Africa) and Levant. It is because of the continuous unrest and turmoil in the country. The present situation of Arab women is far better than some major developing countries in terms of education, living conditions, employment and social rights. The writings of these women are so immense that unfolding the struggle for freedom and responsibility is an impossible task.

Therefore, despite patriarchal and economic restrictions, the contribution of these women to the emerging social political identities is significant. The politics of nationalism was unprecedented by the direct involvement of women in politics in public domain due to the rise of Palestinian Nationalism and Zionism (Katz, 2003). But what is interesting is the fact that women broke their traditional norms for the sake of their nation which did not allow their own rights to flourish. Secondly, their writings and actions created opening for women to enter public spheres. Thirdly, women liberation could not achieve heights because of the national liberation. Finally, due to the traditional and religious beliefs of the society, the rights of women were limited or opposed as subversive.

However, what women of these countries had achieved

during that period is still unreachable for many women of some major developing nations. Egypt, Lebanon, Israel, Algeria, Tunisia, Turkey and Morocco are the pioneering countries where women flourished in all sectors, be it education, employment, household, charity, writings, entrepreneurship, politics or social upliftment. Women of these countries are still doing better in higher education than their male counterparts. Thus, education and literary craft of the Arab women became the building blocks of their empowerment as well as popularity. The influence of Western ideas and indigenous strive, knowledge and learning, navigated the roadmap in the construction of their gender egalitarian society.

References

Al-Ali, Nadje (2002), "Women's Movements in the Middle East: Case Studies of Egypt and Turkey", United Nations Research Institute for Social Development, Geneva.

Badran, Margret (2008), "Islamic Feminism: Current Perspective", Tampere Peace Research Institute, Paper No. 96, University of Tampere, Finland.

Fowcett, Rachelle (2013), "The Reality and Future of Islamic Feminism", available at: https://www.aljazeera.com/indepth/opinion/2013/03/201332715585855781.html.

Hankin, Rachida (1996), "Woman as the other and the other Woman: The Alienation of Muslim Women within Feminism", Durham theses, Durham University, available at: http://etheses.dur.ac.uk/5401.

Hoda, Elsada (1998), "Malik Hifini Nassifal-nisaiyaatt' Hattmannsdorfer", Helena, Cairo, Women and Memory Forum.

Katz, Sheila, (2003), "Women and Gender in the Early Jewish and Palestinian Nationalism", University Press of Florida.

Keddie, Nikki R. and Beth Baron (1993), "Women in the Middle East: A History", Yale University Press.

Moghadam, Valentine (2007), "Feminism and Nationalism in the Middle East", in Neloufer de Mel and Selvey Thiruchandran (eds.), 'At the Cutting Edge: Essays in Honour of Kumari Jayawardena', New Delhi: Women Unlimited/Kali for Women.

Roded, Ruth (2008), "Women in Islam and the Middle East: A Reader", I.B. Tauris & Co. Ltd.: London.

UNESCO (2010), "Arab Muslim Civilization in the Mirror of the Universal Philosophical Perspective", Paris, France.

Whitcher, Rochell (2005), "The Effect of Western Feminist Ideology on Muslim Feminists", Naval Postgraduate School (unpublished thesis).

Zine, Jasmine (2002), "Muslim Women and the Politics of Representation", *American Journal of Social Sciences*, 19:4.

5

Options and Obstacles to Solve Refugee Crisis in West Asia

Lirar Pulikkalakath

The state of the global refugee system is in many ways egregious, marked with an unequal assumption of responsibilities by states, horrible conditions for asylum- seekers and specious incentives for a number of actors.

(David Donnantuono, The Michigan Daily)

Introduction

The history of human civilization is also the history of population movement between different countries and regions. This process is not only a natural phenomenon but also created by people and now by various governments through the process of their political, social and economic activities. In such situations, when some people move voluntarily, most of them leave their territories or homeland forcefully by social, political or economic pressures. For West Asia, such a population movement, especially the displacement, is hardly a new phenomenon. It is the very destiny of the people of the region for centuries especially after the creation of Israel. Nowadays, the post-Arab spring socio-political scenario in various countries in the region acts as a relevant time to analyze and examine the issue of displacement of millions of people and their future.

According to UNHCR (2016), 65.3 million people worldwide are forcibly displaced—roughly equal to the population of France. Among them, 40.8 million are internally displaced persons (IDPs), 21.3 million are refugees and 3.2

million are asylum seekers. That means 1 in every 113 on the planet belong to one of these groups. When the United Nations (UN) officially started its operations specifically for displaced persons after the 1951 Convention and through UN High Commissioner for Refugees (UNHCR), the number of world refugees was just 2.1 million. The latest figure shows above ten times of that number.

The features and flow of Arab refugees are different at different times and it has been a permanent fate of the region for the past some decades. Since West Asia is one of the major theatres of refugee crisis, this paper seeks to analyse the problems and possibilities of solving the regional refugee crisis by discussing repatriation, rehabilitation and resettlement as the major solutions. The search for durable solutions to the protracted refugee crisis in and around the West Asian region is a key humanitarian and development necessity in the current critical situation as millions of people are on their way in search of a better haven. Though the debate over the global solutions to this humanitarian crisis has highly politicized, all the efforts need local, regional and international support and multi-sectoral response that must go beyond the existing humanitarian agenda.

Forced Migration in West Asia: History, Evolution and Contemporary Scenario

Millions of refugees, asylum seekers and internally displaced people in West Asia are one of the major factors contributing to the global displacement crisis. The number of Syrian refugees has increased from around a half a million at the start of 2013 to more than 4 million today surpassing the Afghan refugees as the world's largest refugee community aside from Palestinians (Chamie, 2015). Unending political crisis, military conflicts and social unrest are driving millions of people from their homes. According to various UN estimates, more than 4 million Syrians are refugees, countries in West Asia including Turkey, Iran, Jordan and Lebanon are flooded with forced migrants from Asia and Africa especially from Palestine, Afghanistan, Iraq, Syria and Libya. They have been collectively hosting millions of refugees mainly from the neighbouring countries for the past few decades.

Estimates for 2014 indicate that the countries in the region with the largest numbers of refugees are Jordan, the West Bank and Gaza Strip in Palestine, Turkey, Lebanon, and Iran. In all these countries their number exceeds 1 million and in some countries the number estimates are above 2 million. The region currently hosts around 4.8 million Syrian refugees alone. Massive exodus of people especially the refugee flow in the region has greatly burdened countries like Lebanon and Jordan. The ratios of refugees per 1,000 population in Lebanon and Jordan are about one-third of their resident populations (Arar et al., 2016; Chamie, 2015).

Now, the Arab World, especially countries in the West Asia, share bulk of the globally displaced population both through producing and accommodating them. Domestic political instability due to authoritarian regimes, sectarian violence, frequent foreign intervention, Arab spring and emergence of militant organizations like Islamic State (IS) have resulted in large population dislocations and refugee flows across national boundaries in most of the countries in West Asia. Among the factors that have led to massive human displacement crisis in the region, the Arab Spring and Islamic State (IS) have played a greater role. Both have caused the intensification of the existing phenomenon of intra-regional and inter-regional forced migration.

As of December 2014, the largest number of refugees in West Asia was found in Lebanon. Other major hosting countries included Jordan and Turkey. Currently, the Syrian refugees represent the largest number of forced migrants in any of these countries. In addition to these host countries, Egypt and Yemen accommodate refugees mainly from Somalia, Sudan, and Ethiopia. Zaatari, the largest refugee camp in Jordan, is considered as the fourth largest city in the kingdom and, at one point, the camp accommodated over 150,000 refugees. Such crowded refugee camps have been more or less permanent and common throughout the West Asian region (Cohen, 2014: 5). There are instances of unbalanced and unequal distribution of refugees internationally and especially within the Arab world itself. Among the around 4 million Syrian refugees, 95 percent are located in five countries. With the exception of Turkey, the rest of the countries are among the poorest countries in the Arab West Asian region like Lebanon, Jordan, Iraq and Egypt (MacEoin, 2015).

Durable Solutions for Refugee Crisis

As per the statute of the Office of the United Nations High Commissioner for Refugees, the office should assume the function of providing international protection, under the auspices of the UN, to refugees who fall within the scope of the present Statute and of seeking permanent solutions for the problem of refugees by assisting governments and, subject to the approval of the governments concerned, private organizations to facilitate the voluntary repatriation of such refugees, or their assimilation within new national communities (UN General Assembly, 1950). The Handbook of UNHCR says, there are three options for durable solutions when the world suffers from large movements of people or migration generally. They are: voluntary repatriation or return to the mother country, local integration with the host country and resettlement to third country. Conventionally, these domains have been seen as distinct, or as stages in a refugee 'cycle'. These solutions have traditionally been associated with a single pathway of permanent settlement, whether in the host country, a third country or the country of origin (UNHCR, 2015, Stein).

Voluntary repatriation or return to their home country needs a 'voluntariness', a free decision made by a refugee to return to his or her country based on accurate and objective information that has been provided, premised on the principle of non-refoulement (UNHCR Handbook, 2011). The second option, local integration, can include refugees into the host community through legislation giving them access to public services including education and health, employment, freedom of movement, purchase and disposing of properties and the capacity to travel with valid documentation (Low, 2006: 65). The final solution, that is refugee resettlement, is the planned movement of displaced people through state or international control from their first host country or temporary place of asylum to a different country entirely (Rahmato, 2003: 67).

The evolution of the UNHCR's three durable solutions policy framework reflects this thinking. While earlier eras of mass forced migration gave rise to pragmatic practices of incorporating significant numbers of refugees into receiving societies ("local integration") or enabling self-sorting of people into third countries ("resettlement"), the emphasis in recent decades has been on "repatriation"—the voluntary return of displaced people to their previous home place (Fabos and Cathrine, 2016).

Thus, there are three options available to residents of a refugee camp at the time of its closure: voluntary repatriation to their home country, local integration with the host country and resettlement to a third country. But each option has its own difficulties. The international community, under the guidelines of the UNHCR, has seemingly chosen the first option that is voluntary repatriation as the most politically viable one, but its timing and applicability remain in question. One of the major obstacles to local integration as a solution for refugee crises is the lack of political will of many host states. Many host countries consider refugees a 'burden', and not capable of any meaningful social and economic contribution to their development. They are also seen as a threat to national security (Hansen et al., 2008: 7).

Local integration or rehabilitation to the first asylum country is rarely a welcome option at the receiving end for reasons of political and economic friction. Resettlement, the last option is equally a rarely explored one, as it is not often seen as a 'solution' but rather as another displacement, and difficult to implement, given the high degree of policy and logistical coordination between host countries and the UNHCR, which facilitates the process (Ibid: 4). In reality, these solutions are difficult to apply, as refugee crises are often prolonged and the refugees spend a considerable amount of time in exile (Ibid: 5). It is seen that the feasibility and attractiveness of these three options, has varied over time, partly determined by geo-political considerations: as many commentators have observed, during the Cold War, resettlement or integration were more the norm, because this suited the purposes of the West, while since the end of the Cold War, new imperatives have prevailed and repatriation has become the most desirable durable solution (Chimni, 1999).

Solutions to the West Asian Refugee Crisis: Three Options and Multiple Obstacles

As described above, to have repatriation to mother country, refugees should be able to ultimately return home; once safe return is possible. Practically, refugees would remain in the host countries and continue their lives and livelihoods there in the case of rehabilitation or host-country integration. Through resettlement, the refugees would be relocated to a third country, where they would obtain legal status to pursue education, seek employment, and access public services. Anyhow, there must be proper conditions to have all these durable solutions possible. But it depends on the social, political and economic status of countries dealing with refugees and their policies. West Asia is not an exception in this regard.

As of now, there is absence of a truly regional migration and refugee governance in West Asia, rather it is state driven. It means the countries of the region lack a comprehensive refugee policy. Countries in the Mashreq part of Arab World; Syria, Lebanon, Palestine, Jordan, and Iraq have dealt with refugees for a long time especially since the creation of Israel. As a result of the frequent regional turmoil and unending forced migration, some countries face demographic imbalances or challenges. For instance, Jordan's unofficial population amounts to 60 percent of Palestinian refugees. In November 2015, Jordan was hosting around 630,000 Syrian refugees in addition to the several waves of refugees from Iraq in the 1990s, and after the US-led 2003 invasion.

In Lebanon, Syrian refugees represent one-fourth of the country's population. The presence of large numbers of refugees from neighbouring countries has contributed to many socio-political and economic challenges in these host countries. Increased housing cost, competition between refugees and natives in income-generating activities, over exploitation of scarce resources like water as well as difficulties in health and education sectors to address everyone's needs are some of the challenges the host countries generally face due to the massive influx of refugees (Wolff, 2015). Globally, UNHCR has the mandate to extend protection to international refugees, including the 'search for and implementation of durable solutions for refugees from the available choices of voluntary repatriation, resettlement, or host-country absorption' (Akram, 2002). But how can it be possible in a region like West Asia where political instability and social unrest are regular phenomena?

It is clear that several factors have to be considered before repatriation to home country. According to UNHCR policy, certain conditions must be met that allow refugees to exercise their 'social, economic, civil, political and cultural rights' and enjoy 'peaceful, productive and dignified lives' (UNHCR, 2008). One of the essential things for repatriation to occur is that refugees must be able to return to their mother country fearlessly. In addition to this, infrastructure must be strong enough to protect lives and livelihood. As it is not easy to achieve safety and stability immediately in the troubled areas, several war-torn countries have become safe and stable enough to support repatriation according to UNHCR standards in the past.

Now, the organization is ready to officially announce that Iraq is safe for refugees to return (Tyson, 2016: 24). But in reality, still conflict and displacement go parallel in the country especially in Mosul and other troubled regions. The same situation is there in Syria—perhaps more tragic. Palestinians are in not in a position to return to their mother land in the near future. As long as most of the refugees in West Asia still fear to return to their homeland due to persecution and insecurity, repatriation or voluntary return to their mother country is not at all an easy task. In addition, considering the nature and trend of political instability, military conflicts and social strife in West Asia, repatriation for many is an unrealistic option at least for the near term.

But, the largest factor in favour of repatriation is the fact that it is more likely to be realized than either resettlement or integration. Because, the host state policies and local socio-political and economic issues precluding integration and the minimal international response and assistance to resettlement are highly unlikely to change anytime in the near future. Additionally, there is a strong feeling among refugees to return to their motherland and hope conditions for repatriation will occur at some point in the future. Repatriation is the most likely durable solution available to most of the refugees in West Asia, even if it is still a long way off (Tyson, 2016: 25).

While evaluating the possibilities of local integration to host country as a solution to the refugee crisis in West Asia, it is important to consider the internal policies, the stability and resources of regional host countries. Though historically been welcoming and still accommodating millions of refugees from neighbouring countries, neither Jordan, Lebanon, Iraq and nor Turkey are signatories to the 1951 Convention. It means that regional refugees may not receive treatment according to international standards in these countries.

One of the major reasons behind introducing more restrictive refugee policies by host countries in West Asia is the protracted nature of past refugee crises in the region; be it

Palestinians, Iraqis and now Syrians. As a result, major regional host countries such as Turkey, Jordan, and Lebanon hesitate to offer full legal rights to them. It forces the host state to limit refugees' access to employment, healthcare, housing and education (Krajeski, 2012). Further, it creates troubles for the integration of past and present refugee groups with the host state and society (Tyson, 2016: 23).

For instance, Jordan, one of the leading refugee host country in the world for around seventy years is afraid of a decline in their standard of living and feel the ache of "host community fatigue". This is so because millions of protracted refugees have led to rising costs and crowded schools, streets and hospitals in the kingdom (Arar, 2016). Local integration with the host country also appears to be a difficult process, especially in countries such as Lebanon and Jordan, given the continuous massive influx of refugees from neighbouring countries, limited employment opportunities, scarce resources, domestic demographic considerations, weak economy and destabilizing political repercussions (Chamie, 2015).

Regarding the third option; resettlement of refugees, one of the important elements is that it should be distributed among various refugee groups globally. It cannot restrict or concentrate on a single population or to a particular region. UNHCR reveals that there were 16.7 million refugees in the world as of June 20, 2014. However, the Organization submitted files of only 93,226 refugees in 2013 for consideration and just 71,411 refugees were actually resettled (Tyson, 2016: 23; UNHCR, 2014b).

In addition, as of now, only a small number of countries are ready to accept refugees for resettlement, including the United States, Canada, and Australia. According to its provisions, the resettled countries are expected to ensure the accepted refugees the same rights as guaranteed to its nationals and place the refugees on a path to citizenship. While this option may be only for some particular refugee groups, majority should not be assumed to leave their home country and settle in another place.

This is so because they will have to change their way of life, including acclimatizing to a new culture, learning a new language, and often struggling to find employment. For children, they will have to find and force themselves to fit into the new schools system (Cohen, 2014: 8).

This shows that resettlement will be inadequate for the majority of the displaced community in West Asia especially for the 2 million strong and growing Syrian refugee population. Based on the statistics over the past few years, UNHCR reports that the number of resettled refugees has steadily decreased (UNHCR, 2012). If this is the trend, there will only be fewer chances for resettlement in future. Statistics show that as of April 2014, the U.S. had only accepted 121 Syrian refuges (Acer, 2014). In Europe, Germany has offered 4,000 temporary spaces for Syrian refugees that are not intended for permanent resettlement. Since majority of the developed nations are not ready to intake their due share, resettlement will not be an accessible solution for most of the Syrian refugees (Tyson, 2016: 24).

One of the important features of refugee movement in West Asia is that many of them have been engaging in circular migratory patterns for decades—fleeing their mother country, returning home, and then forced to leave again. For instance, the Iraqi refugees in Jordan often travelled to their mother country for a short period of time from 2006 to 2009, but again returned to Jordan when the crisis escalated (Cohen, 2014: 7). Thus, there are fewer solutions and more troubles since many actors are directly or indirectly part of this game and most of them are not committed to solve the issue. All the scenarios and actors involved in it narrowed the refugee crisis from a human tragedy to a political crisis.

The refugee regime of today is comprised of host States, the UN system, and humanitarian actors and implementing partners, but not refugees themselves. The refugee regime's agreement to support protection spaces for its global "denizens" has the effect of maintaining the temporary status of the "refugee", which in the current situation has the unintended consequence of keeping people's lives on hold. As a result of national policies and serving their own polity, host nations largely have an interest in keeping people in a temporary status. People who are forced to flee tend to occupy marginal spaces because they are considered a threat to the social and political order. The humanitarian organizations and the international refugee regime largely accept this predicament in order to be allowed by host states to be present to assist refugees. The refugee regime is stuck in its own concepts and solutions where people's daily lives are largely being overlooked (Fabos and Cathrine, 2016).

There have been a number of regional and international conventions and frameworks to deal the refugee crisis, from the Convention and protocol related to the status of refugees in 1951 and 1967 respectively to the Bangkok Principles of the Asian-African Legal Consultative Organization in 2001. But it shows that none is effective to solve the global refugee crisis and that of West Asia in particular. Until and unless all the countries especially the developed countries take a proportional percentage of refugees, the crisis would continue indefinitely. They should open their borders to fellow human beings facing persecution and insecurity in their mother country especially to women and children, struggling for life and searching for a safe haven.

Conclusion

In the words of Antonio Guterres, former UN High Commissioner for Refugees and current Secretary General of UN; "the refugee crisis is the consequence of the political dynamics in the state formation, transformation and increasing global interdependence". As a region of origin, destination and transit for many forced migrants including refugees, West Asia and its protracted and other refugee community deserves much attention. The region has produced, and hosted, millions of displaced people including refugees from Palestine, Iraq etc. It was mainly due to the unending Arab-Israeli conflicts, disastrous Gulf Wars and frequent foreign interventions over the past decades.

Recently, the Arab Spring has produced another wave of forced migrants in the region especially from Syria. Now the old and new refugees pose a great threat to the very existence of the entire West Asia. In such critical situations, the region's strong tradition of hospitality and generosity towards affected community was the most powerful assets to dilute and tackle the crises mainly the issue of displacement. But the generosity has a limit to help those who need since refugee crisis in the region has already entered into a more complex situation to solve than ever before. Now the important phenomenon is that a number of countries are producing large number of refugees while most of the host countries are struggling to accommodate these old and new protracted refugees. It needs a full stop otherwise the result would affect the international community too.

Now the world's system for protecting refugees is broken or inefficient—from global to local level. The crisis becomes complex when 75 percent of the total refugees are trapped in protracted situations. Whenever there is massive exodus of population due to conflict, widespread persecution or distress, a common pattern for most people is to become IDPs, for a substantial number will look for refuge in a neighbouring country or countries, and for a smaller number to seek asylum in countries further afield, perhaps in other continents. As UNHCR observes, some of those in neighbouring countries of first asylum may later be resettled further afield, joining those who have gone there directly.

As identified by various international institutions, there are three durable solutions: repatriation, rehabilitation and resettlement. But each has certain limitations and difficulties to materialize. The situation is pretty much complex in West Asia than in any other region. To have repatriation, first of all much effort has to be taken to ensure security and assistance in the refugee producing countries. For that, the governments concerned in the region should be able to protect their citizens from threats and persecution. To achieve this goal, all the states that produce massive exodus of refugees in West Asia should be politically, economically and socially stable and strong to avoid further displacement. Then only the refugees will be ready to return to their home country voluntarily.

Local integration is another complicated solution when 75 percent of the word's refugee resided in the immediate neighbouring countries and most of them are from poor or middle income countries with scares resources in West Asia. UNHCR reveals that top ten major refugee hosting countries together accommodate nearly 60 percent of world's refugees with top three alone receiving 30 percent—Turkey, Lebanon and Jordan come under this category. There are many questions in the air. How is it possible to accommodate more in their land? How long can they accommodate them? What about their depleting limited resources? Above all, there is no idea about the future of the current political crisis in West Asia.

Finally, the rate of resettlement is not sufficient to meet the demand or to solve the issue. It urgently needs willingness of more developed countries to accommodate the displaced across the globe. It is both an opportunity to demonstrate solidarity with poor countries and also a responsibility to share the burden of the refugee crisis. Worldwide, more than 21 million people have been forced to seek sanctuary abroad. It is the duty and responsibilities of governments concerned to ensure protection and assistance to the needy people. But rich countries always treat refugees as somebody else's problem. Nearly 90 percent of the global refugees have been accommodated by countries mainly in West Asia, Africa and South Asia.

Anyhow, this uprooted and unwanted people of West Asia are always in search of a better haven. Their status is also changing accordingly. When they are forced to vacate their home, their identity is homeless, displaced or IDP. When they are forced to flee their mother country or cross the international border they become international citizens and asylum seekers. And once their asylum request is approved they are treated as refugees. When thinking about durable solutions, their identity changes again. It is the destiny of millions of people in the West Asian region for decades. Protracted refugee situation exists when 25,000 or more refugees originate from the same country and seek refuge in another country for at least five consecutive years. They comprise two-third of the total refugees (Hansen et al., 2008).

References

Akram, S. (2002), "Palestinian Refugees and Their Legal Status: Rights, Politics, and Implications for a Just Solution", *Journal of Palestine Studies*, 31(3): 36-51.

Amnesty International (2015), "8 Ways to Solve the World Refugee Crisis", available at: https://www.amnesty.org/en/latest/campaigns/2015/10/eight-solutions-world-refugee-crisis.

Arar, Rawan (2016), "The Real Refugee Crisis is in the Middle East, Not Europe", *The Washington Post*, May 14.

Chamie, Joseph (2015), "Desperate Migration in the Middle East", Yale Global Online and the MacMillan Centre, available at: http://yaleglobal.yale.edu/content/desperate-migration-middle-east.

Chimni, B.S. (1999), "From Resettlement to Involuntary Repatriation: Towards a Critical History of Durable Solutions to Refugee Problems", UNHCR, New Issues in Refugee Research, Working Paper No. 2, available at: http://www.migration4development.org/sites/default/files/bs_chimni.pdf.

Cohen, Elisheva (2014), "Refugees and Forced Migrants", *Middle East Policy Council,* available at: https://csme.indiana.edu/documents/cirricula/MEPolicyCouncil_Refugees_Forced-Migrants.pdf.

Donnantuono, David (2016), "A Solution is Out there for the Refugee Crisis", *The Michigan Daily*, November, 27, available at: https://www.michigandaily.com/section/viewpoints/op-ed-solution-out-there-refugee-crisisa.

Fabos, Anita and Cathrine Brun (2016), "Protracted Refugee Displacement in the Middle East: Making Home in Limbo?", *Middle East Institute*, May, available at: http://www.mei.edu/content/map/protracted-circumstances-refugee-displacement-middle-east-making-home-limbo.

Hansen, Francesca et al. (2008), "Repatriation, Resettlement, Integration: A Study of the Three Refugee Solutions", The Niapele Project/Sciences Po, Summer/Fall, available at: http://www.theniapeleproject.org/files/Niapele-ScPo-Study2008.pdf.

Low, Ana (2003), "Local Integration: A Durable Solution for Refugee?", *Forced Migration Review*, Vol. 25.

MacEoin, Denis (2015), "The Arab States and the Refugees", September 16, *Gatestone Institute,* available at: https://www.gatestoneinstitute.org/6502/refugees-arab-states.

Oli, Ignatius (2016), "The EU and the Burden of Refugee Resettlement", *ZEI Insights*, No. 45 December, available at: https://www.zei.uni-bonn.de/dateien/zei-insights/oli_45.

Rahmato, Dessalegn (2003), "Resettlement in Ethiopia: The Tragedy of Relocation in the 1980s", Forum for Social Studies FSS, Discussion Paper No. 1, Addis Ababa.

Sarah (2015), "Migration and Refugee Crisis in the Mediterranean What Role for International Organizations?", *The Broker*, November 26, available at: http://www.thebrokeronline.eu/Articles/Migration-and-Refugee-Crisis-in-the-Mediterranean.

Stein, Barry N. (n.d), "Durable Solutions for Developing Country Refugees", *International Migration Review,* Vol. XX(2): 264-282.

Tyson, Catherine (2016), "The Syrian Displacement Crisis: Future Durable Solutions", *Oxford Monitor of Forced Migration,* Vol. 4(2): 23- 26.

UN General Assembly (1950), "The Statute of the Office of the United Nations High Commissioner for Refugees", New York: UN.

UNHCR (2012), "Progress Report on Resettlement" June, available at: http://www.unhcr.org/5006a6aa9.html.

UNHCR (2014), "UNHCR: Progress Report on Resettlement, June

2014", June, available at: http://www.unhcr.org/53aa90bf9.html.

UNHCR (2015), "The 10 Point Plan in Action", available at: http://www.unhcr.org/50a4c2b09.pdf.

UNHCR (2016), "Resettlement Fact Sheet 2015", available at: http://www.unhcr.org/524c31a09.pdf.

UNHCR News (2008), "UNHCR: Policy Framework and Implementation Strategy: UNHCR's Role in Support of the Return and Reintegration of Displaced Populations", available at: http://www.unhcr.org/4c2203309.html.

United Nations High Commission for Refugees (2011), "Handbook and Guidelines on Procedures and Criteria for Determining Refugee Status, Geneva, December, available at: http://www.unhcr.org/publications/legal/3d58e13b4/handbook-procedures-criteriadetermining-refugee-status-under-1951-convention.html.

6

Oil as a Tool of Diplomacy in Iraqi Kurdistan

Divya Malhotra

Background

Two issues have been central to the West Asian region; identity and oil. At the intersection of both lies the semi-autonomous province of Kurdistan in Iraq. Kurds, however, were not always a people divided across nations, as seen today. The idea of Kurdish identity was an ethnic notion until 1920. Almost a century ago, the victorious imperial powers in World War I had drawn borders of the modern Iraqi state on sands of West Asia. With a clear eye on oil dispositions, Iraq was placed under the British mandate in 1920 and Iraq was described to be founded as an oil company (Kane, 2010). The fate of Kurds changed when, under the British pressure, the League of Nations unceremoniously appended some of the Kurdish areas to Iraq six years after the country was founded. Since then, Kurds exist as a nation without a nation.

The history of Iraqi Kurds has been a troubled one with a shared sense of suffocation by the successive Iraqi governments and betrayal by Western allies. Their struggle for identity has been mingled with quest for legitimacy. The centrality of oil to the fabric of modern Iraqi state is critical to understanding the depth of the issues involved in searching for agreement on oil legislation (Ibid.). Oil has always been central to the Kurdish plight for international legitimacy. Several scholars have argued that Kurdish leaders have been trying to use oil as a tool to part ways with Baghdad and establish independent diplomatic ties with neighbourhood.

In the words of KRG president Barzani (2012), ever since the discovery of oil in Iraq in the 1920s, successive Iraqi governments have sought to keep oil out of Kurdish hands, blocking exploration and development of fields in Kurdistan. Saddam Hussein's government went even further, using Iraqi oil revenues to finance the military campaigns that destroyed more than 4,500 Kurdish villages and to pay for the poison gas used to kill thousands of Kurdish civilians.

Iraq ranks fifth in the world in proven oil reserves—143.1 billion barrels, according to the BP Statistical Review of World Energy, 2016. The year 2016 saw a rapid rise in global oil production, with production from Iraq rising the highest, that is, 750,000 barrels per day. With a population of 5.2 million (20 percent of Iraq's population) and GDP of US$ 23.6 billion, Kurdistan alone—comprising less than a tenth of Iraqi territory—holds 45 billion barrels of oil and world's largest gas reserves amounting to as much as 5.6 trillion cubic metres (Kurdish Board of Investment, 2012). If the autonomous region were a country, its reserves would rank it tenth in the world, after Libya, according to BP. Kurdistan's oil odyssey has attracted immense international attention and at the same time, has been the centre of conflict between Baghdad and Erbil.

In a near historical perspective, the Kurdistan National Assembly was established in 1992, in the first free and fair elections ever held in the Kurdistan Region or in any part of Iraq. Since then, Kurdistan has its own parliament, president, and civil institutions. Even though independent oil trade from Kurdistan became a reality in 2014, its right to sell the oil that lies beneath its soil remains constitutionally and legally disputed. Reference to Iraqi constitution becomes indispensable to any study of Kurdish oil in order to decipher the conflict from its roots. The differences over revenue sharing have been central to the debate and interestingly, both Baghdad and Erbil have been quoting the constitution to justify their respective positions. The differences over revenue sharing along with loopholes in constitution have given ample space to the Kurdish leaders to initiate independent oil trade in 2014. Placing this issue of oil and diplomacy in the current literature, one may identify certain gaps in analysing the trends.

Although certain countries, particularly Turkey, have recently fostered closer trade relations with the Kurdistan Regional Government (KRG), its historical opposition to an independent Kurdish state will continue. Thus, the contention that the KRG is driven by underlying motivations to establish an independent state remains debatable.

Oil in Kurdistan: Temporal Perspectives

Crude oil has had profound impact on the world civilisation than any single natural resource in recorded history. Oil has become a very decisive element in defining the politics, rhetoric and diplomacy of states. In a public lecture entitled "Oil in World Politics", former secretary of the Organization of the Petroleum Exporting Countries (OPEC), the late Chief M.O. Feyide emphatically stated that, "All over the world, the lives of people are affected and the destiny of nations is determined by the result of oil explorations...The march of progress would be retarded and life itself would be unbearable if the world is deprived of oil. That is why oil has become the concern of governments, a vital ingredient of their politics and a crucial factor in the political and diplomatic strategies" (Pyagbara, 1986).

Kurdistan sits on the intersection of two tectonic plates that created both the high mountains along the Iranian and Turkish borders and small hills of carbonate rock, beneath which crude has been accumulating over the past 50 million to 70 million years. British geologists travelling in the region after World War I discovered oil of the fields of Kirkuk in 1927 (Dabrowska, 2008).

The first oil flowed by pipeline to Haifa in July 1934, and the Kurdish oil industry was born. After the Kirkuk discovery, however, the search for oil in Kurdistan largely stopped. Three subsequent events; outbreak of the Iran-Iraq war, Saddam's gas attacks against the Kurds, and the 1991 Gulf War chased away potential investors. The Kurdish Regional Government was formed in 1991, after the Iraqi military and state apparatus withdrew from the three Kurdish provinces of Erbil, Sulaymaniyah and Dohuk, following Iraq's defeat in the First Gulf War (Voller, 2013). The void created by the Iraqi withdrawal was soon filled by the Kurdish parties, particularly the Kurdistan Democratic Party (KDP), led by Masood Barzani, and the Patriotic Union of Kurdistan (PUK), led by Jalal Talabani. With the establishment of Kurdish Regional Government, the focus was on reconstruction of the devastated semi-autonomous region with the inflow of international aid.

US-led Invasion and Rise of Oil Industry

The US-led invasion of Iraq in 2003 changed the fate of Kurdistan for better. The Kurds consolidated control of their territory and exploitation of untapped resources accelerated. On the eve of US invasion, Kurdistan was a virgin territory from an oil and gas perspective. Oslo-based DNO (Det Norske Oljeselskap) was the first international oil company to start exploration in the Kurdistan region of Iraq in June 2004. In 2004, DNO Iraq entered into two production sharing agreements in Erbil and Dohuk Provinces with the Kurdistan Regional Government, and the first oil well Tawke-1 was drilled and discovered in several layers in 2005 (Wikileaks, 2006).

Evidently, the post invasion period witnessed surge in investor attention towards Kurdish North. The US invasion in 2003 gave the Kurds some room to manoeuvre, as their Sunni and Shiite countrymen battled for control of the government. The instability and violence in central and Southern regions gave the investors a reason to look towards the Kurdish areas. Amidst instability, the first oil drill was promising news to investors eyeing Iraqi oil and with its exploration potential and business-friendly approach, Kurdish Regional Government (KRG) has been aggressively courting international oil companies (Reed, 2012).

Even as semi-autonomous region of Kurdistan started

gaining attention of foreign companies and investors vis-à-vis rest of the country in the post-invasion period, the oil deals for Kurdish oil were negotiated and signed with the central government at Baghdad and Erbil having little autonomy. With these developments, competition over natural resources and animosity over power sharing emerged as the bone of contention between Baghdad and Erbil. The best example to understand the rift could be the disagreement over formulation of a federal hydrocarbon law. Initial deliberations over the hydrocarbon law witnessed the participation of Kurdish representatives alongside Maliki's government.

However, the disagreements over issues such as public sharing agreements (PSAs) eventually led to breakdown of negotiations. In June 2007, the Kurdistan Parliament passed a regional Petroleum Law, ratified as a Hydrocarbon Law in May 2009. Even though the KRG expressed its commitment to sharing the oil income with the central government, six months after the Hydrocarbon Bill was passed in 2007, the president of the region Masoud Barzani threatened, during a visit to the European Parliament, that the KRG would keep for itself revenues from the extracted oil because "they [Baghdad] often use it [oil revenue] against us [the Kurds]" (Baker, 2009). While the words are contentious, the statement is reflective of KRG's perception of its rights over oil extracted from the region.

In 2008, both Shiite and Sunni parliamentarians signed a joint statement expressing "deep concern at individual acts without reference to central government, such as the signing of contracts with foreign companies" (Husari, 2008). Essentially, foreign investments in Kurdistan region were a matter of concern for Baghdad. However, the flow of investments into Iraq's territory was not perceived as a major threat. Threat perception changed when oil was being flown out of Kurdish borders, without consultation of central government authorities.

The question of sovereignty became central. Thus, it can be deciphered that while foreign investments in oil exploration sector boosted the confidence of KRG and set the pace of

Kurdistan's nascent oil industry, the international/cross-border trade of Kurdish oil took Kurdish unilateralism to the next level. Nonetheless, such unilateralism with regard to control and exploitation of oil reserves in the Kurdistan Region has not been acceptable to the government.

At this point in the debate, two ideas need sufficient clarification; the concept of oil diplomacy in order to distinguish between oil investments by foreign companies from oil trade relations, and secondly, Iraqi constitution's respective interpretation by Kurdish Regional Government (KRG) and government at the centre.

Role of Oil in Diplomacy

In the modern political jargon, diplomacy is the art and practice of conducting negotiations between nations through peaceful means. Diplomacy is an essential institution for the conduct of inter-state relations. In the words of Paul Sharp, diplomacy has proved to be a "resilient institution; it is one of the few international institutions that have survived the challenges of popular sovereignty and nineteenth century nationalism" (Sharp, 1999). On the subject of diplomacy, various schools of thought exist and it is not surprising that study of diplomacy displays a variety of conceptualisations rather than scholarly consensus. Most scholars argue that nation-state is the primary actor in international relations and diplomacy is an instrument of state craft. Writings of diplomacy by De Callieres, Satow, and Wicquefort as well as those of Nicolson, Kissinger and Berridge espouse the centrality of states in diplomacy.

Portuguese diplomat Jose Calvet De Magalhaes, in his seminal work "Pure Concept of Diplomacy" defined diplomacy as "an instrument of foreign policy in the establishment and development of peaceful contacts between the governments of different states..." (Jonsson, 2002). Keith Hamilton and Richard Langhorne, in their book titled, *"The Practice of Diplomacy: Its Evolution, Theory and Administration"* (1995) offered an alternate definition of diplomacy as "the peaceful conduct of relations amongst political entities, their principles and accredited agents" (Jonsson, 2002).

While Magalhaes underlines participation of state actors including governments; Hamilton and Langhorne make a rather loose reference to political entities. Clearly, there is an ambiguity regarding nature of actors involved in diplomacy, that is, state or non-state actors. A brief acquaintance with the post-Cold War period shows that there has been notable diplomatic inflation, and more states and new actors have required representation (Sharp, 1999). Thus, there is a justifiable scope to study diplomatic engagements of non-state entities like Iraqi Kurdistan.

Furthermore, the concept of oil diplomacy has not yet been properly theorised in the literature of international relations. Within the broader framework of energy diplomacy and petroleum politics, one may come across cases where oil has been used as a tool to pursue diplomatic goals. Rise of petroleum politics can be traced to the rise of oil industry in West Asia in the early 20th century. Due to long-term economic value, strategic relevance and scarce availability, oil has the ability of being used as a tool to strike partnerships, earn allies and enhance bargaining power in a diplomatic equation.

KRG's Economic Diplomacy

Having stated this, it becomes essential to identify the means of diplomatic engagement in case of Iraqi Kurdistan. Participation of foreign companies started a decade ago and the development of infant oil industry in Kurdish region was possible due to technological expertise and financial investment in exploration, production and marketing of Kurdish oil. Oil sales, however, were not in the ambit of investors. Several oil deals have been signed without the consent or approval of central government in Baghdad. On occasions, Iraqi government has threatened and blacklisted companies for signing independent oil deals with Erbil. Home countries of investors have also warned the foreign companies for signing illegal deals. Despite these pressures, foreign investors have remained undeterred and investments have flooded the Kurdish oil industry (Lando, 2014).

Thus, some degree of autonomy of KRG vis-à-vis Baghdad in oil investments may be implied. Investments are guided by profit motive and foreign companies operate on the principle of free market. Thus, their motive of engagement can, at best, be economic. Secondly, investor engagements involve private parties, and cannot essentially be linked to government's deliberate policy of engagement with foreign nations. So, KRG's independent negotiations with the foreign oil companies in Kurdistan do not qualify to be labelled as independent diplomacy.

Another more recent and controversial route of diplomatic engagement is the oil trade. In 2013, Kurdistan Regional Government (KRG) started independent oil deals with neighbouring countries. Since external oil sales, that is, trade deals are finalised at a government-to-government level, unlike investments, this form of engagement reflects unilateralism in diplomacy. Kurdistan's independent oil trade is being seen beyond the realm of economics and real motives are being questioned. Hence, the question whether oil trade is being used as a tool of diplomacy or not, becomes relevant to the ongoing debate.

Constitutional Interpretation: Views from Baghdad and Erbil

The ideal starting point for understanding Iraq's oil debate is the Iraqi Constitution, which for the Kurds has obtained the status of an almost sacred text (Mills, 2016). Constitution of Iraq is the most valid and authentic reference to comprehend the legitimate provisions made for government at centre as well as KRG with special reference to oil. The view on constitution differs notably from Baghdad and Erbil, and thus reading between the lines becomes a methodological necessity. In October 2005, the constitution of Iraq was approved by referendum and implemented in 2006. The status of the Kurdish Regional Government (KRG) was officially recognised in the Iraqi constitution, enshrining the right of the Iraqi Kurds to localised power over "all administrative requirements of the region" (Anderson, 2010).

Most scholars agree that, within the constitution, an important distinction was made between the right to manage existing and future oil fields, the former falling to the federal government and the latter to the regions (Klich, 2014). Under a longstanding agreement, only Iraq's federal State Oil Marketing Organisation (SOMO) will have the legal authority to market oil and 17 percent of the oil revenue will be shared with KRG. KRG's exclusive right to regulate the oil sector in Kurdistan and particularly, its right to enter into independent contracts relating to exploitation and sale of oil remains disputed. There have been differential views on interpretation of the Iraqi constitution. The subject of oil (and gas) is dealt in Articles 111 and 112 of the Constitution.

According to Article 111, "Oil and gas are owned by all the people of Iraq in all the regions and governorates". Thus, the federal government argues that Iraq's oil belongs to all the people of Iraq, and not a faction, sect or ethnicity. According to Section 1 of Article 112,

"The federal government, with the producing governorates and regional governments, shall undertake the management of oil and gas extracted from present fields, provided that it distributes its revenue in a fair manner in proportion to the population distribution in all parts of the country, specifying an allotment for a specified period for the damaged regions which were unjustly deprived of them by the former regime, and the regions that were damaged afterwards in a way that ensures balanced development in different areas of the country, and this shall be regulated by a law".

According to Section 2 of Article 112,

"The federal government, with producing regional and governorate governments, shall together formulate the necessary strategic policies to develop oil and gas wealth in a way that achieves the highest benefit for the Iraqi people using the most advanced techniques of the market principles and encouraging investments".

Article 111 is rather simplistic and thus largely undisputed. The main source of rift lies in Article 112 which offers scope for discrepancy in interpretation. According to the federal government in Baghdad, the shared authority of regional governorates and centre as prescribed by Article 112 must be restricted in its scope by federal government's power to take the final decision. To substantiate its position, the federal government often refers to Article 110 which defines "those areas where federal government has exclusive authority; formulating foreign, sovereign economic and trade policy, and regulating commercial policy across regional and governorate boundaries in Iraq". In KRG's view, Section 1 of Article 112 gives them the right to govern only the present fields. In ordinary interpretation, present field only includes fields already discovered and under production in 2006, when the Constitution was passed. At that time, there were no oil producing fields in Kurdistan, thus KRG argues that the right over oil fields post-2006, rests with the regional government. Control over new oil fields is clearly contested by KRG, and KRG substantiates its position with Article 115, which states:

"All powers not stipulated in the exclusive powers of the federal government belong to the authorities of the regions... With regard to other powers shared between the federal government and the regional government, priority shall be given to the law of the regions and governorates not organised in a region in case of a dispute".

KRG also quotes Article 126(4) and Article 142 of the Constitution to state that KRG has the right to veto any proposed amendments to the Constitution that affect the powers and rights of Kurdistan. Thus, the perception of deliberate neglect and isolation combined with constitutional ambiguity regarding right over exploitation, exploration and sale of oil from newly discovered fields influences the political behaviour of KRG. Gary Kent, director of the UK All Party Parliamentary Group on Kurdistan stated that "the international community needs to recognise that Baghdad has sold the Kurds short for a decade with broken promises. Even as the security and humanitarian crises accelerated, the Kurds have received no budget entitlements at all and Baghdad has sought to block oil exports which are allowed under the Iraqi constitution" (Denselow, 2014). Having established the idea of oil diplomacy and dilemma of Constitutional interpretation, it can be further analysed whether oil has worked as a tool of diplomacy in case of Iraqi Kurdistan.

Oil and Kurdistan's Foreign Policy Matrix

It is generally argued that establishing credible independent institutions ensures high degree of functional and decisional autonomy in a region, and exhibits a sense of independence from the state. Establishment of a separate Department of Foreign Relations (DFR) in Kurdistan in 2006 signalled its quest for independence from the federal government and was perceived to be directed towards unilateralism. In light of its ethno-nationalist heritage, the KRG's unilateral actions have widely been perceived as part of a broader strategy to gain juridical independence (Klich, 2014). However, equating KRG's economic unilateralism as a move towards secession is too simplistic.

In its brief legitimate history of nearly two decades, semi-autonomous region of Kurdistan claims to have earned a few partners, if not friends. The fact that twenty nine countries have their separate diplomatic representation in Erbil and KRG has official representatives in fourteen countries, at least partially, testifies the argument (Klich, 2014). Since 2006, KRG has been independently managing its relations with the international community within the framework or charter presented by Department of Foreign Relations (DFR). On its official website, the KRG's Department of Foreign Affairs explicitly highlights "promotion of trade, investment, tourism and institutional ties" as one of the key responsibilities. DFR in its present form operates in accordance with KRG's Executive Order number 143 which was signed by the Kurdish Prime Minister Nechirvan Barzani in 2009 (Department for Foreign Relations, 2009).

Since the department falls under the premiership of council of ministers of the Kurdistan Region of Iraq, the foreign relations of Iraqi Kurdistan have the legitimate recognition. Interestingly, the officially documented KRG policy on foreign investment and trade defines its involvement in terms of "strong support to international business, investment and trade in the Kurdistan Region...(by maintaining) a very liberal investment law that reflects its general openness toward the international community" (Department for Foreign Relations, 2014).

The statement made by Karwan Jamal, KRG's Deputy Head of the Department of Foreign Relations (Deputy Minister) also becomes important in this context who, in an interview with the Kurdish Tribune, stated that, "...within these constitutional and legal frameworks, the strategy of the Department of Foreign Relations is to continue its open door policy in order to develop and strengthen relations with the international community in a way that would be mutually beneficial for the Kurdistan Region" (Kurdish Tribune, 2012). From official documents and statements, it is apparent that KRG positions itself in a supporting, co-operational and advisory role than as a decision-making authority. However, developments in 2013 evidently contradict Kurdish statements.

Oil exports from the region started in 2009 and since then billions of dollars have flowed into Iraq's treasury from fields in Kurdistan that have been explored, discovered and developed under the KRG's progressive and investor-friendly regime. Since most export deals were manoeuvred via Baghdad, the tensions were limited to revenue distribution. Relations between Baghdad and Erbil reached its nadir in 2013 in light of Kurdistan's decision to implement independent oil trade to Iran and to Turkey in 2014.

Kurdistan's geography becomes indispensable in order to understand the dynamics of Kurdish oil trade. The Kurdistan Region of Iraq is considered as one of the world's last place for untapped onshore oil. Oil deprived Turkey in north-west and sanction hit Iran in the east become a crucial part of Kurdistan's energy equation. In 2013, KRG started trucking crude from Kurdish fields over the border to Iran's Bandar Imam Khomeini (BIK) export terminal. Speculative reports suggest that at Iran's BIK terminal, the truckloads of crude were pooled in storage tanks and then pumped onto ships for export to Asia or to storage facilities at Fujairah in the United Arab Emirates and elsewhere in the Gulf, where the crude was kept in tank farms, part-owned by European companies (Coles and Finaren, 2013).

The three border gates of Haji Umran, Bashamakh and Broyzkhan constitute the main routes to transport oil via land. While there was immense resistance from the US, rhetorical criticism against Erbil-Tehran trade was not very sharp from Baghdad. Some scholars associate this to Iraq and Iran political intimacy. Given the geopolitical equations, one may contend that US anger was due to involvement of Iran and not merely Kurdish contempt of Iraqi constitution. However, this question may be placed outside the ambit of ongoing discussion.

Turkey has emerged to be the most important lifeline for KRG. Opening of Turkish consulate in Erbil in 2010 and strong energy cooperation exemplify the intimacy at political and economic level. Evidently, Turkey has been an important conduit for Kurdish oil exports. On the Turkish front, the TaqTaq-Khurmala-Fish Khabur pipeline that connects the Taq oil field to the entry point for the Kirkuk-Ceyhan pipeline became functional in 2014 and has been the subject of conflict between federal government and KRG, and Ankara and Baghdad. Turkey connects the land-locked Kurdistan region to European markets and Kurdish oil finds its buyers beyond Turkey, in markets of Israel and Europe.

However, the country which has opposed the Kurdish movement for decades will be careful in extending support to the Kurdish community in its neighbourhood. Iraqi Kurds' rhetoric on autonomy has been strong and KRG in Iraq has been vocally insistent about parting ways with Baghdad. However, to assume that Turkey will be a part of the recipe would be naive and unrealistic. Territorial disintegration of any of Turkey's neighbouring countries will have a domino effect and will increase the danger of secessionist movements by other Kurds. Three aspects regarding Kurdistan's trade pattern need to be highlighted here, Destination of oil, oil pricing strategy and the role of state institutions.

Destination of Kurdish Oil: First factor is the destination of oil; the first tanker, United Leadership, which left the Turkish port in May 2014, was parked off the coast of Morocco and the second one, United Emblem, transferred its cargo to the Liberia-flagged tanker SCF Altai where the tanker offloaded its cargo to Israeli port of Ashkelon (Unal, 2014). Evidently, there are multiple party linkages. Regarding trade with Israel, Kurdish energy minister TanerYildiz's stated, "oil could be sold to any country through the markets...shiploads may be dispatched to Israel or other routes. We do not deal with where the oil will be sent" (Unal, 2014).

This indifference towards trade destination hints that decisions are being guided more by economic considerations, than political, historic and geopolitical compulsions. The third party recipients of Kurdish oil have included European as well as Asian nations like India, Austria and Russia (Nuri, 2014). Similar logic applies to case of Iran, where oil trade deal appeared to be bilateral but benefits extended to multiple parties across continents.

Linking KRG's strategic blueprint to current geopolitical developments is pertinent to this discussion. While KRG and Turkey share close ties, on many occasions the relation came under test after 2014. This created a potential void for new partnerships to flourish. At this point again, reference to Iran becomes relevant. Iran and Iraqi Kurdistan have a long history dating back to Iran's support of Iraqi Kurds in the early 1970s against the Iraqi government. Turkey's reluctance to help KRG while Erbil was under threat from ISIS following the fall of Mosul provided an opportunity for Iran, to use this to improve its leverage in Northern Iraq by offering assistance to KRG in its struggle against ISIS (Linderstrauss, 2016).

On the energy front, the Turkey Ceyhan pipeline—the major functional source of export for Iraqi Kurdish oil—has seen dramatic fluctuations and in February 2016, the Ceyhan pipeline was the target of a bombing by the suspected Kurdistan Workers Party (PKK) in Turkey. The pipeline was temporarily shut down for repairs and cost the KRG US$ 250 million in lost revenues over February-March 2016 (Mawji, 2016). According to a wikileaks document, the Turkish government loaned KRG an amount of US$ 1,150 million in two instalments of US$ 500 million and one instalment of US$ 150 million, and over US$ 3 billion more will be needed to finance KRG's operational and expansion projects (Ekurd Daily, 2016; Mamouri, 2017).

The burgeoning financial debt gave the KRG a reason to move towards "diversification" of trade partners. Over the past two years, a growing segment of the Kurdish oil had been transported through trucks into Iran and used in northern Iranian refineries, and both the partners have been discussing the prospects of building a pipeline since 2014. However, serious deliberations have been happening since March 2016 when Iran proposed a pipeline for bringing Iraqi Kurdistan oil to Iran and meeting was held between KRG's Ministry of Natural Resources and Iran's Ministry of Oil (Mawji, 2016; Rudaw, 2016). As per the details, the new pipeline will carry oil from Kurdish territory to Iran and Iran would refine and then return the oil. Preliminary reports also suggest that pipeline would connect Koysinjaq in the KRG, crossing the border at Parvez Khan and then go to Kermanshah in western Iran, where the crude would be inserted into the Iranian pipeline system and potentially used in the country's northern refineries (Khajehpour, 2016).

KRG's Oil Pricing Strategy: Second is the price factor. It is relevant to highlight that the situation took a negative turn towards mid-2014 when KRG's fiscal debt started mounting on account of three main factors, namely, plunging oil prices, Baghdad's decision in February 2014 to freeze Kurdistan's share of national revenues estimated at US$ 1 billion a month, and a refugee crisis triggered by Kurdistan's war with ISIS, which began in August 2014. With global oil prices having plunged from US$ 130 per barrel in 2013 to US$ 112 per barrel in June 2014 to US$ 31 per barrel in December 2015, the KRG had to revise its strategy and strike new oil deals to finance its economy. Certain reports suggest that Kurds lowered the oil price to strike deals; touching US$ 56 per barrel in June 2014 (Hacaoglu, 2016).

Price discounts are often used as a strategy by new players to enter an established oligopolistic market. However, with oil prices fluctuating in global market, it will be challenging for KRG to strike profitable deals. The fact that KRG, in March 2016, offered to sell its oil fields to Turkey for US$ 5 billion (without Baghdad's consent) to pay off its debts, speaks of KRG's diminishing economic health. In this context, KRG's low-pricing behaviour hints at economic irrationality and myopic vision (Ekurd Daily, 2016; Al monitor, 2017).

Role of State Institutions and Bargaining Power Perspective: Third factor is the involvement of state institutions. Turkey's state-owned Halkbank is managing the receipts from sale of Kurdish oil (Coles, 2014). Thus, there is a state-to-state level coordination at an institutional level. Such engagement apparently hints at financial coordination. The clash of economic logic and political motivation keeps the situation ambiguous.

On the surface, the forging of independent diplomatic ties appears to be a possible gateway for the level of economic and regional autonomy that could support an independent Kurdish state. A holistic understanding compels study of both buyer and seller interests in trade, and relative bargaining power. Oil has been a strategic product and not merely an economic entity. Trade of oil does earn revenue and foreign exchange but its importance is much beyond the money it earns/ financial transaction. Thus, the real price of oil includes a direct monetary cost as well as indirect political cost and the same logic extends to the case of Kurdish oil.

The concept of bargaining power can be employed to understand the costs of trade; direct and indirect, monetary and non-monetary. Trade creates conditions for bargaining, where actors want to coordinate but on different outcomes. In these situations, actors bargain over the distribution of benefits and costs (Slantchev, 2005). In accordance with the popular "Rational Actor Model" of Graham Tillett Allison, bargaining power can be defined as the degree to which an actor is able to influence the expectations of its opponent in a way that is beneficial to the interests of that actor (Slantchev, 2005). To test the proposition in case of KRG, it is important to identify the potential factors guiding behaviour of both the sides.

From a buyer's perspective, the decision to import oil at a lower than market price supports economic logic, since cheaper oil translates into financial benefits. However, the direct monetary benefits are offset by the indirect political cost of engaging with an unrecognised entity such as Kurdistan. In this particular case, Baghdad's blacklist policy is a clear example of a political trade-off which KRG's trading partners faced. Yet, countries have signed oil deals with Kurdistan. In the words of Maria van der Hoeven, executive director of the International Energy Agency, "...the upside of easy oil (from Kurdistan) outweighs the risks of upsetting Baghdad, for large and smaller producers alike" (Swint, 2013).

From the sellers' perspective, oil sales at lower than market price entail a monetary cost. The independent Kurdish oil sales entail a monetary cost on Baghdad. At the same time, Kurdish economy is in infancy. In order to develop the market structures and establish an oil market, Kurdistan needs buyers for its controversial oil. At market price, the buyer nations would have no incentive of signing deals with Kurdistan by offending Iraq. Thus, price cut is a part of strategy to entice potential buyers and create an artificial market space.

It is also advocated that economic self-sufficiency in the short- and medium-run may be used to facilitate autonomy in the long-run. All these political and medium-term economic gains can be labelled as indirect benefits. In this trade equation, it can be stated that for buyers, decisions are influenced by direct monetary benefits and indirect political costs. In case of sellers, there are direct monetary costs but indirect benefits.

Trade will take place only under the condition when benefits are perceived to be higher than costs, in both cases. This logic holds good in case of Kurdish oil trade. Both the parties involved are guided by either monetary benefits or political benefits. The question is whether Kurdistan has sufficient bargaining power to influence its trading partners. From a market economy perspective, the Kurdish oil export is an experiment to identify potential buyers for its controversial oil and estimate price they are willing to pay. And the question for KRG is whether the test of marketability of product is able to increase leverage in negotiations between Erbil and Baghdad, or is this a test to see if they might eventually obtain sufficient revenues to move toward independence (Ahmed and Krauss, 2014).

Assuming that there can be three possible explanations of KRG's behaviour; purely economic desire for self-sufficiency, short-run demand for economic independence directed towards long-term goal of autonomy, and purely political demand for autonomy, KRG's oil trade with Turkey and Iran can be understood using Allison model.

First scenario: Purely economic desire for self-sufficiency is a simplistic explanation given by analysts who view Kurdish policies as a strategy for economic independence. The quest for autonomy in decision-making and greater control over resources is being perceived as a potential threat for independence. Scholars argue that oil trade is being used to extract more concessions from the central government, as a deliberate strategy that will give Kurdistan greater control over its exports and access to more markets (Klich, 2014).

Dispute over Kirkuk, issue of referendum, greater share in budget and autonomy in oil exports are the major issues of contention. Various Western and regional analysts have suggested alike that KRG "attempts to increase its economic autonomy portray a hope for economic independence in the future" (Klich, 2014: 70). KRG's oil trade with Israel is a testimony to the economic motivations. ShwanZulal's analysis becomes important in this regard; "KRG is coy about dealing with Israel because of the controversy and the emotion that Israel brings about in the Muslim world…But if Israel is willing to be supportive, and other countries are not, the Kurds will deal with them" (Carlstrom, 2014).

Shireen T. Hunter of Georgetown University labelled Masoud Barzani as a "good political player", and emphatically stated that he is creating a "current panic of Turkey, Iran, the US and the Iraqi central government to extract concessions that he wants" (Namazi, 2014). Other regional analysts also subscribe to a similar view that "independent oil exports amount to a powerful step for Iraq's Kurdish region to strengthen the economy" (Hacaoglu, 2014). However, the pure economic explanation is rather myopic and incoherent.

Second scenario: Another possible determinant of the Kurdish behaviour could be the short-run demand for economic independence directed towards long-term goal of autonomy. Kurdistan's oil trade is being seen as an "economic platform from which an independent Kurdish state could potentially be launched" and in particular, the intimacy between Erbil and Ankara appears to be a "possible gateway for the level of economic and regional autonomy that could support an independent Kurdish state" (Klich, 2014: 62). There is a valid reason to suspect the real intentions of Kurdistan behind such behaviour. Statements by KRG officials including President Massound Barazani implicitly hint at the Kurdish dream of independence.

In his interview with the CNN, the President stated that, "the time is here for the Kurdistan people to determine their future, and the decision of the people is what we're going to uphold" (CNN London, 2014). The occasional statements by officials as well as analysts have added a degree of conviction to the speculations regarding independence.

However, the actual outcomes will be determined by a set of economic, political, strategic and legal factors in a domestic, regional and global scenario. In fact, economic dependence on Baghdad firmly limits the ability of the KRG to establish its independence. The central government currently supplies Erbil with 17 percent of the federal Iraqi budget, equating to US$ 10 billion annually, or about 95 percent of its revenue (Natali, 2013).

Third scenario: The most contentious of all the possible explanations is the purely political demand for autonomy. This would imply that signing independent oil deals is directly driven by desire for autonomy from federal government, and independent oil exports are being used to tie diplomatic knots. Various regional analysts suggest that oil trade with Turkey or Iran is an important step toward independence (Hacauglu, 2014).

Certain Western analysts also subscribe to a similar view that exploration and export of Kurdish oil will be a "geopolitical game changer" (Swint, 2009). Rhetoric by Kurdish officials exhibits a rather confusing picture. According to KRG Prime Minister Nechirvan Barzani, "We do not view this issue as a path towards Kurdistan's independence, but rather as the expression of our constitutional rights" (Hacauglu et al., 2014). In hindsight, sustainability of such relations remains highly questionable and KRG's energy ties with Turkey and Iran can be studied to understand this.

KRG-Turkey Oil Trade: Prism of Price Elasticity

This peculiar partnership with Iraqi Kurds can be understood in the light of two factors; firstly, the partnership ensures easy movement of low priced Kurdish oil to oil deprived Turkey. Secondly, Turkey is aware that it offers the only accessible market to landlocked Kurdish region. Perhaps the most important thing to note, given Baghdad's and Ankara's anxiety amidst Kurdish unilateralism, is the fact that the Kurdistan region, being landlocked, must depend on Turkish infrastructure to export oil in commercial quantities to markets in Europe (Voller, 2013). This suggests that by becoming an irreplaceable stakeholder in Iraqi Kurdistan's economic development and Iraq's future, Turkey can buy KRG's assurance that any action by Kurds in Iraq should not cause domestic disturbances in Turkey and ambition of establishing a wider Kurdistan can be checked. Thus, Turkey is buying both Kurdish oil and Kurdish assurance in return of its economic aid and assistance.

The micro economic concept of price elasticity can be applied to understand the bargaining power equation between KRG and buyers of Kurdish oil (Turkey, Iran, and other third parties). As an energy poor country which produces only ten percent of its demand, essentially Turkey's 'oil imports' are highly inelastic, and in absence of any substitutes, demand for oil imports will continue to be inelastic. However, Turkey's imports of 'Kurdish oil' are largely driven by the price incentive and thus 'oil imports from Kurdistan' are highly elastic because Turkey is not solely dependent on Kurdish oil and can shift to other oil exporting nations. That is, in worst case scenario, Turkey can exercise the option of substituting its oil imports from Kurdistan to its traditional suppliers like Iran, Russia, Saudi Arabia, Kazakhstan etc. (Energy Information Agency, 2014). KRG's geographic and geopolitical compulsions make it dependent on Turkey for its oil sales and evidently, Turkey enjoys a greater bargaining power in this equation.

Iraqi Kurdistan's international relations have been rapidly

increasing, but this does not necessarily translate into tangible and practicable support for an independent state (Klich, 2014). Besides this, it needs to be seen how the partnerships advance in situations when market prices fall further or when price of Kurdish oil is raised to market levels. Operating at lower than marginal cost is not an economically feasible strategy, and price rise is inevitable. Also, KRG has been trying to diversify its pipeline portfolio. Similar examination of KRG and Iran's relation suggest that KRG has started looking eastwards towards post-sanction Iran as a substitute or supplement to Turkey in order to reduce its dependence.

On the other hand, sanction hit Iran is seeking new partnerships in the neighbourhood and is equally desperate to revive its economy. In this case, KRG might exercise equal or higher bargaining power since Iran is manoeuvring its re-entry in the energy market.

However, Iranian Oil Minister Bijan Namdar Zanganeh plans to visit Iraqi Oil Minister Jabbar al-Luaibi to discuss an oil pipeline proposal from the province of Sulaimaniyah in Iraqi Kurdistan to Iranian territory which signals Iran's tilt towards Baghdad, and threatens KRG's plans of establishing monopoly over the oil trade (Mamouri, 2017). At best, we can conclude that KRG's actions seem to be directed towards greater economic concessions and political accommodation from Baghdad, rather than independence in short-term.

Conclusion

Economic autonomy is a promising prospect for a conflict zone like Iraqi Kurdistan, whose existence is rooted in the unfulfilled promise of a homeland. KRG's diplomatic success based on independent oil deals has sparked scepticism and triggered a serious debate on the real agenda behind its economic autonomy. Such unilateralism is being associated with Kurdish desire for secession. However, this explanation is rather weak. KRG has a proven capacity for 'inter-state' relations, but there are many overt opponents of Kurdish secession, including US and Turkey.

The recent developments in Kurdish oil sector need to be understood in conjunction with constitutional provisions and the diplomatic signals. KRG's actions can be labelled as a strategy designed to achieve a higher degree of economic self-sufficiency directly; by raising revenues from oil deals and indirectly, by bargaining with Baghdad for budgetary concessions. However, one cannot overlook the fact that its desire for a separate national identity lacks international legitimacy. Thus, oil is being used as a tool of diplomatic expansion and there is little in support of the argument that oil-based diplomacy essentially hints at independence.

Temporal perspectives on Kurdistan help one to understand that over time, Kurdish struggle for autonomy has moulded itself as per developments in Iraq, and from an ethnic struggle of Kurds, Iraqi Kurds have focused on their desire for a state. KRG's unilateralism emerged as a potent threat to Baghdad in post-2003 scenario when Kurdish areas witnessed a surge in investor attention. With shift in policy from foreign investments to independent oil trade, the case of desired secession of Iraqi Kurdistan has gained ample scholarly attention. The assessment in this paper suggests that KRG's policies are headed towards economic autonomy.

However, its linkages to independence are missing. Based on Graham Tillett Allison's Rational Actor Model and micro economic concept of elasticity of oil demand, one can decipher that KRG's vision is infested with strategic myopia and is rather unsustainable. Oil based diplomacy is not likely to garner support for autonomy, especially when it is engaging with an anti-Kurd Turkey. Bargaining power analysis confirms that in KRG's oil equations, the oil buyers enjoy a higher bargaining capacity and thus KRG's independent oil trade does not guarantee political gains. Thus, clearly, KRG lacks the international support, legitimacy as well as the bargaining power to pursue its goal of independence by using oil for diplomacy, and analysis suggests that KRG is aiming at economic self-reliance to negotiate with Baghdad for budgetary concessions and higher powers.

References

Ahmed, A. and Krauss, C. (2014), "Oil Gives Kurds a Path to Independence and Conflict with Baghdad", *The New York Times,* October 25.

Alves, A. (2011), "China's Oil Diplomacy: Comparing Chinese Economic Statecraft in Angola and Brazil", Ph.D. thesis, London School of Economics and Political Science, London.

Anderson, L. (2010), "Internationalizing Iraq's Constitutional Dilemma", in R. Lowe and G. Stansfield (eds.), 'The Kurdish Policy Imperative', London: Chatham House/Royal Institute of International Affairs

Baker, L. (2009), "Iraq's Kurds Will Hold on to Oil Revenues", available at: http://www.reuters.com/article/2009/11/10/idUSLA726993.

Barzani, M. (2012), "Kurdistan is a Model for Iraq", *Wall Street Journal.*

British Petroleum (2016), "BP Statistical Review of World Energy, 2016", available at: https://www.bp.com/content/dam/bp/pdf/energy-economics/statistical-review-2016/bp-statistical-review-of-world-energy-2016-full-report.pdf.

Carlstrom, G. (2014), "Iraqi Kurdish Oil Tanker Anchors Off Israel", *Al Jazeera,* available at: http://www.aljazeera.com/news/middleeast/2014/06/iraqi-kurdish-oil-tanker-anchors-off-israel-2014623103411252699.html.

CNN London (2014, June 23), "Iraq Falls Apart: Miscarriage of Justice; Imagine a World" [transcript], Interview with Massoud Barzani by Christiane Amanpour, available at: http://edition.cnn.com/TRANSCRIPTS/1406/23/ampr.01.html.

Coles, I. and Finaren, D. (2013), "Iraqi Kurdistan Opens Official Crude Oil Trade Route via Iran: Sources", *Reuters*, available at: http://www.reuters.com/article/2013/08/07/hold-kurds-oil-iran-idUSL6N0FU4LG20130807.

Constitution of Iraq (2005), available at: http://www.iraqinationality.gov.iq/ attach/iraqi_constitution.pdf.

Dabrowska, K. and G. Hann (2008), "Iraq Then and Now: A Guide to the Country and its People", England: The Global Pequot Press Inc.

Denselow, J. (2014), "The Kurdish Kingmakers", *Al Jazeera*, Qatar.

Ekurd Daily (2016, December 27), "Documents Reveal Iraqi Kurdistan Attempts to Sell Oil Fields to Turkey", available at: http://ekurd.net/kurdistan-sell-oil-fields-turkey-2016-12-27.

Energy Information Agency (2014), "Turkey Analysis Report", Washington D.C.

Gunter, M. (1999), "The Kurdish Predicament in Iraq", New York: Palgrave Macmillan.

Hacaoglu, S. (2014), "Turkey Allows Unilateral Kurdish Oil Exports as Iraq Ties Fray", *Bloomberg News*, available at: https://www.bloomberg.com/news/articles/2014-05-26/turkey-allows-unilateral-kurdish-oil-exports-as-iraq-ties-fray.

Hacauglu, S., Fair-weather, J. and Razzouk, N. (2014), "Oil Odyssey Offers Glimpse of Kurdish Independence in Iraq", available at: https://www.bloomberg.com/news/articles/2014-06-18/half-price-kurdish-oil-threatens-iraq-breakup-with-turkish-help.

Husari, R. (2008), "Iraq: Sunni and Shiite Lawmakers Sign Fragile Pact against Kurds", Energy Intelligence Group, available at: http://www.highbeam.com/doc/1G1-173971531.html.

Jonsson, C. (2002), "Diplomacy, Bargaining and Negotiation", in 'Handbook of International Relations', New York: Sage Publications Ltd.

Kane, S. (2010), "Iraq's Oil Politics: Where Agreement Might Not Be Found", United States Institute of Peace Report, 64(8), Washington D.C.

Khajehpour, B. (2016, June 29), "Iran's Pipeline Politics Reaches Iraqi Kurdistan", *Al Monitor: Iran Pulse*.

Kissinger, H. (1994), "Diplomacy", London: Simon & Schuster.

Klich, S. (2014), "Dependent yet Defiant: The Implications of Unilateralism in Iraqi Kurdistan", *The Australian National University Undergraduate Research Journal,* 5(13).

Kurdistan Board of Investment (2012), "Investment Factsheet: Kurdistan Region-Iraq", available at: http://www.iraq-jccme.jp/pdf/arc/04_krg_Investment_factsheet_en.pdf.

Kurdistan Tribune (2012, August 18), "KRG Department of Foreign Relations Will Continue Open Door Policy", available at: http://kurdistantribune.com/krg-department-of-foreign-relations-will-continue-open-door-policy-karwan-jamal.

Lando, B. (2014), "Chevron Undeterred by Baghdad Blacklist", Iraq Oil Report, available at: http://www.iraqoilreport.com/politics/oil-policy/hold-2-8405.

Linderstrauss, G. (2016), "Turkey Bets, Yet Again, on Barzani: Turkey-KRG Relations in Light of the Regional Turbulence", *Turkey Analyst,* available at: http://www.turkeyanalyst.org/publications/turkey-analyst-articles/item/504-turkey-bets-yet-again-on-barzani-turkey-krg-relations-in-light-of-the-regional-turbulence.html.

Mamouri, A. (2017, January 6), "Iraqi Kurdistan Oil: A Slippery Issue", *Al Monitor*, available at: http://www.al-monitor.com/pulse/originals/2017/01/iran-iraq-turkey-oil-ceyhan-sulaymaniyah-barzani.html.

Mawji, O. (2016), "Iraqi Kurdistan's Rise as an Independent Energy Player", *Geopolitical Monitor*, available at: https://www.geopoliticalmonitor.com/iraqi-kurdistans-rise-as-an-independent-energy-player.

Mills, R. (2016), "Under the Mountains: Kurdish Oil and Regional Politics, The Oxford Institute for Energy Studies, available at: https://www.oxfordenergy.org/wpcms/wp-content/uploads/2016/02/Kurdish-Oil-and-Regional-Politics-WPM-63.pdf.

Namazi, M. (2014, August 7), "Iran Fears an Independent Kurdistan in Iraq", *Iran Wire*, available at: http://en.iranwire.com/features/5931.

Natali, D. (2013, February 20), "Who Will Pay IOCs in Iraqi Kurdistan?", *Al Monitor*, available at: http://www.al-monitor.com/pulse/originals/2013/02/iraq-turkey-pipeline-reduce-tensions-between-baghdad-ankara.html.

Nuri, A. (2014, June 23), "Kurdish Oil to Israel: A New Mid-East", *The Times of Israel,* Jerusalem.

Pyagbara, L. (2007, August 27), "The Adverse Impacts of Oil Pollution on the Environment and Well-being of a Local Indigenous Community: The Experience of the Ogoni People of Nigeria", paper presentation, International Expert Group Meeting on Indigenous People and Protection of the Environment, Russian Federation, Khabarovsk, Russia.

Reed, S. (2012, July 20), "Chevron Makes Oil Exploration Deal in Iraqi Kurdistan", *New York Times.*

Sharp, P. (1999), "For Diplomacy: Representation and the Study of International Relations", *International Studies Review,* 1(1), 33-57.

Slantchev, B. (2005, April 19), "Introduction to International Relations Lecture 4: Bargaining and Dynamic Commitment", available at: http://slantchev.ucsd.edu/courses/ps12/04-bargaining-dynamic-commitment.pdf.

Swint, B. (2009, June 13), "New Oil Pipeline Boosts Iraqi Kurdistan: The Region Made of Three Northern Provinces", *The Washington Post.*

Swint, B. (2013), "Kurdistan's Oil Ambitions", *Business Week.*

Unal, A. (2014), "Turkey's Halkbank Collects the Revenue of Kurdish Oil", *Mesopotamia Kurdistan Daily Independent News Service*, available at: http://www.mesop.de/2014/06/24/mesop-ankaras-oil-revenues-no-oil-to-israel.

Voller, Y. (2013), "Kurdish Oil Politics in Iraq: Contested Sovereignty and Unilateralism", *Journal of Middle East Policy Council,* 20(1).

Wikileaks (2006), "Activities of Norwegian Oil Company Subsidiary cable 06BAGHDAD4734", available at: http://wikileaks.org/cable/2006/12/ 06BAGHDAD4734.html.

7

Water Scarcity in Jordan: Demand and Supply Side Factors

P.R. Kumaraswamy and Manjeri Singh

Water scarcity in Jordan is a stark reality. Being the second 'poorest and driest' country in the world, the Hashemite Kingdom faces water scarcity not only due to anthropological issues but also because of low water supplies. Around 93 percent of the country receives less than 200 mm of rainfall annually while only two percent gets around 400 mm. In addition to this, Jordan has only one major river system, namely, River Jordan, after which the country bears its name. Even though one of the largest river systems in the region, River Jordan is not the major supplier of freshwater and it accounts for only 50 MCM of total freshwater available annually. Groundwater is also not replenished because of over-abstraction, water theft, low rainfall, lower soil water retention capacity and high evaporation rate. In 2014 alone, there were about 140 illegal wells discovered in the country (MWI, n.d.). It is important to delve into the sources of water available in Jordan to understand the water scarcity its population is facing.

Sources of Water

The three major sources of water in Jordan are the surface water, ground water, and reclaimed waste water. In 2013, Ministry of Water and Irrigation estimated the annual water availability at 892 million cubic metres (MCM). Out of these, renewable freshwater accounts for 275 MCM or 28 percent (of which 50 MCM comes from Israel as part of the 1994 Peace Treaty). Renewable groundwater supplies 433 MCM or 51 percent while non-renewable fossil groundwater is about 75

MCM or 9 percent. Added to these natural sources, Jordan has to rely on artificial sources mainly by reclaiming wastewater which supplies about 102 MCM or 12 percent of the total water available in the country (MWI, 2013).

The surface water comes from three major river systems, namely, Jordan, Yarmouk and Zarqa and except for River Zarqathe the other two are international waterways. The water supplies from these have been highly unreliable due to upstream diversions and over-pumping in countries that share these river systems; for instance, Syria draws most of the water from Yarmouk River and its tributaries while Israel over-pumps from River Jordan. These directly affect the water availability in Jordan in a negative way.

In the past, Jordan River has been the major source of water supplies to the Kingdom with a base flow of 1.3 billion cubic metres per year (BCM/year). After Israel had built the National Water Carrier in 1953 and diverted waters from Lake Tiberius to its coastal plains and southern desert, the flow of the Lower Jordan River dropped significantly. Israel agreeing to provide 50 MCM/year to Jordan as a part of the 1994 Peace Treaty was meant to compensate this loss. The treaty specifies that Israel may extract 12 million cubic metres (MCM) of water during summer and 13 MCM in winter from the Yarmouk River. In exchange, Jordan is allowed to "store" twenty MCM of its water in Lake Tiberius in Israel during winter. Israel agreed to help Jordan find additional water using desalination technology (Susskind and Islam, 2012). However, a study conducted by the Government of Jordan found that the Lower Jordan River has been reduced to 2 percent of its historic flow (Bromberg, 2007). Added to these issues, even the water quality of the River has deteriorated sharply, with high levels of salinity and pollution from agricultural fertilizers and untreated wastewater upstream in Israel and in the West Bank.

Yarmouk River is the another important source for Jordan which had a base flow of 450 MCM/year but over the years,

Syria built about 45 dams over it and the flow rate has reduced to 50-100 MCM/year thereby considerably reducing Jordan's share. The third surface water source to Jordan is River Zarqa which is a seasonal stream and is mostly fed by rainfall and reclaimed wastewater. The water of this system is highly polluted mostly because the industrial areas of Jordan and around 70 percent of the small to medium sized industries are located closer to it. About 50 percent of the water to Zarqa River comes from Al-Samra wastewater treatment plant and hence the water drawn from this system is not used for domestic or municipal purposes.

Since surface water resources are unreliable in terms of quality, quantity and availability, the Jordanian population relies mainly on *groundwater* for its domestic needs. However, the groundwater supply is not adequate to meet the growing domestic demands. Farmers also use this groundwater for crop irrigation and hence domestic and agricultural sectors are competing for the same resource. In 2013, the agricultural sector consumed about 53 percent of the water resources while contributing only about 6 percent of GDP (MWI, 2015). However, this was an improvement from the 2010 levels when about 68 percent of the water was used for agriculture.

Groundwater (both renewable and non-renewable) accounts for about 60 percent of the annual water budget, or about 508 MCM/year (MWI, 2015). There are two main types of groundwater resources, namely, renewable and non-renewable (or fossil) resources. Renewable groundwater aquifers can be recharged by natural and artificial recharge. Rainfall, surface water and irrigation are natural sources of recharge, while processed fresh water (through leakages in the delivery systems) or treated wastewater fall can be identified as artificial resources. Twelve groundwater basins have been identified in Jordan (Ghneim, 2011). It has been estimated that the safe yield that allows for recharge of groundwater supplies of renewable groundwater resources across the country is about 275 MCM/year. However, water stealing practices through illegal wells has made the country to withdraw water far more than the safe yield (MWI, 2013).

The unreliability of supply through natural sources has led the country to opt for *unconventional methods* of water resources. Two most important non-conventional sources are treated wastewater and water attained through desalination process. Because of transportation and pumping costs, these options are still not exploited to their full capacity. Moreover, desalination requires costly and modern technology and given Jordan's economic conditions, it is not a viable option. Treated wastewater, on the other hand, is becoming an increasingly important resource, contributing around 12 percent to the national water budget in 2013 (Yorke, 2013). Around three-quarters of this water is used in the agricultural sector; for instance, in 2013 more than 75 percent of the approximately 102 MCM of treated wastewater produced was used for agricultural purposes (Ghneim, 2011).

Most of the treated wastewater is released from treatment plants near the major population centres (and also the major wastewater sources) of the country. Jordan currently uses about 55 MCM of its treated wastewater for restricted irrigation purposes which can only be used for certain crops. According to the Ministry of Water and Irrigation (MWI), the government plans to increase the use of treated wastewater for irrigation to 232 MCM/year by 2020, mostly in the Jordan Valley. It is to be noted that the amount of wastewater has increased over the years, mainly due to the significant increase in population (partly contributed to refugee influx) which has resulted in the existing wastewater treatment plants being used beyond their original design capacity and this, in turn, has reduced the quality of treated wastewater to drop.

As a result of this reduced quality, the treated wastewater cannot be fully exploited to progressively replace the freshwater resources in all agricultural uses (Mohsen, 2007). These contribute to the absolute shortage of water in the country. Added to this, Jordan has a relative scarcity of water regarding its sectorial distribution.

Distribution of Water

The country is a classic example of the mismanagement of water in the sense that sectors which offer low yields regarding employment or GDP are given more water than the sectors which have been performing better in both the aspects and can perform better if given more water. The competition between agricultural, domestic and industrial sectors is strong and constantly growing, especially as the availability of fresh water decreases. According to a report published by MWI in 2015, while the water resources in Jordan continue to be limited, the demand by domestic, industrial and agricultural sectors, as well as environment would continue to increase.

Regarding distribution (Table 7.1), the agricultural sector has always been the main water user (ranging from 70 percent until about 2000 to 68 percent in 2010 and 53 percent in 2013) followed by the domestic sector which uses about 41 percent water. The industrial sector comprising of mainly potash and phosphate industries consumes about 5 percent of water and the emerging tourism industry—the major income generator—uses only 1 percent of the water. In 2010, 605 MCM or 67.9 percent of water went for agricultural use, 250 MCM or 28.1 percent for drinking and domestic use and 35 MCM or 3.9 percent for industrial use (MWI 2010). Moreover, regarding revenue generation, industrial and tourism industries are more beneficial as water supplied to these sectors are charged at high rates while agricultural as well as municipal water is highly subsidized. For domestic use, the price is 25JD (around US$35.30) for six cubic metres of water and is much higher for industrial use (GOETHE, n.d.).

A water rationing is used to control distribution in different parts of the country. The day when running water is available in the kingdom, it is popularly known as the "water day". For urban areas, "water day" is twice in a week for 24 hours while in rural areas it is only once a week or twice in two weeks. However, after a "significantly poor winter" in 2015, the MWI decided to reduce the already limited household water supply as part of a strategic emergency plan to cope with the increasing demand for potable water (MWI, n.d.). Moreover, water deficit which is currently over 500 MCM annually, increased in 2014 with a 30 percent deficit in drinking water and 50 percent in irrigation (The Jordan Times, 2014).

Table 7.1: Water Uses in Jordan, 2013

Sector	SW	RG	NRG	TW	Total (MCM)	Percentage
Agriculture	104	216	34	100	454	53
Domestic	122	197	34		353	42
Industry	13	20	7	2	42	5
Total	239	433	75	102	849	
Percentage	28	51	9	12	100	

SW = Surface Water; RG = Renewable Groundwater; NRG = Non-Renewable Groundwater; TW = Treated Wastewater.

Source: MWI, 2013.

There are anthropogenic factors that trigger the already scarce water in Jordan. These include growing population, rapid urbanization, and industrialization which are further accompanied by leakage, water loss and water theft. An estimated 40 percent to 80 percent of the water supply is lost in the network, depending on the location. Inefficient administrative processes, out-dated infrastructure, and inadequate maintenance are the main factors responsible for this huge waste. Administrative issues include unbilled water use, illegal extractions and metering issues.

Jordan is characterized by a rapidly expanding population, caused largely by periodic influx of massive refugee immigration. After the establishment of the State of Israel in 1948, Palestinians of the West Bank which was annexed by Jordan, were granted citizenship. The refugees from Iraq since 2003 and Syria since 2011 have contributed to immense increases in Jordan's resident population. While its water supply has largely remained at a fixed level, Jordan's population has increased exponentially, thereby forcing the country to spread its resources in an attempt to provide water for all its citizens and residents.

Poor governance and inefficient implementation have plagued Jordan in its efforts to effectively allocate and use water. The government has put measures in place aimed at reducing demand and increasing supply, but these have barely proved beneficial. Peace Treaty with Israel signed in 1994 guaranteed Jordan an additional 215 MCM of water annually through various infrastructural changes. Even within the Peace Treaty, both countries "recognize that their water resources are not sufficient to meet their needs. More water should be supplied for their use through various methods, including projects of regional and international cooperation" (Susskind and Islam, 2012).

Efforts at imposing policy to alleviate the crisis could not take off due to "joined-up government" between involved parties (Ibid). A good example of how a "promising local project" can be stalled by conflict is the Disi Water Conveyance Project, which aimed to transport water to Amman from underground resources the Kingdom shares with Saudi Arabia. Its construction has been greatly affected by disagreement between the local tribes (Dziuban 2012). Moreover, even after being functional, the project did not take into account the growth in population in the wake of the Syrian crisis. Therefore, when in 2014, the project was eventually started, there were about 1.4 million Syrian refugees in the country already.

The misallocation of water resources has resulted in a lower than ideal economic returns. Generally, agricultural uses offer a lower value of returns compared to municipal and industrial uses, but since much of Jordan's water is of poor quality, more of it is allocated to irrigation and agriculture. Even in cases where fresh and clean water is found, they are located far from urban areas and are therefore consumed by agriculture to avoid high pumping and transport costs. Without a significant flow of water for municipal purposes, drinking water is limited, and people throughout the country are feeling the impact.

Challenges to Sustenance

This growing scarcity has driven the Jordanian government to develop a water demand management strategy to maximize water use efficiency and minimize wastage. The strategy includes measures to increase irrigation efficiency, broaden the use of treated wastewater in the agricultural sector and in the longer term, carry out seawater desalination at Aqaba, possibly as part of the Red Sea-Dead Sea Project. As water demand in Jordan continues to increase, stress on the country's natural water resources continues to grow and widen the demand-supply gap. As Jordan can no longer depend only on its natural water resources, it is necessary to look for alternative sources of water. One of the sources already being harnessed is domestic wastewater, which is treated and reused as an alternative water supply, especially for agricultural irrigation. In 2013, the agricultural sector used around 53 percent of the country's water supplies and treated wastewater provided a fifth of a quarter of this amount to agriculture.

Therefore, in present times, the growing water scarcity in Jordan is managed through a combination of supply and demand-driven approaches. The demand-driven approach (also called demand management) implements water saving measures and reducing demand for water from the source. Technical measures, such as repair of leaking water pipes in a distribution network and the use of perforated tubing for crop irrigation (drip irrigation) result in water savings. Legal, administrative and financial measures can also help reduce demand. Setting a higher price for water, for instance, would make people more cautious in their use of water. Demand management approaches emphasize economic and social aspects of water use to a greater degree than supply management approaches do (Khaleq, 2008).

To conclude, Jordan has been using survival methods to address its water scarcity issue either by reallocation of water within the sectors, lowering the demand for further reduction in supply to households or by increasing the supply by treating wastewater. All of these are good strategies for management of water in present times but would be insufficient to secure water supplies for future. Therefore, Jordan needs to sustain water by adding more water to its reservoirs or through supply side management such as water harvesting, wastewater treatment and above all desalination.

References

Abu-Sharar, T.M. et al. (2003), "The Use of Treated Sewage for Irrigation in Jordan: Opportunities and Constraints", *Water and Environment Journal*, Vol. 17, No. 4, 232-238.

Ghneim, A. (2011), "Wastewater Reuse and Management in the Middle East and North Africa: A Case Study of Jordan", M.Sc. dissertation, published by Universitätsverlag der TU Berlin.

Al-Ansari, Nadher, Alibraheim A., Alsaman M. and Knuttson, Sven (2014), "Water Demand Management in Jordan", *Scientific Research*, [published online in January], Vol. 6, 19-26.

Bromberg, G. (2007), 'Will the Jordan River Keep on Flowing?", *Yale Environment*, 360.

FAO (Food and Agriculture Organization of the United Nations) (2008), "Irrigation in the Middle East Region: AQUASTAT Survey 2008", FAO, Rome, available at: www.fao.org/nr/water/aquastat/countries_regions/jordan/jordan_cp.pdf.

FAO Aquastat (2013), "Countries, Regions, Trans-boundary River Basins, Jordan", available at: http://www.fao.org/nr/water/aquastat/countries_regions/JOR/index.stm.

Hadadin, M. (1998), "Environmental Letter, World Water Day, Jordan", 6-8.

Hadadin, Nidal, Qaqish, Maher, Akawwi, Emad and Bdour, Ahmed (2010), "Water Shortage in Jordan-Sustainable Solutions", *Desalination*, No. 250, 197-202.

Mohsen, M.S. (2007), "Water Strategies and Potential of Desalination in Jordan", *Desalination*, No. 203, 27-46.

MWI (Ministry of Water and Irrigation) (2008), "Water for Life: Jordan's Water Strategy 2008-2022", available at: http://web.idrc.ca/uploads/user-S/12431464431JO_Water-Strategy09.pdf.

MWI (Ministry of Water and Irrigation), "Annual Report, 2010".

MWI (Ministry of Water and Irrigation), "Annual Report, 2011".

MWI (Ministry of Water and Irrigation), "Annual Report, 2013".

Subah, Ali (2012), "Water in Jordan: Water Security and Protection", Ministry of Water and Irrigation, available at: http://www.envirosecurity.org/essmed/june2012/presentations/II-B_Jordan_Ali_Subah.pdf.

UNESCO (2012), "Managing Water under Uncertainty and Risk", United Nations World Water Development Report 4.

Yorke, V. (2013), "Politics Matter: Jordan's Path to Water Security Lies through Political Reforms and Regional Cooperation", NCCR Trade Regulation, Working paper 2013/19.

8

Hostage-Prisoners Swap: Israel's Experience

Minakshi Sardar

Introduction

Protection of the civilians has always been an important concern for the state. Taking of civilian/s as hostages has been a major threat to individual lives, the society and the state at large. The incidents of hostage taking are old phenomenon and can be traced through ancient texts. However, the recent era has made such acts easier with the use of modern technologies and other equipment.

Hostage taking can be explained as an act, of taking person/s by force in order to fulfil certain political demands, aimed towards the state. Such incidents pose severe challenges to the state security. The targeted person can be identified as the hostage, while the person/s performing the act is/are the hostage taker/s. The ultimate motive of the hostage taker is to use the hostage as a bargaining tool to compel the government to meet their demands. Any hostage taking scenario involves three major actors, the hostage, the hostage taker and the rescue unit. States being a victim to such incidents have often relied on negotiation to release the hostage. Be it the Kandahar crisis of 1999 or that of Laju hijacking in 1974, negotiation strategy has helped the state to secure the lives of the hostages.

Israel with its stated policy of 'no negotiation' with hostage takers have often agreed to negotiated settlements to secure the life of the hostages or sometimes their bodies or simply even their body parts. Israel has not negotiated with the hostage takers directly; these negotiations have always allowed involvement of another state. The several wars fought between the Arab states and Israel, like the 1948 war, the 1956 war, the

1967 war, the 1973 war or the 1982 war allowed for the capture of several combatants as prisoners of war. Unlike hostage taking where a non-state actor illegally captures a civilian, prisoner's exchange is legal and often practiced among the states. In case of Israel, several non-state actors have often used the hostages to release such prisoners of war captured by Israel.

A study of Israel's experience with hostage taking, suggests that hostage taking has been used as a common tactic to release prisoners from Israeli jails. Israel has strongly supported the use of military and has strictly followed the policy of not surrendering to the hostage takers. However, such incidents of releasing prisoners to secure the hostages have often given scope to differences in opinion among people. Israel's swap between hostage and prisoners has often led to internal tension and have raised questions over time on the price it had paid (even though indirectly) by striking deal with the hostage takers. The focus of this paper is to find the relevance of such negotiations for Israel in hostage scenario and the rationale behind such decision-making. The paper will discuss the negotiated settlements which have continued over a long period of time.

Hostage Taking

According to Gary Noesner, a hostage incident can be defined as one in which "a subject holds other people in order to force a third party to comply with his or her substantive demands" (McMains and Mullins, 2010: 463). American Heritage Dictionary defines hostage as "a person held as a security for the fulfilment of certain terms" (American Heritage Dictionary, 1980).

The ultimate motive of the attacker is to use the hostage to compel the third party to respond to their demands which would not be possible otherwise (Noesner, 1999; McMains and Mullins, 2010:13). Taking of hostages has not been limited to specific territories or people. It is a global threat that creates common fear and concern for human lives all over the globe. Such actions, which risks civilian lives has been criticized by the international community. Article 1 (Clause 1) of the International Convention against the Taking of Hostages of 1979 which came into force on June 3, 1983 states,

"Any person who seizes or detains and threatens to kill, to injure or to continue to detain another person (herein after referred to as 'hostage') in order to compel a third party, namely, a state, an international intergovernmental organization, and natural or judicial person, or a group of persons, to do or abstain from doing any act as an explicit or implicit condition for the release of the hostage commits the offence of taking of hostages ('hostage-taking') within the meaning of this Convention (International Convention Against the Taking of Hostages, 1979)".

The convention strictly makes it clear that hostage taking acts are against the international law. However, several organisations over time have violated the convention by taking recourse to such actions (Hoffman 2006: 26-27). Hostage taking incidents like Munich massacre of 1972, Moscow theatre crisis of 2002, the Iran embassy siege in 1979, and the hijacking at Entebbe in 1976 have not just been limited to territories but have been a global threat leading to concerns for the international community.

A severe consequence of such incident is the impact on the life of the hostage. The psychological impact on the victim limits the person's capacity to lead a normal day-to-day life. The degree of impact may vary from person to person, but the psychological impact makes the hostage a victim of fear and stress. The stress level might lead to mental damage, physical break down and in severe cases, may lead to sickness like headache or nervous breakdown. Sometimes the stress may also lead to hallucination (Lanza, 1986; Siegel, 1984; McMains and Mullins, 2010: 472). It becomes difficult for the victim to regain normalcy in daily life.

A major drawback in hostage crisis is the Stockholm syndrome, the term first introduced in 1973 by Nils Bejerot, after an incident of bank robbery in Stockholm. The syndrome refers to a situation where the hostage prefers to side with the captors. The hostage assumedly develops some degree of sympathy or compassion for the captors gradually and hence sides with them to achieve their demands (Bejerot, 1974: 486). The impact is not just harmful for the victim, but also makes the task of the rescue unit very difficult. Gary Noesner stressing on the importance of life argues, "In most hostage incidents, the explicit threat is to the hostage's life. It is not the loss of property, status, or belonging to a community that is at stake...life itself is at stake" (McMains and Mullins 2010: 464).

The mainstream debate that has developed in hostage studies has been on how a state should response in hostage situations. While several scholars like Isabelle Duyvesteyn (2008), Michael Bar-Zohar (2012), Nissim Mishal (2012) and Daniel Byman (2011) have advocated the reliance on military in such situations, scholars like Suleyman Hancerli (2007), Mitchell R. Hammer (2007), Ozgur Nikbay (2007), Michael McMains and Wayman C. Mullins (2010) have stressed on negotiation tactics in dealing with hostage situations. While some states prefer to use the military to rescue the hostages, many states prefer negotiations as the possible strategy to secure the release of the hostage. States have often experimented with such tactics but still there has been no universal acceptance of any specific policy to deal with the hostage crisis.

Negotiation Strategy

The word negotiation refers to a process involving communication through series of discussion between two or more actors in order to reach a common agreement. The purpose of the process is to settle the problem through peaceful means that would be mutually accepted by the involved parties. According to Herb Cohen, negotiation is the use of power and information to affect the behaviour, which is in a web of tensions where people try to maximise their gains and minimize their losses (Cohen, 1982). Instances are not rare to show how negotiation as a strategy has often been used to strike a deal. In any negotiation process, the willingness of the party to get into negotiation is very important. At the same time, the settlement cannot benefit all the parties equally. It is a bargaining process through which some manage to gain more than the others. However, every party tries to strike a deal that would bring in maximum gain. Negotiation is not limited to specific time-frame rather the process may involve from few hours to several years.

In hostage negotiation, there are three major elements, the victim, the hostage taker and the negotiator. Communication plays a major role in the entire process. The outcome of the bargaining process depends on how well the messages are communicated between the parties. The most important element to the entire process is the role of the mediator. Hence, it is vital that the mediator is well skilled in the communication process. The task of the mediator is to bring the involved parties into common agreement. Adam Dolnik and Keith M. Fitzgerald (2008) suggest that negotiation is a process of communication through which the minds and thoughts of the hijacker can be influenced. They argue that it is through the communication skill that the state can influence the decision-making of the hostage taker (Dolnik and Fitzgerald, 2007: 9).

It is also important that the negotiator is well aware of the credibility of the hostage taker to harm the hostage. So, it is crucial for the negotiator to have a good understanding of the background of the hostage, so that it is easier for the negotiator to communicate with the hostage (McMains and Mullins, 2010:474). Negotiation as an evolving field of study, has gained prominence since the 1970s. Several scholars like Randall G. Rogan, Mitchell R. Hammer and Clinton R. Van Zandt opine, "hostage negotiation is rapidly emerging as a field of behavioural science application, poised to move beyond largely anecdotal accounts of effective and ineffective negotiation strategies towards increasing efforts at systematically incorporating alternative disciplinary perspectives and employing more rigorous methodological approaches for analysing the dynamics of crisis negotiation" (Hammer, 2007: 7). There have been two major models developed to negotiate with the hostage takers, the REACT model and the SAFE model (McMains and Mullins, 2010).

Israel and Hostage Negotiations

Since the formation of the state of Israel, it has been a victim of several hostage taking incidents. Such activities have often been carried out by non-state organizations like Black September, Fatah and its factions, the Hamas and the Hezbollah. Some of the most prominent hostage situations include the 1968 hijacking, the 1970 hijacking, the 1972 Munich massacre, the 1976 Entebbe hijacking, 1978 Coastal Road massacre, the 1980 Misgav am incident, 1988 Mother bus hijacking, 1994 kidnapping of Nachshonwachsman, kidnapping of Elhanan Tannenbaum in 2000, the three soldiers in 2006, abduction of Gilad Shalit in 2006 and the three teenagers in 2014. The state has often pursued its offensive policy in such crisis situations. For example, in the wake of hostage taking, Prime Minister Yitzhak Rabin, in spite of several losses caused by military response strictly advocated the slogan "No Surrender to Terrorism" (Inbar, 1999: 100). Israel with its policy of not negotiating with any non-state actor/s (Inbar, 1999; Kauffmann, 2008: 64; Boltz et al., 2012: 262) has also materialised hostage prisoner swap to secure the release of the hostages under certain situations.

The act of hostage taking has mostly been executed under the leadership of the several Palestinian groups and the Hezbollah. Most of the incidents have involved members of the Arab Liberation Front (ALF), PLO, Black September Organisation (BSO), Democratic Front for the Liberation of Palestine (DFLP), Popular Front for the Liberation of Palestine (PFLP), Palestine Liberation Organization (PLO), Hamas and Hezbollah. While Fatah and its factions have been involved in aerial hijacking or hostage taking of group of people, the hostage taking of individual civilian or military personnel has been the common tactics for Hamas and Hezbollah. Israel has always relied on its military power to secure the lives of the hostages. Negotiation has only taken place in instances where the military has failed to release the hostage. In case of Israel, two trends can be observed. Negotiation used as a strategy of buying time which can be termed as proxy negotiation and negotiation that have taken place over a prolonged period of time to secure the release of the hostage or even its body parts.

Instances are also not rare where Israel has negotiated for prisoners exchange, for example in November 1983, Israel had released more than 4,500 Palestinian prisoners in return of 6 IDF soldiers who were kept as captives by PLO in Southern Lebanon. Similarly, in 1985, Israel released 1,150 Palestinian prisoners for the bodies of 9 IDF soldiers. This is famously known as the Jibril deal. Any hostage negotiation should be discussed taking two factors into consideration: the time taken for negotiations and the price paid by the state. Proxy negotiation has been a common tactic for Israel in hostage taking situations. In instances like the 1972 hijacking of Sabena Flight, or that of 1976 Entebbe hijacking, Israel convinced the captors that it would negotiate with the captors, but the ultimate motive was to secure some time (few hours) for the military to launch its attack on the hostage takers. This strategy has often helped Israel to use its military in rescuing the hostages.

All negotiations to exchange the prisoners of war or hostage prisoner's swap, has a theological linkage. According to Judaism, every Jew should be given some honourable burial. This traditional practice has often made Israel to bargain for bringing back the Jew or its body part to Israel for the burial. While Israel has been strict on the use of force there are few incidents of Israel's experience with hostage negotiations. These include the 1968 El Al Flight 426 hijacking, the 2000 kidnapping of Elhanan Tannenbaum, 2006 abduction of two IDF soldiers and the 2006 abduction of Gilad Shalit. The relevance of such hostage-prisoners swap is dependent on two factors: firstly, the time taken for the settlement and secondly, the price paid by the state for the swap.

Hijacking El Al Flight 426, 1968

The hijacking of the Flight 426 took place on July 23, 1968 by members of PFLP (Laqueur, 2002: 108). The flight was initially scheduled from Rome to Israel but was hijacked and diverted to Algiers (Byman, 2011: 29). The flight carried 48 passengers with Odeb Abarnell as their pilot. Immediately at Algiers, the passengers were divided into Israelis and others. While the Israelis (12 in number) were kept back as hostages the remaining passengers were immediately set free. The 12 Israelis consisted of 5 crew members and 7 passengers. It was after this incident that Israel came out with a special department concerning the aviation security (Hasisi et al., 2012: 14).

The captors demanded the release of around 1,000 Palestinians kept as prisoners in Israeli jails. However, with the policy of no surrender, Israel immediately declined the proposal and preferred to refer the case to the UN. The incident of hijacking made the Airline Pilot Association (ALPA) boycott Algiers. Algeria finally agreed to negotiate in order to release the hostages and this was done with the mediation of Italy. Finally, on September 12, all the hostages were released and in return Israel had to release only 16 Palestinian prisoners. However, this incident created much havoc amongst the international community. Though the lives of the hostages were secured, the incident made Israel adopt its retaliatory policy and make its security system stronger (Price and Forrest, 2013: 49).

Kidnapping of Tannenbaum, 2000

Elhanan Tannenbaum was a citizen of Israel and by profession a businessman. Apart from that, he had also served as a colonel in the Israel Defence Force (IDF) (Melman, 2001). He was accused of being involved in drug trafficking along with his friend identified as Kais Obeid. He was kidnapped in 2000 from Dubai and then taken hostage to Lebanon by the Hezbollah group (BBC News, 2004). Hezbollah would use Tannenbaum as a bargaining chip against Israel (Harik, 2005: 155).

Since Israel would not negotiate directly, it was Germany that helped Israel to strike a deal with the hostage takers (Libel, 2013: 5). The two Germans who actively participated in the negotiations were Gerhard Conrad and Ernst Uhrlao. One reason that can be assumed for Germany's initiative was perhaps to regain its prestige at the international level that was lost during the 1972 Munich massacre. It was only in 2004 when Tannenbaum was brought back to Israel through prisoner's swap. Along with Tannenbaum, Israel also bargained for the body parts of 3 Israeli soldiers from the Hezbollah (Levitt 2013: 246). Apart from releasing 435 Palestinian prisoners, Israel also had to set free one German. The list of prisoners released through the deal included names like Mustafa Dirani and Sheikh Abdel Karim. Israel also had to give the body remains of 60 Hezbollah fighters (Levitt 2013: 225; Levi, 2014).

Abduction of Gilad Shalit, 2006

The most debated negotiation in the history of Israel experiences has been that of the incident of Gilad Shalit. To quote Daniel Byman, "The Shalit kidnapping highlighted an area of intense Israeli vulnerability, as well as a motive that terrorist organizations well understand: the Israeli's desire to rescue their own prisoners" (Byman, 2011: 185). Gilad Shalit with a dual citizenship (Israeli-French) had joined the Israel Defence Force in 2005. Serving in the Israeli military has been of social prestige and the state of Israel will always make every possible endeavour to secure the release of its soldier from the hostage takers (Schweitzer 2010: 32). On June 25, 2006, Shalit was abducted from the Israeli borders near Gaza Strip. The abductors were later recognized as members of the Hamas militant group. The members had used the tunnel to reach to the Israeli soldiers and took over the soldiers stationed there by surprise. The attack by Hamas wounded Shalit and other members stationed there. Hamas managed to carry Shalit along with them inside Gaza. However, it managed to keep the location of captivity a secret.

As usual, the prime objective of the Group was to compel the Israeli Government to release prisoners from Israeli jails. The Government with its strict policy of no surrender immediately refused to respond to their demands. The then Prime Minister Ehud Olmert expressed its decision of not giving in to the demands of the Hamas. The statement of the Israeli Foreign Ministry Spokesperson Mark Regev also made it clear that Israel would not negotiate with Hamas to release the hostage. He stated "We will not negotiate with hostage-takers" (Young, 2006; Harel, 2011).

Israel immediately launched its military campaign to rescue back the soldier, but this attempt could not bring out any fruitful result. A series of attack and counter attack took place with the launch of Operation *Summer Rains* by Israel Defence Force on June 28, 2006 in Gaza. The purpose of the attack was to compel Hamas to return back the abducted soldier. A major drawback of Shalit affair was the lack of knowledge about the location of the captive. Hamas managed to keep the affair under secret, to the extent that even the Red Cross Society was denied any access to Shalit. The Israeli intelligence also could not gather any concrete information of the location (Estrin, 2012; Melman, 2011; Levy, 2011).

In 2007 and in 2009 consecutively, Hamas released 2 video tapes to convince the people and the Israeli Government that Shalit was still alive. In exchange of the tape, Israel had to release 21 female prisoners from Israeli jails (Schweitzer, 2010: 31). The Israeli social activist Gershon Baskin, the co-director of Israel Palestine Centre for Research and Information initiated negotiations to release the hostage in 2006. Baskin was the mediator between the Hamas official and Israeli Envoy David Meiden. The negotiation process continued for several years and finally in 2011 Shalit was brought back to Israel though the deal under the mediation carried out by Egypt and Germany. Most of the time, the deal could not materialize because of the varied opinion on the release of Palestinian prisoners.

For example, the mediation came to a standstill in 2007 when Israel took control of the Gaza Strip. Similar was the case in 2009, when Prime Minister Olmert refused to release 125 heavy weight prisoners from the demand list put up by the captors (Schweitzer, 2010: 30). The list included names of prisoners like Samir Kuntar and others who were involved in several violent activities. Israel though agreed to the demands partially, it was reluctant to release those specific prisoners. It was in 2011, under the leadership of Prime Minister Benjamin Netanyahu that a deal was reached with Hamas with the help of Egypt and Germany. An emergency cabinet was called for to support the release of Shalit. It was on October 18, 2011, that Shalit was brought back to Israel after spending 5 years as hostage under Hamas.

The negotiation deal that secured the release of Shalit, released 1,027 Palestinian prisoners. The deal materialised in 2 phases, first the release of 477 prisoners on October 18 along with transfer of Shalit to Israel and the second phase included the release of 550 prisoners from Israeli jails (Katz, 2011; Jewish Virtual Library, 2011). In the first phase, the 477 prisoners included 280 prisoners serving life sentence. Among the prisoners, 96 of them were released to West Bank, and 14 prisoners to Jerusalem (east Jerusalem). This also included 6 Arab Israeli prisoners along with 27 female prisoners. In the second phase, Israel released 550 prisoners. Among them, 505 prisoners were from West Bank, 41 prisoners from Gaza, 2 from East Jerusalem and 2 from Jordan (IMFA, 2011; Ha'aretz, 2011).

The deal no doubt had created much tension inside Israeli society but it was able to bring back the soldier alive. Netanyahu on return of Shalit stated that, "Today, I can say on behalf of all Israelis, in the spirit of the eternal values of the

Jewish people: Your children shall return to their own border" (Jewish Virtual Library 2011; MFA, 2011). The mediation of Egypt under Omar Suleiman could not bring about any concrete result and this paved the way for the involvement of Germany in the negotiation process. The success of the negotiation helped Germany to come out as an important regional player.

The deal created differences in opinion. While some section of the society advocated the release of the soldier, others were against the deal. It should be kept in mind that those rejecting the deal were not against the release of the soldier but against the price that Israel had to pay to secure the release. Some sections of the society that rejected the deal views the deal to be futile because the prisoners when released would again take re course to such violent activities (Ginsberg, 2011; Phillips, 2011). These sections were mainly the families of soldiers who had sacrificed their lives just to capture these prisoners.

In spite of all the opposition, a large section of the society supported the Shalit deal. Several news agencies played an important role in broadcasting the final stage of negotiation. Support for the release of Shalit was also carried out by the social media. It helped in mobilising the people to unite for the release of the hostage. There were also several non-profit organizations formed to support the cause and the mass mobilisation highlighted the solidarity of the movement to release Shalit (Harman and Izikovich, 2011).

The Ynet news agency on October 16, 2011, conducted a survey of 500 Israeli citizens regarding their opinion on the Shalit deal. The report suggested that 79 percent of the poll supported the deal while only 14 percent were against it (Ahronoth, 2011; BBC News, 2011). Similar survey was conducted by the Ha'aretz news agency with a total survey poll of 600 Jewish Israeli adults. Among them, 63 percent supported the deal while 19 percent were against the deal and the rest 18 percent were indifferent to the deal (Khoury, 2011).

However, with all the criticism and support, the deal could bring back the soldier alive and at the same time the price paid by Israel opened a new chapter of debate inside the Israeli society.

Abduction of Two IDF soldiers, 2006

After the abduction of Gilad Shalit, there were a series of attacks and counter attacks between Israel and Hamas. Added to this was the firing of rockets and counter attacks between Israel and Hezbollah at the Israel-Lebanon border. On June 25, 2006, the Hezbollah attacked on the border killing 3 Israeli soldiers and also abducted 2 IDF soldiers. The two soldiers were later identified as Ehud Goldwasser and Eldad Regev. They both were used as a bargaining chip by Hezbollah to release Samir Kuntar from the Israeli prison. The abduction of the two soldiers sparked the launch of the second Lebanon war by Israel (Byman, 2011: 9). The military campaign could no way bring back the 2 soldiers (Lambeth 2012: 46). Shlomo Brom writes, "At the start of the war there was an expectation, nurtured by the political leadership, that the IDF would defeat Hezbollah and rescue the hostages ; the aim of disarming Hezbollah was presented as a realistic objective" (Brom, 2007: 13).

Hezbollah demanded the release of Lebanese citizens in Israeli jail along with the release of other Palestinian prisoners. It also demanded the release of Shamir Kuntar. Initially, it was assumed that the 2 abducted soldiers were alive but gradually the Israeli intelligence suspected that the 2 soldiers were killed by the captors. Israel agreed to most of the demands except releasing Samir Kuntar (Schweitzer, 2010: 27). It was finally through the mediation of Germany under Gerhard Conrad that Israel agreed to reach an agreement with the Hezbollah. The protracted negotiation took two years to reach an agreement. In 2008, Israel released Kuntar along with 4 Lebanese fighters and the bodies of few other fighters including Lebanese fighters in exchange of the bodies of the 2 abducted soldiers (Witte and Ibrahim, 2008; Libel, 2013: 7).

Conclusion

The state of Israel has always used its military as a response to hostage incidents. This follows the simple logic that negotiating with hostage takers will encourage the captors in taking recourse to such activities. However, there are instances where the military has failed Israel and protracted negotiations with non-state actors were undertaken in order to secure the release of the hostages. Such protracted negotiations took place only with the help of the third party which mediated between the state and the hostage takers.

A close observation of the hostage-prisoner swap infers that in the negotiation process, the situation is not under the control of the state unlike in case of military operations. In any hostage negotiation, the state has to meet the demands at two levels: firstly, the demands of the hostage takers and secondly, that of the mediators. Since Israel does not negotiate with the hostage takers directly, this makes the state dependant on the mediator. The longer the time taken for negotiations the more exposed is the vulnerability of the state. The process of negotiation when continues over a long period of time, allows the hostage takers to put up more demands at the table, making it a more complex process.

In all the instances of negotiations, Israel has released several soldiers in order to secure the hostage or its body parts. For example, to secure the release of Tannenbaum, Israel released 400 prisoners along with the bodies of 60 Hezbollah fighters. Similarly, during the Shalit deal, Israel released 1,027 prisoners in exchange of one hostage. The price that Israel has paid in the negotiation process has been qualitatively higher than what it has achieved.

Moreover, the negotiations have in no way reduced the occurrence of such incidents. Such incidents have convinced the hostage taker to use the hostages as a mere bargaining tool to release the prisoners. In case of Israel, hostage taking has become a common technique by the hostage takers. In such circumstances, relying on negotiations does not serve the national interest of the state rather makes the state suffer greater losses at the hands of the captors. However, owing to its domestic pressure and the theological baggage, Israel has often paid quantitatively a high price in its indirect negotiations with the hostage takers and has been successful in bringing back the body parts or the hostages alive.

References

Ahronoth, Yedioth (2011), "Poll: 79 Percent of Israeli's support Shalit Deal", *Ynet News,* available at: http://www.ynetnews.com/articles/0,7340,L-4135847,00.html.

Bar-Zohar, Michael and Nissim, Mishal (2012), "Mossad", New York, NY: Harper Collins.

Bejerot, Nils (1974), "The Six Day War in Stockholm", *New Scientist*, 61(886), 486-487.

Brom, Shlomo and Meir, Elran (2007), "The Second Lebanese War: Strategic Perspective", Tel Aviv: Institute For National Security Studies.

Byman, Daniel (2011), "A High Price: Triumph and Failures of Israeli Counterterrorism", New York, NY: Oxford University Press.

—(2005), "Deadly Connections State that Sponsor Terrorism", UK: Cambridge University Press.

Cohen, Herb (1982), "You Can Negotiate Anything", New York (NY): Bantam Publication.

Dolnik, Adam (2007), "Understanding Terrorist Innovation Technology, Tactics and Global Trends", New York (NY) and London: Routledge.

Duyvesteyn, Isabelle (2008), "Great Expectations: The Use of Armed Force to Combat Terrorism", *Small Wars and Insurgencies*, Vol. 19(28), 328-351.

Estrin, Daniel (2012), "A Year After his Release, Freed Israeli Soldier Discloses Details of Hamas Captivity in Gaza", *National Post,* available at: http://news.nationalpost.com/news/world/israel-middle-east/a-year-after-his-release-freed-israeli-soldier-discloses-details-of-hamas-captivity-in-gaza.

Ginsberg, Johanna (2011), "Analyst Sees Mixed Reaction to Shalit Exchange", *NJJN,* available at:

http://njjewishnews.com/article/6867/analyst-sees-mixed-reaction-to-shalit-exchange#.WP7zUPmGPIU.

Hammer, Mitchell R. (2007), "Saving Lives: The S.A.F.E. Model for Resolving Hostage and Crisis Incidents", London: Praeger Security International.

Haaretz (2011), "Second Stage of Shalit Swap Complete as 550 Palestinian Prisoners Released", available at: http://www.haaretz.com/israel-news/second-stage-of-shalit-swap-complete-as-550-palestinian-prisoners-released-1.402168.

Harik, Judith Palmer (2005), "Hezbollah: The Changing Face of Terrorism", United Kingdom: I.B. Tauris.

Hasisi, Badi et al. (2012), "Ethnic Profiling in Airport Screening: Lessons from Israel, 1968- 2010", *American Law and Economic Review*, Oxford University Press, 1-44.

Harmon, Danna and GiliIzikovich (2011), "Foreign Media Flock to Israel Ahead of Shalit Exchange Deal", *Haaretz,* available at: http://www.haaretz.com/foreign-media-flock-to-israel-ahead-of-shalit-exchange-deal-1.390333.

Hoffman, Bruce (2015), "Anonymous Soldier: The Struggle for Israel, 1917-1947", New York: Alfred A. Knoff.

——(2006), "Inside Terrorism", New York: Columbia University Press.

Inbar, Efraim (2008), "Israel's National Security: Issues and Challenges since the Yom Kippur War", Oxon: Routledge.

——(1999), "Rabin and Israel's National Security", Washington D.C.: The Woodrow Wilson Centre Press.

International Convention against the Taking of Hostages adopted by General Assembly of United Nations on December 1979, available at: http://www.un.org/en/sc/ctc/docs/conventions/Conv5.pdf.

Israel Defence Force official blog, available at: https://www.idfblog.com.

Israel Ministry of Foreign Affairs, available at: http://mfa.gov.il/MFA/Pages/default.aspx.

Katz, Yaakov (2011), "The Schalit Deal: 1,027 Prisoners to be Freed in 2 Stages", *The Jerusalem Post*, available at: http://www.jpost.com/Diplomacy-and-Politics/The-Schalit-deal-1027-prisoners-to-be-freed-in-2-stages.

Kauffmann, Mayeul (2008), "Building and Using Datasets on Armed Conflicts", NATO Science for Peace and Security Series,

Amsterdam: IOS Press.

Keith, Fitzgerald M. and Adam Dolnik (2007), "Negotiating Hostage Crises with the New Terrorists", London: Praeger Security International.

Khoury, Jack (2011), "Poll: Majority of Israelis Support Release of 1,000 Palestinian Prisoners for Shalit", *Haaretz*, available at: http://www.haaretz.com/poll-majority-of-israelis-support-release-of-1-000-palestinian-prisoners-for-shalit-1.368791.

Laqueur, Walter (2001), "A History of Terrorism", New Jersey: Transaction Publishers.

—(1999), "The New Terrorism: Fanaticism and the Arms of Mass Destruction", New York: Oxford University Press.

Levi, Yaakov (2014), "Terrorist Released in Tannenbaum Deal Killed", *ArutzSheva*, available at: http://www.israelnationalnews.com/News/News.aspx/181070.

Levitt, Mathew (2013), "Hezbollah: The Global Footprint of Lebanon's Party of God", Washington D.C: Georgetown University Press.

—(2006), "Hamas: Politics, Charity and Terrorism in the Service of Jihad", USA: The Washington Institute for Near East Policy.

Levy, Elior (2011), "Hezbollah Instructed Hamas on Shalit Talks", *Ynet News,* available at: http://www.ynetnews.com/articles/0,7340,L-4135263,00.html.

Libel, Tamir (2013), "Hostage of Foreign Interests: German Intelligence Involvement in Arab-Israeli Hostage Deals: 1980-2010", *Journal of Intelligence History.*

McMains, Michael J. and Wayman C. Mullins (2010), "Crisis Negotiations: Managing Critical Incidents and Hostage Situations in Law Enforcement and Corrections", New Jersey: Mathew Bender and Comp.

Melman, Yossi (2001), "Tannenbaum Family Awaits News of Missing Businessman", *Haaretz,* available at: http://www.haaretz.com/tannenbaum-family-awaits-news-of-missing-businessman-1.73334.

—(2011), "The Best-Kept Secret", *Haaretz,* available at: http://www.haaretz.com/weekend/week-s-end/the-best-kept-secret-1.391255.

Phillips, Melanie (2011), "Has Israel Made a Deal with the Devil?", *Daily Mail*, available at: http://www.dailymail.co.uk/debate/article-2048141/Gilad-Shalit-freed-Has-Israel-deal-devil.html.

Price, Jeffrey and Jeffrey Forest (2013), "Practical Aviation Security: Predicting and Preventing Future Threats", United Kingdom: Butterworth-Heinemann.

Schweitzer, Yoram (2010), "Israel: Hostage to its Soldiers Captors", in 'Strategic Survey for Israel 2010', Shlomo Brom and Anat Kurz (eds.), Tel Aviv: INSS.

Suleyman, Hancerli and Ozgur, Nikbayeds (2007), "Understanding and Responding to the Terrorism Phenomenon: A Multi-Dimensional Perspective", NATO Science for Peace and Security Series, Vol. 21, Amsterdam: IOS Press.

Witte, Griff and Alia Ibrahim (2008), "Israel Mourns, Hezbollah Exults", *The Washington Post*, available at: http://www.washingtonpost.com/wpdyn/content/article/2008/07/16/AR2008071600282.html.

Young, Annette (2006), "Israeli Army Turns on Lomert", *Information Liberation*, available at: http://www.informationliberation.com/?id=13068.

9

Saudi-Iran Rivalry and its Effects on West-Asian Stability

Syed Jaleel Hussain

Introduction

West Asia is one of the most volatile regions in the world today. Almost all the countries in the region, especially the powerful ones, are directly or indirectly involved in conflicts that are either intractable or bloody. With the renewed American involvement in the region after September 11 attacks and the resulting quick fall of Iraqi dictator Saddam Hussein, the regional politics became more unstable due to a sudden change in the balance of power in the Gulf region. The political uncertainty, especially in a post-Saddam Iraq, became a breeding ground for terrorist groups like Al-Qaeda which soon had a formidable presence in other countries like Yemen. However, the biggest shock to the regional stability came in the aftermath of the failure of the Arab spring in 2015 with the sudden rise of Islamic State (Obaid, 2005) of Iraq and Syria (ISIS) which later adopted the name Islamic State (IS).

The Islamic State not only represented the most extremist version of all the Islamist terrorist organizations but it also shockingly upturned the geopolitical realities in the region. In a span of months, the Islamic State controlled huge swathes of the adjoining territories of Iraq and Syria, posing a severe threat to the very survival of the two states. The battle between IS and these two states is going on even today. However, the situation has inverted now. The equation is now in the favour of the states of Iraq and Syria and IS now is fighting for its survival.

One of the most important reasons for the re-emergence of these two states is the unconditional Iranian support to the regimes in Syria and Iraq. Iran committed not only the weapons worth billions of dollars but also military advisors and even fighters. It also involved groups like Hezbollah, for example, to sustain the Syrian regime of Bashar-al Assad. The heavy Iranian involvement was not only an attempt to prevent the collapse of friendly regimes in the two states, but it was a strategic battle for influence in West Asia fought against Iranian archrival Saudi Arabia.

The dynamics of politics in West Asia can be summed up as this battle for power and influence between Saudi Arabia and Iran. Both states use the ideological and sectarian differences to achieve their strategic goals in West Asia and beyond. The ideological dimension of this tussle took an unprecedented turn with the arrival of an Islamic revolutionary regime in Iran in 1979 under the charismatic cleric Ayatollah Khomeini. The revolutionary zeal of the new Iranian regime and its insistence on exporting the revolution to other countries alarmed the Arab gulf monarchies who all have a sizeable Shia population. These Arab countries came together to form the Gulf Cooperation Council (GCC) in 1980 as a measure to check the growing Iranian influence in the region and preclude the possibility of its military interference in any Arab gulf country. Iran is the only regional military power that can pose a formidable military threat to the stability in the Gulf (Cordesman and Obaid, 2005: 14). The formation of GCC was the first collective effort by the Gulf monarchies to build an organization aimed against Iran. The primary driver of the formation of GCC was the security dilemma faced by Saudi Arabia—the biggest and the richest Gulf state. [1]

The political situation in West Asia has now boiled down to the political and strategic competition between Saudi Arabia and Iran. The turbulent civil wars in Yemen, Iraq, Bahrain and Syria are all the offshoots of this rivalry where these two powerful states support opposite groups, thereby prolonging the conflicts in the region. Most of the scholarship on the subject deals with the ideological and the sectarian nature of the Saudi-Iran confrontation and there is little focus on the strategic nature of the rivalry. The effects of this confrontation on the regional stability have also not been studied in detail so far. [2]

There is a lot of scholarship on the defence and military capabilities of Saudi Arabia and Iran (Eisenstadt, 1996; Cordesman and Obaid, 2005), their national security apparatus and institutions (Bayman et al., 2001), the process of decision-making (Chubin, 2002), and war fighting capabilities and nature of the state and the government systems (Keddie, 2003; Chubin, 2000). Since both the states are not completely transparent about their overall defence inventory, most of the literature is based on the secondary sources. [3] There is, however, a dearth of literature on the effects of the Saudi-Iran rivalry on the regional stability and the exact nature of the strategic interests of these two states in the region. [4] Because of the focus on the sectarian dimensions of their confrontation, this rivalry is seen as zero-sum and irresolvable (Halliday, 2005). The focus of this paper is to show the exact nature of the strategic interests of the two states in the region and their mutual interest in regional stability. The study will look at the probable alternatives to the zero-sum scenarios portrayed in the literature on the subject.

The literature on Iran's defense and foreign policy looks at the ideological nature of the revolutionary government and its interest in keeping the revolutionary zeal alive in the region by raising the slogan of 'neither east nor west' (Ehteshami and Zweri, 2008: vii). This involves the funding of proxy groups to destabilize other states with the ultimate aim of installing Shia regimes or pro-Iran regimes in these states. Some of the scholarship focuses on the strategic nature of the Iranian support for the proxy groups in the region or its political support for minority Shia groups in other countries in the region as a rational move to increase its influence in the region and gain considerable bargaining leverage while dealing with other states in the region.

Ehteshami and Zweiri (2008) maintain that Iran has been toiling to portray itself as the heart of the Muslim world since the Islamic revolution of 1979. This is not a purely ideological aspiration of the Islamic republic but rooted in a conscious assessment of its national interest. By using the language of Islamic resistance against the oppressors of Muslim rights, Iran attempts to 'gain worldwide Muslim support, which gives it more legitimacy in the face of regional and international challenges (p. xiii)'. It is this struggle for influence in the Muslim world that fundamentally pits it against Saudi Arabia which seeks the same place for almost the same strategic and security reasons.

The Saudi state is seen as perennially caught in a security dilemma in the region. It sees potential security threats emanating from Yemen in the south, and Iran and Iraq from the east and the perpetual dilemma of a pro-Iran regime in the Kingdom of Bahrain. Internally, the Saudi regime faces the pressures of an increasing presence of Sunni extremist groups like Al-Qaeda (Dekmejian, 1994) and greater resistance against unfavorable policies from minority Shias. The internal asymmetric threats are more urgent than ever before as these groups challenge the moral and political legitimacy of the Saudi regime itself (Cordesman and Obaid, 2005: 109-136).

Thus, the Saudis see the increasing influence of Iran in Yemen, Bahrain, and Iraq as a form of strategic encirclement and a direct threat to the Saudi state. Hence, Saudis would not hesitate to use extreme force to resist the status quo in these states. The brutal crackdown on the democratic protestors in Bahrain by the Saudi army and the use of full military capabilities against a change in regime in Yemen led by the Houthis (International Crisis Group [ICG], 2016) show the extent of Saudi paranoia associated with a growing Iranian influence in the region. Saudi insecurity about the growing Iranian clout in the region in the aftermath of the successful conclusion of the nuclear agreement between Iran and the west is already evident (Sanger and Gordon, 2015). It has intensified its support for extremist groups in Syria and Iraq and is pursuing the goal of routing Houthis in Yemen more vigorously. The apparent failure of Saudi strategy in the region is only exacerbating its security dilemma.

Explaining Instability in West Asia

Structural realism offers a powerful explanation of the behavior of states in a hostile environment wherein a state is surrounded by rival and hostile states. Since the basic goal of a state is ensuring its survival by defending its territorial integrity and sovereign decision-making, there are two ways of achieving this quintessential state goal: arming and allying. In the realist logic of self-help, armament is the first preference of any state. Every state wants a strong army with the most sophisticated and up-to-date weaponry in its military inventory. Since the state is never sure of the exact size of the arsenal that the other states possess, it becomes impossible for it to determine the size of its own arsenal that should be sufficient to deter an enemy state or turn a war decisively in its favor. Therefore, when a state starts investing in building up its military arsenal, the need for more sophistication and numbers keeps increasing gradually.

This, in turn, leads to a self-perpetuating atmosphere of uncertainty and mistrust among other states leading to a beefing up of their own military hardware. This aggravates the dilemma of the first state which sees the military build-up by others states as a threat to its own security. In this way, the act of securing a state by arming itself makes it insecure forever. Security dilemma thus becomes a self-fulfilling ending.

The other way of ensuring the security of the state is by entering into an alliance with another state that has a formidable interest in its security and the necessary power to protect it from aggression by other states. By entering into a formal alliance with a great power, a state gets a security guarantee necessary for its security and vital interests.

In such an environment, nuclear weapons are indispensable and ultimate guardians of a state's sovereignty and its territorial integrity. Any state that possesses nuclear weapons cannot be attacked by any other state, however powerful in conventional military terms that state be. [5] The fear of nuclear retaliation and mutually assured destruction deter states from launching a military offensive against the states possessing nuclear weapons. Notwithstanding the high cost of manufacturing and maintenance of the nuclear weapons, including the crucial delivery systems, this immense value of deterrence makes them indispensable in any state's defense inventory.

There is a colossal amount of evidence to prove that West Asian conflicts and the resulting instability proceed through realist logic. For instance, the security dilemma faced by Saudi Arabia has consistently pushed its defense budgets to disproportionate levels. Saudi military expenditures have been one of the highest in the world. It spent close to 20 percent of its budget on defence during the late eighties and peaked at 27-29 percent of the GDP during the Gulf War I. The percentage dropped to below and around 14 percent during the early 2000s (Cordesman and Obaid, 2005: 172). Owing to its involvement in different conflicts in West Asia, Saudi Arabia has become the largest military spender in the region, with an estimated US$ 87.2 billion in 2015 that amounts to 13.7 percent of its GDP. [6] Its defence spending doubled between 2006 and 2015.

However, Iranian military expenditures have been comparatively limited. This is in line with the goal of self-help propounded by the realist theory. Iran has been reeling under severe US sanctions since the revolution of 1979 and has been unable to procure parts for its aging and obsolescent weapons and aircraft of the shah era (Cordesman and Klieber, 2007: 30-39). Due to a lack of access to modern military technology, Iran has tried to rebuild its conventional capabilities by using domestic defence capabilities. This has resulted in successful production of an array of ballistic and cruise missile capabilities that include medium range and long range ballistic missiles.

Various sectors of its defense industry are continuously developing especially the sectors for missiles and guided weapons. In 2015, Iran unveiled the *Soumar* cruise missile based closely on the Russian Kh-55 which has a range in the order of 2,500 km that could hit targets not only throughout the Middle East but in Eastern and Southern Europe as well (Pfeffer, 2015). Its successful deployment in considerable numbers would provide a valuable complement to Iran's medium-range missile inventory. The successful completion of the nuclear agreement with the P5+1 and the European Union has also begun to open the way for Iran to refurbish its conventional arms capabilities. Following the nuclear agreement, Tehran and Moscow re-engaged on the sale of a version of the S-300 (SA-10 *Grumble*/SA-20 *Gargoyle*) medium-to-long-range surface-to-air missile system that can change the nature of Iran's missile defense capabilities.

Saudi Arabia overtook Russia to become the third largest military spender owing to a sharp increase in military spending in Yemen. As predicted by the realist theory, the Saudi state invested heavily in the belligerent campaign, codenamed Operation Decisive Storm, leading a coalition of nine Arab states. This campaign is costing the coalition about US$ 200 million a day and the Saudi contribution alone has been so far been estimated to be around US$ 5.3 billion (Perlo-freeman et al., 2016: 5).

Though the Saudi army is the best-equipped force in the Gulf region, the sheer size and scale of the Iranian power threaten Saudi rulers. The continuing arms race in the region, along with growing Iranian capabilities is causing a huge concern among Saudi strategists. This is only increasing the instability in the region. Though the realist logic of self-help and arms race escalates a conflict inevitably towards confrontation or war, [7] it seems to be ill-equipped to offer policy suggestions for conflict resolution so that actors may get out of the vicious circle of security dilemma in West Asia.

The nature and scope of conflicts and their potential processes of resolution in West Asia are better explained by Benjamin Miller's theory of regional war and peace (Miller, 2007). He divides the regional peace and war outcomes into four types according to their intensity: Hot war, Cold war, Cold peace and Warm peace. Rather than the simple dichotomous understanding of war and peace—that is too broad and imprecise— this typology serves better to explain the patterns of conflict and peace in West Asia.

Hot war represents the most intensely conflictual outcome and warm peace the most peaceful. In a hot war, the two sides resort to violence to resolve the conflict between them. The use of force is aimed at destroying the offensive military capabilities of the adversary. In a cold war, there is no use of force but the hostilities may break at any time. It is characterized by 'recurrent military crisis and a considerable likelihood of escalation to war, either in a premeditated way or inadvertently'. In cold peace, the conflict is reduced but not resolved and the parties still feel threatened by an increase in other's power. Parties focus on diplomacy and not military force for conflict management. In warm peace, the conflict between the parties is resolved and the chances of violence are extremely low. Parties reach formal agreements to resolve the crisis and the relations between them develop beyond the intergovernmental level.

The most important variable in Miller's theory is the "regional state-to-nation balance" (Miller, 2007: 54-60). An imbalance in this variable is 'an underlying cause of regional wars' and explains the variation in war-proneness of different regions. A region is said to have a state-to-nation imbalance if it contains some weak states and a degree of incompatibility exists between regional states and national sentiments of the populations in that region. This creates both the secessionist and nationalist groups challenging the authority of the state and increases the power of the revisionist states which sponsor such groups. Both these factors result in lowering the level of state coherence, thereby weakening the state institutions. This increases prospects for irredentism and secessionism that threaten the territorial integrity of such states and intensifies the security dilemma of other neighboring states in the region.

The more powerful the nationalist/revisionist forces and weaker the state, the higher is the regional war-proneness. In fact, revisionism and state failure are the twin products of the state-to-nation imbalance that reinforce each other. A revisionist state sponsors nationalist groups in other states which undermine the political legitimacy of such states and undermines their internal coherence. A revisionist state may also take advantage of such states' domestic weaknesses and intervene militarily to change the territorial status quo. Hence, the state-to-nation balance exercises important independent effects on the balance of power in a region.

The great powers that have an interest in the region can only affect the cold outcomes, that is, cold war and cold peace and cannot cause hot outcomes (hot war and warm peace) on their own. The great powers, owing to their superior capabilities are in an asymmetric relationship with the regional actors and can powerfully influence the cold outcomes in the region. Cold outcomes are directly related to the cost-benefit calculations of the regional actors which may—under the great power influence—motivate them to move from hot war to cold war or from cold war to cold peace. Great powers cannot induce a state to wage a hot war or accept a warm peace because both of these outcomes are related to the survival of the state itself. A state can only wage a war or accept the resolution of a conflict if it satisfies its needs and interests. Great powers are unable to affect such outcomes on their own.

A combination of realism and Miller's theory offers a powerful theoretical tool to analyse the specific patterns of conflict and instability in West Asia. As predicted by Miller's theory, West Asia contains some weak states and a high degree of incompatibility exists between regional states and national sentiments of the populations in that region. These include Kurds in different states in the region, Shias in most of the Gulf Arab monarchies and Baluchis in Iran. This has created both the secessionist and nationalist groups challenging the authority of their respective states. This has created opportunities for leading powers in the region to sponsor such nationalist of irredentist groups in the rival states or their allies in order to weaken them. The political support offered by Iran to the Houthis in Yemen, Shias in Bahrain, Iraq and Saudi Arabia is aimed at weakening Saudi state and curtailing its influence amongst its allies.

Iran is particularly focused on Iraq for three closely interconnected reasons. First, a stable and democratic Iraq allied to Iran will remove its strongest security threat in the gulf. Historically, Iraq, owing to its resources and manpower, has been the only state in the region that has the potential to militarily threaten Iran's territorial integrity. [8] Second, a friendly Iraq will remove the terrorist and irredentist threats historically emanating from Iraq. Such terrorist groups like the Mujahhedin-e Khalq Organization (MKO), [9] that seeks the overthrow of the current Iranian regime, have been a huge cause of concern for Iran and their removal from Iraq has been one of its priorities. Third, Iran would get another strong Arab ally, after the neighbouring Syria, helping to greatly increase its influence and say in policymaking in the region. Saudi Arabia is concerned about a pro-Iran regime in Iraq for the same reasons. A stronger Iraq would be a grave threat to its security than Iran. It should be noted that Iraq shares a vast 814 km. border with Saudi Arabia and most of its critical oil fields, oil export facilities, power and desalination plants are within five minutes flying time from air bases in southern Iraq. This is exacerbating the Saudi security dilemma.

Saudi leaders see the developments in the region having the potential negative effects both for internal security and its foreign policy. As predicted by Miller's theory, Saudis fear that a Shia revival in Yemen and Bahrain, like Iraq could create a potential for irredentism in disaffected Shia Ismailis of Najran that are close to its southern border with Yemen and Shias in eastern province where bulk of Saudi oil is located. [10] This can create an internal security challenge that may take decades to pacify. On the other hand, this could mean a changed geopolitical scenario for Saudi Arabia. It would be encircled by pro-Iran regimes on its east (Bahrain), north (Iraq) and south (Yemen). This has unnerved the Saudi regime to a far greater extent. The potential of a replication of an Iraq-like situation in Yemen where Iran may gain larger influence after Houthis came to power, led to a highly disproportionate response from Saudi Arabia. Saudi fears that if it does not deal with the potential of a pro-Iran regime in Yemen, it may end up seriously jeopardising its security. This explains why Saudis are putting everything into the Yemen.

Contrarily, Saudi support for rebels in Syria is aimed at curtailing the growing Iranian influence in the region. Since Syria is the only Iranian ally in the region, a regime change would install a less friendly regime that would have the potential of isolating Iran completely from the regional policy dynamics. Since Syria is the only conduit for any Iranian material support to Hezbollah in Lebanon, this would also weaken its influence there. This explains why Iran has committed so much of its resources, manpower and Hezbollah fighters in Syria to keep Assad regime in power.

Conclusion

One of the important causes for concern for Arab states including Saudi Arabia is the nature of Iran's regional policy. Iran is perceived to be an aspiring hegemon that wants to dominate the region politically and strategically. Most of the available literature is based on these assumptions about Iran's foreign policy. There is however, a caveat that has not been sufficiently explored in the literature. The Iranian constitution speaks about four core principles for crafting the foreign policy of the Islamic republic: rejection of external domination, preservation of sovereignty and territorial integrity, defence of the rights of all Muslims and the maintenance of peaceful relations with all the non-belligerent states. The Iranian elites see the American-led West (Pollack, 2004: 4-5) and not Saudi Arabia as the hegemonic and oppressor state and recognize any confrontation with it as zero-sum. [11] In its interaction with Saudis and the other Gulf states, an increasingly 'pragmatic approach has been adopted by decision-makers in Iran that tends to be driven by regional and international developments' rather than strict ideological considerations (Ehteshami and Zweiri, 2008: xiii).

For example, the member countries of the Gulf Cooperation Council including Saudi Arabia shifted their belligerent stance against Iran and tried to normalize relations with it after the reformist president Mohammad Khatami came to power in May 1997 (Ibid.: 115). This proves to an extent that the animosity between these countries is driven by domestic and regional factors and can be drastically changed by investing adequate political will to energise the cooperation.

Iranian foreign policy, especially after 1997, has proven that its relations with Saudi Arabia depend on how it conducts its foreign and defence policy. Khatami was successful in improving relations whereas his successor Mahmud Ahmadinejad could not take relations to a higher level. However, Ahmadinejad did improve relations in many areas of mutual interest. For example, he became the first leader to attend the GCC heads of state summit in Doha in December 2007 (Ehteshami, 2008: 133). Iran has also been interested in new security arrangements in the Gulf including the proposal for a collective security pact between Gulf littoral states. Except Oman, no other Arab country has shown any interest in Iran's military overtures.

The conclusion that can be drawn from these facts is that Iran needs to provide a degree of reassurance to Arab countries about regional security and its positive role in it and on the other hand Arab states in the region must acknowledge the role of Iran as a regional power with a stake in the stability in West

Asia. This alone can help remove the trust deficit between the two groups and help stabilize the region in the long-run. Failure to cooperate on these vital issues will only push Iran away from Arab countries with a lot of negative consequences for regional stability.

Endnotes

1. For a comprehensive assessment of the Saudi security dilemma and the measures taken by the Kingdom see, Cordesman and Obaid (2005).
2. Most of the literature focuses on the confrontation between United States and Iran and the role of Saudi Arabia in this rivalry. The clash is shown as ideological with strategic underpinnings. See for example, Sadeghinia (2011).
3. These sources include, for example, *SIPRI Fact Sheet* published by Stockholm International Peace Research Institute, *Military Balance* published by IISS, London, *Jane's Defence Weekly* and *Jane's Armour and Artillery* published by Jane's Information Group.
4. Some notable exceptions include Halliday (2005).
5. This is in accordance with the proponents of existential deterrence. Recent scholarship has questioned the deterrent value of nuclear weapons saying that it is not the mere possession of nuclear weapons that deters conflict and coercion but the specific operationalization of nuclear arsenal, that is the nuclear posture, that deters aggression by other states. Different nuclear postures have varying effects on the degree of deterrence. Some postures deter more whereas others deter less. For an original treatment of the effect of postures on deterrence, see Narang (2014).
6. These figures are according to *SIPRI*. *Military Balance* puts the figure at US$ 81.9 billion that amounts to 12.9 percent of its GDP. See IISS, *The Military Balance* (2016), pp. 19-20.
7. For a correlation between the realist logic and escalation of crisis to war, see the seminal study by John A. Vasquez, *The War Puzzle Revisited* (New York: Cambridge University Press, 2009) especially chapter 5 "The Realist Road to War" in which he concludes: 'How states react to the policies and actions of their rival is not determined simply by what the other side does at any given moment, but by the entire history of their relationship, as

interpreted by general lessons of history, which have become embedded in the folklore of the system...Since realism is part of the system's folklore that has shaped behaviour, it does provide observers with a rough description of the kinds of behaviour that one would expect to be associated with the onset of war. What is crucial to understand is that against equals, these practices do not produce peace and security, as realists maintain, but increased insecurity, coercion, and entanglement in a process and series of steps that may lead to war. Each step leads decision makers further and further into a trap (both globally and domestically) where they have little choice but to fight' (pp. 213-214).

8. According to the 2004-05 statistics, the size of the Iraqi military forces, immediately before USA disbanded the Baathist army, were 424,000 compared to Iran's 540,000 and Saudi's 219,500. It possessed 2,200 battle tanks, 316 combat aircraft with six bombers, 400 SAM launchers compared to Iran's 1,613 tanks, 306 combat aircraft with zero bombers, 250 SAM launchers and Saudi's 1,055 tanks, 291 aircraft with zero bombers and 106 SAM launchers. The balance is clearly skewed toward Iraq. For comparative figures, see Cordesman and Obaid (2005), pp. 185-189.
9. For an overview of the organization and its goals, see Garduño (2011). For as assessment of the group's activities after 2003 US invasion of Iraq, see Goulka et al. (2009).
10. Ismaili Shias are a majority in Najran province and constitute about 33 percent of the population of Eastern province. For a comprehensive analysis of the degree of disaffection in Ismailis in Saudi Arabia, see Human Rights Watch, *The Ismailis of Najran: Second-class Saudi Citizen.* 2008, available at: https://www.hrw.org/sites/default/files/reports/saudiarabia0908 web.pdf.

    For an analysis of Shias in eastern province, see International Crisis Group, *The Shiite Question in Saudi Arabia*, Middle East Report N°45, September 19, 2005.
11. For instance, see the statement by Brigadier General Zolqadr on the nature of American threat to Iran in Anoshiravan Ehteshami, 'Iran and its Immediate Neighbourhood' in Ehteshami and Zweiri (eds.) (2008), p. 138.

References

Bayman, D. (2001), "Iran's Security Policy in the Post-Revolutionary Era", Santa Monica: Rand.

Chubin, S. (2002), "Whither Iran? Reform, Domestic Politics and National Security", London: IISS.

Chubin, S. (2000), "Iran's Strategic Predicament", *The Middle East Journal*, 50(1).

Cordesman, A.H. and Obaid, N. (2005), "National Security in Saudi Arabia: Threats, Responses and Challenges", London: Prager Security International.

Cordesman, A.H. and Klieber, M. (2007), "Iran's Military Forces and War fighting Capabilities: The Threat in the Northern Gulf", Westport: Prager Security International.

Dekmejian, R.H. (1994), "The Rise of Political Islamism in Saudi Arabia", *Middle East Journal*, Vol. 48(4).

Ehteshami, A. and Zweri, M. (eds.), (2008), "Iran's Foreign Policy: From Khatami to Ahmadinejad", Berkshire: Ithaca Press.

Eisenstadt, M. (1996), "Iranian Military Power: Capabilities and Intentions", Washington, DC: Washington Institute.

Garduño, M. (2011), "The Collective Action of Mujahedeen-e Khalq Organization (MKO): Evolution, Interests and Current situation", paper presented at conference on State, Society and Economy in the Modern Middle East, London Middle East Institute, SOAS, May 7.

Goulka J. (2009), "The Mujahedin-e Khalq in Iraq: A Policy Conundrum", Rand Corporation.

Halliday, F. (2005), "The Middle East in International Relations: Power, Politics and Ideology", Cambridge: Cambridge University Press.

International Crisis Group (2005), "The Shiite Question in Saudi Arabia", Middle East Report N°45, September 19.

Keddie, N. (2003), "Modern Iran: Roots and Result of the Revolution", New Haven: Yale University Press.

Miller, B. (2007), "States, Nations and the Great Powers: The Sources of Regional War and Peace", New York: Cambridge University Press.

Narang, V. (2014), "Nuclear Strategy in the Modern Era: Regional Powers and International Conflict", Princeton, NJ: Princeton University Press.

Perlo-freeman, S., Fleurant, A., Wezeman, P. and Wezeman, S.

(2016), "Trends in World Military Expenditure, 2015", SIPRI Fact Sheet.

Pollack (2004), "The Persian Puzzle: The Conflict between Iran and America", New York: Random House.

Sadeghinia, M. (2011), "Security Arrangements in the Persian Gulf with Special Reference to Iran's Foreign Policy", Reading: Ithaca Press.

Vasquez, J.A. (2009), "The War Puzzle Revisited", New York: Cambridge University Press.

10

Major Issues in the New Cold War in the West Asian and North African Region

A.K. Pasha

Historical Background:

Jawaharlal Nehru was the first major Asian leader who identified the implications of European imperialism and set about to work for Asian identity, development and cooperation. He was conscious of the emerging challenges as well as the opportunities available to work towards a new vision, greater role for Asian countries to maintain security, stability and peacefully resolve emerging conflict situations primarily created by European colonialism. As a mark of respect, the INC observed September 27, 1936, as the Palestine Day by holding meetings and demonstrations throughout the country as an indication of support for the Arab cause. To Nehru, it was abundantly clear as to who was the real culprit behind the Arab-Zionist conflict.

The British had laid the foundation for a conflict in the holy land for its own gains to further its imperialistic goals. He also saw a similarity between the imperialist policies pursued in India and in West Asia. In a speech delivered in London in July 1938, Nehru said, "This (the problem of Palestine) is a peculiar problem and we are apt to think of it too much in terms of conflict between the Arabs and the Jews…It is fundamentally a problem created by British imperialism in Palestine and unless you keep that in mind, you will not solve it" (Pasha, 1999 A). After the Second World War, the UN decided to partition Palestine in 1947. Although Nehru continued to resist the idea of according recognition to Israel established in May 1948, yet eventually decided to recognize the Jewish state on September 17, 1950. But he opposed Western-backed military alliances. His approach to secure peace through regional cooperation, Panchshila, and non-aligned policy received a rude shock when the US intervened in Iran in 1952-53 to overthrow Dr. Mohammed Mossadeq over the issue of oil nationalization.

Genesis of New Cold War

During the Iranian revolution, Ayatollah Khomeini mobilized his people on the basis of Islam to overthrow the Shah of Iran. This was a major blow to the US influence. Soon after, the House of Saud was shaken by the Mecca Mosque takeover in November 1979. The US, in Saddam Hussein, found an ally and encouraged him to invade Iran and was supported by the GCC [formed in 1991] states. The US dual containment policy led to the Iran-Iraq war for eight years starting September 1980.

In the midst of this war, Israel bombed the Iraqi nuclear reactor at Osirak near Baghdad. US tried to win over Saddam Hussein to its side but the Iraqi ruler had his own independent ideas. Although the Iran-Iraq war came to an end in July 1988 but Saddam Hussein's concerns multiplied due to fall in oil prices in view of over production by UAE, Kuwait, Saudi Arabia and others. Iraqi domestic position had become precarious and with no funds coming from GCC or elsewhere, Saddam Hussein invaded Kuwait in August 1990. For the US, Saddam Hussein's blunder came as a big gift. The US administration mobilized over thirty countries for a grand coalition of countries to expel Iraq from Kuwait. UN economic sanctions were imposed on Iraq and coalition forces led by US launched an attack on Iraq and expelled the Iraqi forces. Kuwait was liberated by the end of February 1991. It must be mentioned here that the US undermined all peaceful efforts by Arab League, OIC, UN and others to get Iraq out peacefully from Kuwait. From the very outset, the US was determined to destroy Iraq's military which would lead to the overthrow of Saddam Hussein.

Around this time, it was clear that the Cold War was coming to an end with the disintegration and collapse of the USSR. Earlier, after suffering heavy losses, Moscow had decided to withdraw from Afghanistan. Although Iraq was a close ally of Moscow, the new Russian leaders had no inclination to come to the rescue of Iraq as they needed Western support to tide over their own economic problems. Despite Iraqi expulsion from Kuwait, defeat at the hands of US and acceptance of UNSC Resolutions on WMD's, and its new border with Kuwait, the UN sanctions on Iraq remained. The civil war in South Iraq involving the Shias and the Kurds in northern Iraq provided the US-UK combine to impose no fly zones on much of the Iraqi territory. Under the pretext of protecting the Kurds and Shias, both the Western countries resorted to daily (almost) bombing of Iraqi facilities—both military and civilian—which had already been devastated in the 1991 war.

By early 2001, West Asia and the Gulf region had come to see violence on a large scale not only due to the Palestinian Intifada but also as a fallout from Afghanistan's Taliban and other groups opposed to US, Israel and its Arab allies. Even countries like Saudi Arabia had come to witness greater violence within its territory especially with the rise of Al-Qaeda. All this led to the 9/11 events in the US, which linked global violence/terrorism to the WANA region. US response was to invade and occupy Afghanistan. After Afghanistan, Iraq became the next target of the US. It was invaded in March 2003 and Saddam was toppled on the pretext of WMD's, human rights violations and support to terrorism. All of it was in violation of UN and International law. The US invasion and occupation of Iraq and Afghanistan gave a new boost to Islamic groups who resorted to violence. Shia-Sunni-Kurdish sectarianism also led to civil war in Iraq following the fear of its disintegration. Regime change which was applied in Libya, Iraq, and Afghanistan is being implemented in Syria. This had led to greater violence in Iraq as well as in Syria. Iran and its ally Hezbollah of Lebanon support the Syrian President Assad. Religious groups from Hamas, Hezbollah, Islamic Jihad, Al-Qaeda and now ISIL and many more have emerged which preach violence to counter the US-Israeli hegemony. Regional powers like Saudi Arabia, Turkey, Iran, UAE, Qatar and others are now involved in many of the regional problems leading to violence, terrorism, extremism, death, destruction and refugee problem.

Lack of Democracy in the GCC States

The struggle for democracy and people's demand to replace autocracy with democratic structures is a recent phenomenon in the Gulf [Arab] societies. The huge oil revenues, at least since 1973, enabled the six Gulf ruling families in Kuwait, Saudi Arabia, Bahrain, Qatar, United Arab Emirates and Oman to embark on rapid modernization of their societies. Focus on infrastructure, oil based industrial development and on education has led to the emergence of a middle class, desirous of playing a role in the decision-making process. Massive economic development taking place in the GCC states is actually transforming the political fabric in these states. Thus, the process of political change has intensified due to a number of internal and external factors. The Gulf Cooperation Council was established in 1981 largely as reaction on the part of the Gulf monarchies to the Iranian revolution of 1979 in which people's power mobilized by Ayatollah Khomeini under the banner of Islam toppled the strongest monarchy in the Gulf region aligned with the US/West.

In the wake of the 1979 Iranian revolution, fall in oil revenues in the 1980's and especially after the 1991 US-led liberation war over Kuwait, one can notice growing demands for political participation. Before the Iranian revolution, the prospects for democracy in GCC states were dim but the revolutionary changes in Iran prompted Gulf rulers to initiate modest political reforms and promise democratization of their absolute monarchies. But soon this enthusiasm waned as the Iranian revolution was contained and confined within its borders. The eight year Iran-Iraq war further neutralized the revolutionary zeal of the Iranian clergy.

In the Kuwait crisis, Iraqi President Saddam Hussein not only challenged the legitimacy of the GCC rulers, like Ayatollah Khomeini had done earlier, but also presented them as dependent on outside help as the GCC States rushed to seek US military help to safeguard their family rule. Since 1991, two significant changes of far reaching consequences to the area have taken place: the collapse of the Arab unity; and the other is the "explosion of questioning process" that has spurred the incipient process of democratization and test the legitimacy of Arab regimes in the Gulf area. The presence of outside forces [mainly US military] posed a challenge to the legitimacy of the GCC rulers where the political process is a family enterprise. It also exposed their fragility and their inner weakness despite their enormous oil wealth.

The dependence of the GCC rulers on outside help is mainly due to the present processes of governance in these states and to their linkages with the US. The authoritarian nature of the political system and the domestic dynamics of power, place the state structures at a very advantageous position, while relegating public institutions to the periphery. In other words, the regime for all practical purposes has replaced the state. For reasons of regime security, the rulers have pushed their human resources to the sidelines and thus have gradually strengthened their ties with the US-the most dominant power in the Gulf region. Due to this dependency syndrome, the GCC rulers unfortunately demonstrate and use their power, authority and military capability against most of their own citizens, who unfortunately thus largely cease to be productive participants in its political process and also in the overall social and economic development. This has also deprived most of the people of their role in the process of political development.

The rulers instead of trying to anchor political development and stability in the concept of legitimacy seek that anchor in US protection. Foreign protection, thus, becomes a substitute for legitimacy and hence people's participation and human rights have become casualties. It needs to be stressed that both domestic and external factors coalesce in the interest of the status quo, resulting in virtual political paralysis. The GCC rulers still largely unwilling to share power and basically opposed to people's participation in the decision-making process of the political system and having a largely narrow social base, in order to retain power, have established very effective coercive institutions and widely use coercion and repression against their own people.

Thus, fear dominates the lives of most citizens in GCC States. Additionally, oil revenues are also used to neutralize opposition and consolidate the grip of the ruling families. The real meaning of the consolidation of the family rule was the entrenchment of central decision-making of the highest bureaucratic level in the ruling elite. Since the loyalty of the state is viewed as personal loyalty to the ruling family, any criticism or dissent is seen negatively. Any group or social force calling on these families to share real power are thus opposed and repressed except in Kuwait where periodic elections since 1963 to the national assembly are held and power is shared by the Al Sabah family with others, even though in a limited manner. Like in the wake of the 1979 Iranian revolution, Iraqi invasion of Kuwait in 1990 also convinced some GCC rulers to initiate political change and work for limited people's participation in the political system. In their perception, a "democratic deficit" in their states undermines their capacity to withstand political shocks, but sadly even after a lapse of 28 years since the invasion of Kuwait one can still discern their strong determination to remain absolute rulers.

Even though the odds are against democratic change, but now all the GCC states have their own middle class who wish to play a role in the political system. This could become the credible basis on which to democratize their largely authoritarian systems. But it is not clear whether the GCC rulers, due to domestic, regional and global factors, would match public aspirations for greater political participation in the political system. Many citizens, civil society groups, associations and other democratic groups in the GCC states want the US to speak for democracy in their states. They are convinced that democracy in all its forms and dimensions will come soon if the US acts quickly and decisively because the US has accumulated enormous leverage over the GCC rulers and families. Many Arabs feel there is an excellent chance now at this critical juncture to bring genuine democracy in the GCC states. Although many in the GCC are convinced that the US wants to see democracy in their states, they find fault with it because they suspect the attitude of the US is not to push things, but to wish that things will go in the direction of democracy.

Iraqi invasion of Kuwait represented the greatest challenge to the established order in the Gulf. It not only challenged the legitimacy of the GCC ruling families who have anchored their stability in US protection and through which US corporate interests are in turn protected, but also presented them to the Arabs as in fact, working against Pan-Arab interests. Thus, the close nexus between the US and the GCC rulers was exposed successfully. That at first sight of crisis, the GCC ruling families had to cry out to the US for help, raises the pertinent question as to what happened to the billions of dollars which the GCC rulers have spent for decades on acquiring weapons from the US and others for defense.

Most of the Gulf Arabs are aware that bulk of the arms were purchased to make money and not to seriously build a strong military machine as these autocrats are afraid of coups. Beyond doubt, it has been established that the ruling elites have bungled. Not only the Gulf rulers could not defend the country and invited foreign forces on their land but some also want long-term presence of these foreign forces [mainly from US] as a deterrent for potential trouble makers [internal and external]. This dependency syndrome which has become endemic can be directly attributed to the existing process of governance in the GCC states and to their linkages with the US.

The reason for the lack of democracy in GCC states cannot be wholly attributed to the US and to the self-interest of the ruling family members. One opinion is that we should not overlook the fact that these are relatively nascent political systems and democratic structures need time to take roots. Democracy is a process that goes on continuously at varied paces and that it need not move in the direction of the West. The emphasis of the current leadership consisting of Amirs, Sultans and Kings is on gradualism and how to preserve continuity while at the same time introducing inevitable change. No doubt they are apparently playing a crucial role in the nation building and state formation process during which they claim power according to them has to be concentrated and centralized. They face a clear dilemma in unleashing the dynamism associated with rapid growth and globalization while at the same time working hard to preserve their own family rule, stability and identity and also having to contain tensions flowing from this process. The dichotomy of economic development and relative political stagnation stares at the rulers in all the GCC states.

Saudi rulers, since the establishment of their Kingdom by King Abdul Aziz in 1932, have been promising their people that they would introduce a representative assembly. King Abdullah has promised to hold municipal elections. But the sad reality is that despite greater political development there is very little input from the general public in running the state affairs even though there is demand for political reforms and popular participation in decision-making. One major reason why political conflict was virtually absent in the Kingdom was the manner in which the Saudi Kings showered their subjects with money and so no political opposition was serious. In the aftermath of the Arab Spring and in the wake of overthrow of dictators in Tunisia, Egypt and Libya in 2010-11, many Saudis have called for political reforms.

Undoubtedly, ensuring the security of the monarchies has been the principal reason for the establishment of the GCC. It has become crystal clear with the GCC-military intervention in Bahrain to put down the demand for genuine political participation and to widen and deepen democracy movement and prevent the freedom contagion from spreading to other parts of the GCC states. There is no doubt that the Saudis are quite apprehensive of the Shia majority coming to power in Bahrain because of the adverse impact it could have on its own restive Shia minority in the oil-rich Al-Hasa part of the country. The House of Saud is also concerned about the impact of a regime change in Bahrain on the balance of power between Saudi Arabia and an assertive Shia Iran in the region. But these are secondary explanations.

The primary concern of the Arab autocracies in the Gulf is the suppression of democratic movements regardless of the sectarian character of the populations engaging in democratic struggles. They are worried that if any of the monarchies fall or even reach a substantial compromise with democratic movements, it will have a domino effect in all the GCC states. The GCC was established as an instrument to protect and prolong autocratic family rule on the Arabian littoral of the Gulf. Its military operation in Bahrain has clearly shown these true colors and is clearly a setback to political development (Hudson, 1988).

The wandering Arab tribes of Al Sabahs, Al Khalifahs, Al Thanis, and others were given flags by the British and provided protection and when the ruling families were given political independence they gained formal legitimacy and international recognition as Arab Gulf states. However, the historical incongruity was that this weakened the traditional legitimacy of the ruling families which had already been eroded over a period of time by resistance and organized opposition movements. Thus, the greatest deterrent possessed by these ruling families especially after they got massive oil revenues, was the monopoly of authority and wealth. The distribution of oil money necessitates the creation of state structures to distribute it among the citizens in the shape of state expenditure.

Unfortunately, the first step invariably was the consolidation of the ruling families and their transformation into political institutions which owned the state. This has actually meant full concentration of power in the hands of the ruling tribal elite's. As these states were created around the families and by virtue of this fact other structures were functional extensions to the point that loyalty to the state was translated as personal loyalty to the ruling family. Under the circumstances, the GCC ruling families evinced strong opposition to the very idea of sharing power with any group or social force.

Even the merchant families which are very old and on whom the present ruling families were financially dependent before oil was discovered have been virtually sidelined. But all the GCC rulers are aware [as literacy has spread rapidly, together with other factors] that their citizens wish to exercise public control on government and curtailment of almost unlimited power of the ruling families. But the sad and harsh reality is that the ruling families have systematically prevented the rise of new social and political forces autonomous of the state and desirous of expressing the interests of various segments of the population especially the middle class.

This has meant the prevention of the rise of political parties, banning social and political movements or groups not seen as loyal to them, suppression of trade unions, direct and debilitating supervision over professional associations, and bureaucratic and other hurdles towards the growth of civil society, rigorous censorship, control of mosques, religious and many other institutions. The domination, intimidation and repression by the ruling families have in turn led to increasing friction, tension, subversive activities and political violence.

Legitimacy is thus side stepped in favor of coercive power, itself dependent on an unequal relationship with the US. In all likelihood, the much suspected link with the US will continue to promote repressive policies and discourage genuine political participation until at least abundant oil and its revenues are available. The GCC regimes with US support have become confident, bold and thus more repressive. They use security and intelligence apparatus to perpetuate their authoritarian and undemocratic rule. This structure of the state presided over by the Minister of Interior [invariably by a ruling family member] in most cases, is the most modern, efficient and perhaps highly developed and widely used or abused.

The technology of repression has been upgraded by leaps and bounds with severe implications for popular participation and human rights. Thus, democracy is a victim of a political process in which legitimacy and consensus politics are truly wanting. Under such circumstances, dissent is seen as unacceptable. They often use oil revenues to stifle any dissent—either benevolently, by buying off any opposition, or forcefully, through the all-pervasive mukhaburat—intelligence services that penetrate the entire system. The concept of a loyal opposition is not even known in GCC states. Suspicion, paranoia, fear of assassination and of being overthrown are leading to expulsion, assassination, repression, incarceration, including torture and in some cases execution of dissenters under fake trials. To a very large extent, this sad state of affairs is also due to the ongoing Arab-Israeli conflict.

More and more people in the Gulf now believe that their governments due to the authoritarian nature of the political system and also under the US influence cannot do anything to relieve their humiliation and improve their lot. Hence, the emergence of Islamic groups which employ violence and suicide bombings. Moreover, the secular groups also follow this strategy under popular support. One writer says, "suicide bombings take root because they free the desperate from the need to rely on governments. Rather than being sponsored by states, this form of violence challenges states". Al-Qaeda and other religious groups may be ultimately contained but newer groups would emerge and may follow their methods. Lack of democracy and suppression of political opposition invariably drives people to join Islamic groups and repression alone cannot eliminate terrorism. Any successful counter terrorism strategy must thus address both the opportunities available to militants and the level of their motivation.

To summarize the above discussion, it is clear that there is no such thing as a 'perfect democracy' but all democratic forces should support and encourage the process of political change and modernization in the GCC States because once the Arab [Gulf] regimes become democratic and responsive to popular demands, not only their legitimacy would be enhanced but more significantly their dependence on outside states especially the US would come down and this may lead to reduction in outside military and political intervention which has periodically undermined peace, security and stability in the region. Genuine political reforms would give the politically oppressed people a stake in the running of the political system as also the much needed political stability and smooth transition. The abundant oil resources could then be used to advance economic development so as to engage the Arab people in the process of political and economic progress.

Prince Turki al Faisal, Saudi Ambassador to the US said, Americans wanted reforms and change in Saudi society but noted, "we don't mind being criticized. There is a well-known saying in Arabic: Your true friend is one who tells you the truth rather than one who simply agrees with you. But it is the way in which Americans criticize, whether it is politicians or public figures or a thought leader that causes us concern. We often hear political rhetoric and bombast and not constructive commentary". He acknowledged that the Saudi leadership is very much conscious of bringing about reforms in the Kingdom in a gradual manner, "but we're not going to change just because you tell us to. Making dictums leads nowhere. Constructive comments, on the other hand, are more helpful" (Kidwai, 2010).

Along with the steps towards democratic transformation, steps to resolve the thorny AIC would also be debated, and discussed at all forums thereby allowing Arab leaders to take initiatives for meaningful steps along with serious US-Israeli steps (which are very essential). Both these steps would reinforce the momentum for change and India could then look forward to greater peace, security and stability in the Gulf region in future.

In certain Gulf countries like Bahrain, Kuwait and elsewhere, the Islamic parties have gained significant number of seats in legislature or come to share power through democratic process but such groups have fairly soon learnt how to be responsible and accountable. It is apparent that it is far easier to control terrorism and religious extremism in liberal democratic political systems which have high level of legitimacy and strong domestic control than the present political set up where the rulers want to remain in total control of all state affairs. The long overdue change has now become inevitable and if delayed, internal and regional violence and terrorism may be directed against such autocratic regimes unwilling or unable to initiate reforms. Instability, religious extremism and terrorism could then spill over into other regions like South Asia as security and stability in both the regions are mutually interlinked through a number of factors (Naqeeb, 1990).

The Rise of Islamic State

The single most important reason for the rise of Islamic State is US invasion and occupation of Iraq. Despite opposition from UNSC members Russia, France, Germany, China, Syria and others, the Anglo-American leaders invaded Iraq. Many also questioned the allegations against Iraq especially disarming or liberating the Iraqi people from the dictatorship of Saddam Hussein. Many felt Iraq posed no threat to any one especially since 1991 when UN sanctions had crippled Iraq's military capability severely. US invasion of

Iraq through *Operation Iraqi Freedom* and the so-called '*shock and awe*' policy was believed would bring to an end the Saddam Hussein regime. Initially, the Iraqi military put up stiff resistance in some places but soon they simply melted into the civilian crowd. There were massive civilian causalities on the Iraqi side during and after the war.

The US occupied Baghdad on April 9, 2003 and soon there were daily demonstrations and fierce resistance by the Iraqis' demanding the withdrawal of US forces from Iraq. US inability to restore basic services in most of the Iraqi cities fuelled protests throughout the country but it was most intense in the so called Sunni triangle. To neutralize the mounting Iraqi resistance, the US began to play the sectarian card. They used Shia national guards to suppress Sunnis and also Peshmergas or the Kurdish guards as well to kill Sunnis and silence them. The US could not find WMD's and any links between Saddam Hussein and Al-Qaeda.

With escalating Iraqi resistance and mounting criticism of US brutality against Iraqis at places like Abu Ghraib prison, the US could not control and subjugate the Iraqis through its representative Paul Bremer. He was forced to hand over power to an interim Iraqi government led by Prime Minister Ayad Allawi in June 2004. Elections were again held on January 30, 2005 amidst mounting violence and boycott by Sunni Arabs. The Shias and Kurds who were favored by the US since 1991 voted in large numbers and under the proportional representation system gained a majority of seats in the National Assembly. The above elections and the subsequent elections which brought Ibrahim el Jafaari and Nouri-el Maliki as Prime Ministers widened the differences between the Shias, Sunnis and Kurds which led to more sectarian violence.

Moreover, the sectarian divide in Iraq further widened due to US policy of divide and rule with religious groups and parties gaining ground thereby undermining secularism which was the basis of Iraqi political system under the Baathist rule. Shias undoubtedly dominated the new Iraqi political system and the Kurds strived to achieve maximum autonomy apparently without provoking Turkey. The oil rich region of Kirkuk virtually came under Kurdish control. The US found political sectarianism very useful to control Iraq. Iraqi central governments have become weak and are unable to assert authority over the entire country. Iraqi security forces are unable to contain escalating violence in which more Iraqis are dying and suffering thereby further destroying the country.

The US forces after their withdrawal towards the end of 2011 have now returned in modest numbers in Iraq apparently to provide security and training to the Iraqi forces at the government's request to combat the ISIL forces. From Iraq, the US plans to implement its regional strategy towards Syria, and others. Soon, Iraq has become more dangerous and a frightening place than Afghanistan. This led to more violence, wars, instability and terrorism spreading to the whole region and the world.

Despite being promised freedom, protection of human rights and all the rhetoric about "building a new democracy", most ordinary Iraqis are still being killed on a daily basis and the army has become a mute spectator as most Iraqis still struggle for survival, with human rights violations being a daily phenomenon. Iraqis felt that with the end of Saddam regime, an era of calm, democracy and respect for human rights would begin. But US atrocities on Iraqis continued on a daily basis. The US used warplanes, helicopters, artillery, APC's, and Special Forces with banned weapons to crush any resistance by Iraqis to US occupation.

The US also used clusters, phosphorus and chemical bombs to eliminate Iraqi resistance. Thousands of innocent Iraqis routinely got killed when US forces raided towns and villages and at road blocks and check points with no investigation. In fact, most killings went unreported. Thus, Iraq saw more stability due to weak central governments. Apart from the massive loss of civilian lives, most Iraqis still struggle for their basic needs. The Iraqis now face for the third time [apparently to contain and degrade ISIL] indiscriminate daily bombardment by the US planes and helicopters of their residential areas. It has become obvious that as more Iraqis were killed by US and its trained Iraqi forces, there was more violence, terrorism and resistance. As the suffering, pain and agony of Iraqis increased; more prolonged will be the process to bring stability to Iraq.

Thus, US's reckless post-9/11 policy of "regime change" and the global war on terror [against so-called militant Islam] toppled the Taliban and then Iraqi regime on the false pretext that his regime was developing WMD's that could be used for terrorism. The collapse of the Iraqi Baathist regime, de-Baathification, and dissolving of the military and security forces opened the flood gates for Jihadi groups to infiltrate into Iraq and from there move on to Syria and other parts of the region (Al Rasheed, 1998).

The capture of Mosul and large areas in Iraq and Syria in early 2014 by ISIL and declaration of Caliphate undoubtedly poses a grave challenge to Iraq, Syria and the region if not to the world, with far reaching implications especially to its neighbors and others. It clearly illustrates the collapse of governance across a broad expanse of territory, endangering lives, creating chaos and forcing the evacuation, deportation, arrest and even execution of those not "inclusive" of the new "state". There are also other attributes at play: the mosaic of ethnicity, tribes, religion and secularism that are at war with each other on multiple levels that allows Salafist-Jihadists to come to power.

The Caliphate is a unique alternative state structure that excludes everyone but the pious. But there are other more subtle attributes that make these Caliphates—more dangerous for the entire region and perhaps the world. This can be directly traced to the US invasion of Iraq in 2003 which soon disbanded the Iraqi military and Baathist dominated administration. This alienated bulk of the Sunnis who had ruled Iraq for centuries. The bombing and destruction of

Fallujah and other Iraqi cities by US-led forces had paved the way for the civil war in Iraq. Al-Qaida in Iraq [AQI] also played a role in the growing violence in Iraq. In October 2006, it was renamed as Islamic State of Iraq, with focus on Iraq with its goal to set up an Islamic state. The Iraqi governments dominated by Shias accentuated the division between Shias and Sunnis and Kurds. Iraqi PM Nouri el Maliki and now Hayder el Abaddi especially cracked down hard on the Sunnis.

The US military withdrawal in 2011 saw increased tensions beginning to fray the coalition governments underscoring Iraq's fragile political, military and economic challenges. It also made it easier for Shia dominated governments to consolidate power. The US was able to contain Sunni violence in Iraq's Al Anbar province by pouring huge sums of money and arms plus promise of induction of Sunnis in the Iraqi military. But the Iraqi Shias neutralized US promises which gradually paved the way for the emergence of ISIL. This led to growing violence including car and suicide bombings, kidnappings and targeted assassinations. In this connection, Iran continued to support the Shia-dominated governments in Baghdad whereas Saudi Arabia and other Gulf States supported with money and weapons the disaffected Sunni groups in Iraq.

The civil war in Syria since 2011 supported by Saudi Arabia, Qatar, Turkey, Jordan, Iran, Russia, US-EU and many others enabled the Islamic groups to regroup/align, especially the Sunni groups. Unable to bring down the Bashar el Assad regime, ISIL focused on North East Syria and North West Iraq. The West/Gulf states like Qatar, Saudi Arabia, UAE plus Jordan and Turkey supported the anti-Assad groups with men, money, intelligence and guns. In its ruthless operations, ISIL expanded its control to parts of Iraq especially Mosul, Ramadi and Der-erZoor and Raa'qa in Syria.

In this they received substantial support from Turkey, Jordan, Saudi Arabia and other Gulf States, Israel and the West. It will not be easy to overthrow the Caliphate merely by air strikes. The US needs the cooperation of Syria, Iran, Iraq,

Turkey as also of Russia and other players to contain, degrade and ultimately destroy ISIL which appears to have a clear political vision, well-organized military structure, motivated fighters [including large number of foreign fighters], money, weapons and good control over social media. The growing sectarianism raging in the West Asian region from Iraq, Syria, Lebanon, Bahrain, Yemen, Saudi Arabia and other Gulf States has come to the surface mainly after US invasion of Iraq.

Many believed that it came to the fore since the Iranian Revolution in 1979 but the Islamic republic rarely used the Shia card in its foreign policy as it is now using it so effectively, much to the surprise of Sunni Arab states. The systematic persecution of Sunnis by the Nour el Maliki government in Iraq basically led to the emergence of Caliphate. Also the US which had promised the Iraqi Sunnis a fair deal in political system, military and economic cake was thwarted by the Maliki government and Iran was a mute spectator to the suppression and persecution of Sunnis.

The power struggle in Bahrain involving the ruling Sunni al Khalifa family and majority Shias made the Saudis nervous about Iranian intentions. This convinced the House of Saud to contain Iran's growing regional influence by sending GCC troops to crush Shia uprising in Bahrain. This also prompted them to support anti-Assad Sunni forces in Syria and work against Muslim Brotherhood in Egypt, Houthis in Yemen and Hamas in Gaza. The other GCC states like Qatar and UAE also got involved in the Syrian civil war along with Turkey which wishes to expand its influence in Syria—its close neighbor. ISIL also covertly receives support of all kinds from Turkey.

On top of all this, the US/West was also behind the emergence of ISIL which now controls huge territories in Iraq and Syria. In effect, ISIL has blunted the Iranian influence in the region, especially Iraq and Syria. However, the Lebanese party Hezbollah by involving itself in Syria to save the Assad regime has become over stretched and has lost many fighters.

About 60 countries have come together to contain and degrade the ISIL but it will not be defeated by air attacks only as all of them are not willing to send soldiers to commit on the ground to fight the Caliphate. The US/West, Iran, and GCC states were opposed to the continuation of Maliki as Iraqi PM and instead opted for Haider al Abadi who was quickly supported by the Grand Ayatollah Ali al Sistani, the supreme religious authority in Iraq. Al Abadi has of course formed a new government but he faces huge challenges from ISIL, Kurds, Sunnis, Shia militias, and foreign pressures—particularly from the US—falling oil prices, corruption and other issues. Iraq also has a new President Fouad Massoum in place of Jallal Talibani.

Although Iran is worried about ISIL and possibly Iranian air strikes and some of its troops may have been involved against the Caliphate forces but more worried are the GCC states which fear from the radical Wahhabi outfit as a mortal danger. Despite Russian air strikes in ISIL and coordination with Syrian military to defeat ISIL, support from Turkey, Saudi Arabia, Qatar and others is leading to more violence. It was said that ISIL had more than 50,000 foreign fighters. The British PM David Cameroon had said that ISIL may intensify its violent activities [like the 2015 Paris attack] in future with more countries [over 60] getting involved militarily in efforts to defeat ISIL.

It is also becoming clear that under the garb of fighting ISIL, the parties want to clearly overthrow the Assad regime and reorder the map of the region. Saudi Arabia has also formed a 34 nation Islamic alliance to fight ISIL and other forms of terrorism. Energy gas pipelines from Qatar to Turkey and rival gas pipelines from Iran to the Mediterranean are also complicating the Syrian civil war. The present turmoil in the region would continue in future, bringing more surprises, renewed threat of domestic, regional and global terrorism, suicide attacks, harsher repression, brutal killings, people fleeing as refugees, human rights violations, military interventions, and possible overthrow of well entrenched regimes including the GCC monarchies.

Resolution of Palestine issue, end to foreign interventions, democratization of political systems, respect for human rights and fair distribution of resources may give some relief to the people who are tired of wars, revolutions, coups, uprisings, and killings all of which are pushing them towards terrorism and embracing extremists groups to get justice and security (Dekmejian, 1998).

Violence/Terrorism as Normal

As we have seen earlier, soon after the 9/11 events, the US led a global campaign against terrorism and especially the Al-Qaeda network with its attack on Afghanistan. Although Al-Qaeda appears to have been disrupted as its members were either killed, imprisoned or they fled to safer places, but terrorists means have increasingly become legitimate and popular in the perceptions of most people in West Asia. It is interesting to note that those carrying out terrorist acts in West Asia and elsewhere (not just Al-Qaeda) are claiming to do it in the name of Islam. If seen objectively, Islam is not central to the terror issue, although one cannot say that religion plays no role. Some groups in the West Asian region may be dangerous not because of their Islamic character but due to their violent methods and intolerant ends. The actions of a few (misguided) radical Muslims should not be seen as a general phenomenon flowing from Islamic faith.

It is interesting to note that Hezbollah, Hamas and Islamic Jihad were treated by the US as local movements fighting against occupation, and not as part of the global terrorist networks like Al-Qaeda and so not included in the list of 27 terrorist organizations whose assets were frozen by the US Congress. No wonder, Arafat and most secular Palestinians distanced themselves from Al-Qaeda and even Saddam Hussein. Bin Laden's struggle against the West was essentially a religious war whereas the Palestinian struggle against Israel is a national liberation movement. While the former uses mindless violence and terrorism, the Palestinians resort to violence in self-defense.

Much of the world sees Israeli violence against Palestinians as violation of international law, Geneva conventions, UN Resolutions and hence illegitimate because the Israeli goal is to continue its occupation of Palestinian land and the Palestinians have a legitimate right to resist Israeli occupation. Netanyahu's policy of territorial expansionism will not end the confrontation but will increase terrorism in Palestine and in other parts of the region and elsewhere and people would get inspiration from these activities.

Early resolution of the Israeli-Palestinian issue is crucial to avoid the specter of terrorism spreading worldwide. Here, it must be mentioned that US State Department reports had identified that West Asia was not the leading region in the number of terrorist incidents throughout the 1990s. It was also not the leading area as far as the number of attacks against US targets was concerned. Five years before the 9/11 incident, terrorism in West Asia had significantly declined every year and by 2000, West Asia had emerged as a region with the fewest terrorist attacks. This global trend must be kept in mind to counter the futile attempt to link Islam with terrorism.

The phenomenon of suicide attacks and its effectiveness especially by Hamas, Islamic Jihad, Hezbollah, Al-Qaeda, and others began to be emulated by the ISIS. Since the secular groups could not recruit the number of members as the Islamic groups did, no wonder they began to emulate the suicide method. The suicide bombing phenomenon has thus become secularized. This is born out of the hopelessness and humiliation at the hands of Israeli and other oppressors. Since the Islamic doctrine prohibits suicide, the perpetrators and their sympathizers may have used religion to suit their ends. It must also be stressed that suicide bombing is not confined to Islamic groups in West Asia only.

Although many Israeli civilians have fallen victims to Palestinian violence inside Israel and OAT's but thousands of Palestinians have been killed by Israeli military forces, many thousands injured and a large number permanently crippled. Many have called Israeli attacks against innocent civilians as savage, barbaric and state sponsored terrorism. Several human rights groups worldwide have condemned Israeli use of excessive violence against Palestinians in clear violations of international law, Geneva Conventions, UNSCR's and other global conventions.

Mounting Palestinian casualties due to excessive and disproportionate violence by the Israeli forces caused much anguish and anxiety to America's faithful allies in the region like Egypt, Saudi Arabia, Jordan and others. Saudi Arabia after the 9/11 events, despite accusations that 15 out of 19 pilots who crashed with aircraft's at WTC and Pentagon were Saudi nationals, has managed to keep its pro-American image but has been "staunchly anti-Zionist", despite King Abdullah's peace plan to resolve AIC which was endorsed by the Arab Summit in early 2002. He advised the US to examine the roots of terrorism:

"*We see Palestine children being shot at, buildings being destroyed, trees uprooted, people encircled, and territories closed and women killed, unborn babies delivered at check points. They are very painful images. And when we worry about the future, and we worry about the causes that lead people to become violent, the reasons that lead people to become violent, the reasons that lead people to become suicide bombers, these are the reasons they do so*" (Pasha, 2014).

One must recall here that Osama bin Laden was largely a US creation. Due to the Cold War and the need to expel the USSR from Afghanistan in 1980s, propelled the US to cultivate Islamic groups worldwide. The US mobilized Muslim fighters in the name of Jihad or holy Islamic struggle against Communism. Saudi Arabia, Egypt, Sudan and others were pressurized to send fanatically religious people like

Osama bin Laden who came from a wealthy family. Bin Laden was very much a part of the Saudi establishment. His point of departure came when he objected to the presence of American troops on Saudi soil when King Fahd invited US troops to defend the Kingdom in the wake of Saddam Hussein's invasion of Kuwait in 1990. Osama bin Laden focused his attention on expelling US forces from Saudi Arabia and creating an Islamic political order across the Muslim World.

Even though Saudi Arabia is a fundamentalist state with most of the laws based on the Shariah, it still became a target of Osama bin Laden when he began to highlight Islamic issues that resonate with the public, especially the Palestine issue and sanctions against Iraq. Osama bin Laden said, "Let there be no two religions in Saudi Arabia"–based on a Hadith. According to one writer in a classified survey, it was found the 95 percent of the Saudis agreed with Bin Laden regards the presence of American troops in Saudi Arabia. Dilip Hiro in his book *War without End* opined, "the US war on terrorism is a war without end". He emphasizes the need to go to the root cause of terrorism, and argues that US threats to Iraq—an established government—amounts to terror.

According to him, "Americans always blame others, never themselves. Whatever happens to America, it is their own fault. Americans won't like to hear that. This war (on terrorism) will go on because of the definition Bush has put on it. He himself is threatening established governments: so long as anybody is terrorizing established governments, there needs to be a war". More and more people in West Asia now believe that their governments due to the authoritarian nature of the political system and also under US influence cannot do anything to relieve their humiliation and improve their lot. Hence, the emergence of more radical Islamic groups that employ suicide bombings. Moreover, the secular groups also follow this strategy under popular support.

According to one writer, "suicide bombings take root because they free the desperate from the need to rely on governments. Rather than being sponsored by states, this form of violence challenges states". Al-Qaeda, ISIS and other terrorist groups in West Asia may be ultimately defeated but newer groups would emerge and may follow Al-Qaeda's methods. Lack of democracy and suppression of political opposition drives people to join Islamic groups and repression alone cannot eliminate terrorism. "Any successful counter terrorism strategy must thus address both the opportunities available to militants and the level of their motivations" (Pasha, 2016).

Historic Nuclear Deal

The much anticipated moment finally came with the nuclear deal announced in Vienne, Austria, on July 14, 2015 between Iran and the P5+1 Group known as the Joint Comprehensive Plan of Action [JCPOA]. President Obama told Saudi King that the deal "will verifiably prevent Iran from obtaining a nuclear weapon by cutting off all the potential pathways to a bomb while ensuring the peaceful nature of Iran's nuclear program going forward" (Pasha, 2010). He said it is not based on trust but on verification and also "underscored that the US is as committed as ever to working with our Gulf partners to counter Iran's destabilizing activities in the region and promote stability as well as resolutions to the region's crises". The US expects Iran to be a responsible regional power that should contribute to regional peace, security and stability. It is also very clear that the US will not be held prisoner by its regional allies [KSA or Israel] if its national interests cross their path. In a word, the nuclear deal became a reality largely because a 'military option' perhaps no longer existed for the US and Israel (Hiro, 2002).

Hardening of Saudi Position on Iran

But the ground reality was quite different as the nuclear deal did not enhance relations between Iran and Saudi Arabia. The Saudis themselves have been speaking openly that the deal will lead to the "eruption of small wars because it is a non-proliferation agreement which will not change Iran's behavior in the region". In fact, bilateral talks between Iran and KSA have come to a halt due to break in diplomatic ties and the *status quo* is becoming too dangerous with the killing of Ayatollah Nimr al Nimr on January 2, 2016, who was in custody since 2012 [clearly a provocative step towards Iran], burning of Saudi embassy in Tehran, and giving Riyadh a chance to break diplomatic ties with Tehran [few supporters of KSA also followed and some in GCC recalled diplomats from Tehran].

Clearly, Riyadh is exhibiting its nervousness and this partly explains its decision to increase tensions with Iran, hoping to involve the US on its side [old ally vs. new friend] if there is a showdown with Iran on any issue. The fall in oil prices has aggravated Saudi concerns as the decline has been quite sharp from US$ 110 a barrel in 2014 to less than US$ 30 in January 2016 which forced the Saudi rulers to cut subsidies and increase prices of oil and other items.

All of these economic woes have forced the Saudi regime to privatize their oil company Aramco. This is gradually bound to undermine their legitimacy and absolutist rule questioned in coming years as these issues are not only economic but would eventually impact the country's political economy and carry geopolitical overtones as well. There are growing concerns about the new direction of Saudi foreign policy positions towards Iran and Yemen and attempts to calm the Saudi people who are divided on sectarian lines which may spiral out of their hands, although the tension between Iran and KSA has little to do with religion (Pasha, 2007).

Lifting of Sanctions on Iran

Under the nuclear deal, Iran quickly decommissioned the Arak plutonium facility by removing the reactor core, reduced its stockpile of enriched uranium by 98 percent and shipped most of its low-enriched uranium to Russia and reduced the number of centrifuges installed at the Fardow and Natanz facilities by two-thirds and converted the Fardow facility into a research center. It also allows for unprecedented robust intrusive inspections of Iran's remaining nuclear facilities by the IAEA. These steps prevent any possibility of Iran taking either the uranium or the plutonium route towards the acquisition of nuclear weapons [Persian Nuclear bomb] in the near future. The deal was passed unanimously by UNSC and it has become legally enshrined. Moreover, the IAEA announced on January 16, 2015, its verification report to the effect that Iran has met all obligations under the JCPOA.

Iran had taken these steps with unusual speed hoping to get the sanctions lifted quickly. The lifting of nuclear-related economic sanctions imposed by UN, US and EU was announced by US-EU on January 17, 2016 [known as the 'Implementation Day'] after Iran fulfilled all conditions under the nuclear deal, including clean certificate by IAEA, release of US$ 100 billion of frozen assets, and Iran's ability to pump oil and to sell to international buyers, and use the international banking system for financial transactions and normalization of its ties with the West.

As one analyst pointed out, "relations between Iran and the rest of the world are going to change dramatically, and their nature and quality will serve as a guarantee for the agreement's fulfillment". In other words, Iran has been re-integrated into the world economic system as a normal member of the international economic system. All of this has added to Saudi worries as Riyadh would have preferred an ostracized Iran over a competitive oil producer. Having utterly failed to scuttle the nuclear deal between Iran and US, the Saudis swiftly responded by forming an "Islamic Alliance against Terrorism"—anti-terrorist front of 34 states excluding Iran. Thus, it became clear that the Saudis did not like to be put in a corner and if they were, they will fight (Pasha, 2008).

Meanwhile, Iran assured the GCC states that it has no intention of interfering in the internal affairs of its neighbors and that it wants friendly relations with all the GCC states (Pasha, 2013A). However, the Saudis were not impressed by Iranian assurances. Saudi Arabia needs a protector and for long US has done that—oil for security. King Salman visited US in September 2015, his first visit to US since ascending to the throne in January 2015 and comes after a period of tensions due to the nuclear deal US signed with Iran in July 2015.

Whereas Obama judged the deal as important or even a victory [as it helped avoid a war] with the US, the KSA perceives it as a substantial challenge to its interests, because it immensely strengthens a country that is perceived by Riyadh as a source of an imminent threat to KSA and the region. Saudi foreign minister Adel al-Jubeir said, a "new strategic partnership" was discussed and that Mr. Obama made assurances that the nuclear agreement prevents Iran from acquiring a nuclear weapon, includes inspections of military and suspected sites, and has a provision for the snapback of sanctions if Iran violates the agreement. In order to placate the Saudis, Israelis and others critical of the nuclear deal, Obama announced new sanctions on Iran—individuals and companies involved in Iran's ballistic missile program when Tehran tested new missiles in 2015 capable of carrying nuclear weapons. This step was taken on the 'Implementation Day' when the sanctions were lifted. But the new sanctions are by the US-EU and have no UNSC mandate (Pasha, 2009).

Interestingly, both Iran and Saudi Arabia have ruled out war as an option to settle their differences and the US is advising/counseling Riyadh against taking rash actions or to avoid stoking the fires in the Gulf. The US has sought to involve Iran in finding a solution to the raging civil war in Syria and also to stabilize Iraq and to contain the Islamic state in Syria and Iraq. President Rouhani on a visit [January 25-29, 2016] to Europe—in Italy and France—after sanctions were removed, not only criticized KSA on Yemen, Syria, Bahrain and on killing of dissident Sheikh al-Nimr [who was an outspoken critic of the House of Saud and played a prominent role in the 2011 uprisings in the Shia-dominated Eastern Province] but also talked about de-escalation of situation in the region and to work for peace and stability in the Gulf region.

As pressure mounts on militants of ISIL due to Russian bombing and Syria's military makes advances to recapture lost territories, the Caliphate forces will march towards KSA. This ground reality should compel Saudis to work with Iran to defeat the ISIL forces as soon as possible. In any case, the Saudis at the moment and in the immediate future do not expect a change in Iran's behavior due to accumulated animosities and also because they believe people in Tehran, "have a mix of nationalist supremacy, rigid religious beliefs, and old images of a great empire that the time of its resurrection is upon us". In the final analysis, both KSA and Iran have to live as neighbors and work for rapprochement and be content with their spheres of influence. The US for the foreseeable future will continue to be the arbiter in Gulf affairs and will not allow the power balance to tilt either way (Al-Rashed, 2015).

References

Adib-Moghaddam, Arshin (2016), "The Tension between Iran and Saudi Arabia has Little to do with Religion", *The Independent*, January 5.

Al Rasheed, Madawi (1998), "The Shia of Saudi Arabia: A Minority in Search of Cultural Authenticity", *British Journal of Middle Eastern Studies*, Vol. 25, No. 1.

Al Saud, Turki Faisal bin Abdul Aziz, (2013), "Saudi Arabia's Foreign Policy", *Middle East Policy*, 42.

Al-Rashed, Abdulrahman (2015), "Opinion: Is the Gulf's Relationship with Washington a Mistake?", *A-Sharq Al-Awsat*, August 1.

Anderson, Lisa (2001), "Arab Democracy: Dismal Prospects", *World Policy Journal*, Vol. 18, No. 3, 53-60.

Bhadrakumar, M.K. (2016), "Obama Speaks on Iran Shakes up Middle East Politics", *Indian Punch line*, January 18.

Brynen, Rex, Bahgat Korany and Paul Noble (1995), "Political Liberalization and Democratization in the Arab World: Theoretical Perspectives", Boulder and London: Lynne Rienner.

Cheema, Sujata Ashwarya (2015), "Saudi Arabia's Nuclear Plans: Progress, Prospects and Politics", in Gawdat Bahgat (ed.), 'The Changing Energy Landscape in the Gulf: Strategic Implications', London: Gerlach Press, 93-123.

Dekmejian, R.H. (1998), "Saudi Arabian Consultative Council", *MEJ*, Vol. 52, No. 2 , Spring, 204-218.

Ehteshami, Anoushiravan (2003), "Reform from Above: The Politics of Participation in Oil Monarchies", *International Affairs*, Vol. 79, No. 1.

Eickelman, Dale F. (2002), "Bin Laden, The Arab Street, and the Middle East's Democracy Deficit", *Current History*, January.

Gause III, F. Gregory, (2014), "Beyond Sectarianism: The New Middle East Cold War", *Brookings Doha Centre Analysis*, No. 11.

Dietl, Gulshan (2009), "Iran, Saudi Arabia and the Bomb", in Anwar Alam (ed.), 'Iran and Post-9/11 World Order: Reflections on Iranian Nuclear Program', New Delhi: New Century Publications, 154-181.

Hiro, Dilip (2002), "War without End: The Rise of Islamist Terrorism and Global Response, New Delhi: Roli Books.

Hudson, Michael C. (1988), "State, Society and Legitimacy: An Essay on Arab Political Prospects in the 1990's", in Hisham Sharabi (ed.), 'The Next Arab Decade: Alternative Futures', Boulder: Westview, 22-27.

Ilias, M.H. and P.J. Vincent (eds.) (2007), "India-West Asia Relations: Understanding Cultural Interplays", New Delhi: New Century Publications.

Kidwai, M. Saleem (2010), "US Policy towards the Muslim World", Maryland, University Press of America.

Khalil, Asad Abu (1997), "Change and Democratization in the Arab World: The Role of Political Parties", *TWQ*, Vol. 18, No.1, 14-63.

Mabon, Simon (2016), "After Years of Proxy war, Saudi Arabia and Iran are finally Squaring up in the Open", *The Independent*, January 5.

Menon, Shivshankar (2015), "It's Time for India to Start Looking West Again", *The Wire*, October 15.

Milan, Rai (2002), "War Plan Iraq: Ten Reasons against War on Iraq", London: Verso.

Naqeeb, Khaldoun Hasan (1990), "Society and State in the Gulf and Arab Peninsula: A Different Perspective", London: Routledge.

Obaid, Nawaf (2013), "Saudi Arabia Shifts to More Activist Foreign Policy Doctrine", *Al Monitor*, October 17.

Pasha, A.K. (1999 A), "India and West Asia: Continuity and Change", Delhi: Gyan Sagar Publications.

——(2012), "India's Historical and Cultural Relations with the Arab World", in Priya Singh and Susmita Bhattacharya (eds.), 'Perspectives on West Asia: The Evolving Geopolitical Discourses', New Delhi: Shipra and MAKAIAS, 184-246.

——(2014), "India and Saudi Arabia: Retrospect and Prospects", in Fazal Mahmood and Rafiullah Azmi (eds.), 'Foreign Policy of India and West Asia: Change and Continuity', New Delhi: New Century Publications, 187-216.

——(1995), "Kuwait: Strategies of Survival", New Delhi: HarAnand, Publications.

——(2008), "Democratization in the GCC States and India", in R.M. Abhyankar (ed.), 'West Asia and the Region: Defining India's Role', New Delhi: Academic Foundation, 581-608.

——(2013 A), "India's Changing Threat Perception from West Asia," in Mohd. Moazzam Ali Muztarib (ed.), 'Threat Perception in a Globalizing World with Special Reference to India', New Delhi: Gyan Publishing House, 198-216.

——(2013 B), "Turmoil in West Asia and India's Quest for Energy Security", in Mohanan B. Pillai (ed.), 'India's National Security: Concerns and Strategies', New Delhi: New Century Publications, 133-177.

——(2014), "Iraq in Turmoil: Foreign Intervention, Sectarian War and Caliphate", in R.S. Vasan (ed.), 'Security Imperatives in a Changing Global Order: Recent Developments in Middle East and West Asia', Chennai: Center for Asia Studies, 46-98.

——(2016), "Violence in West Asia: Emerging Threats to Domestic, Regional and World Peace", in Sekhar Basu Roy (ed.), 'Terror in West Asia: Threat to Global Peace', Kolkata: New Approach, 145-178.

——(2009), "Iranian Nuclear Program: Regional Responses", in Anwar Alam (ed.), 'Iran and Post-9/11 World Order: Reflections on Iranian Nuclear Program', New Delhi: New Century Publications, 113-153.

——(2006), "Globalization, Politics and Identity in the Arab World", in John W Fox, Nada Mourtada Sabbah and Mohammed al-Mutawa, (eds.), 'Globalization and the Gulf', London; Routledge, 127-140.

——(2012), "India and the GCC States: Political, Economic and Foreign Relations", in Kingshuk Chatterjee (ed.), India and the Middle East: Problems and Prospects', New Delhi: Knowledge World Publishers, 25-66.

——(2013 C), "Euro-Asian Maritime, Trade and Security Issues and the West Asian/Gulf Factor", in K.S. Pavithran (ed.), 'Foreign Policy and Maritime Security of India', New Delhi: New Century Publications, 207-254.

——(2011), "Violence in West Asia: Implications for India's Federalism and Security", in G. Gopa Kumar (ed.), 'Foreign Policy, Federalism and International Treaties', New Delhi: New Century Publications, 192-254.

——(1999 C) (ed.), "Contemporary Gulf: State, Society, Economy and Foreign Policy", New Delhi: Détente.

——(2000) (ed.), "India, Iran, and the GCC States: Political Strategy and Foreign Policy", New Delhi: Manas Publications.

——(2014) (ed.), "India's Political and Foreign Relations with the Gulf Region", New Delhi: Wisdom Publications.

——(2003), "US Invasion of Iraq and Aftermath in War on Iraq", Gulf Studies Program, CWAAS, SIS, JNU, New Delhi, 1-18.

——(2014) (ed.), "India and the Gulf Region: Maritime History, Trade, Security and Political Reforms", Delhi: Wisdom Publications.

——(2010), "11 September 2001 Attack on US and West Asia", in M. Saleem Kidwai (ed.), 'US Policy towards the Muslim World: Focus on Post-9/11 Period', New York: University Press of America, 77-177.

——(2013 D), "India and the GCC States: Political Relations, Changing Geopolitical Spectrum and Foreign Relations", in Ranjit Gupta and Christian Koch (eds.), 'GCC-India Relations', Dubai: Gulf Research Centre Foundation, 43-72.

——(2014), "India and the GCC States," in Shaji Varkey (ed.), 'Globalization, State and Governance', New Delhi: New Century Publications, 23-49.

——(2000) (ed.), "Arab Israeli Peace Process: An Indian Perspective", New Delhi: Manas Publications.

——(1999 B) (ed.), "Perspectives on India and the Gulf States", New Delhi: Détente Publications.

——(2003), "Iraq: Sanctions and Wars", New Delhi: Sterling Publications.

Pradhan, Prasanta Kumar (2016), "The Widening Gulf: Arab Spring and the Saudi-Iranian Divide", in P.R. Kumarswamy et al. (eds.), 'Contemporary Persian Gulf', New Delhi, K.W. Publishers, 101-116.

Raphaeli, Nimrod (2005), "Demands for Reforms in Saudi Arabia", *MES*, Vol. 41, No. 4, July.

Saleh, Al-Mani (1996), "The Ideological Dimensions in Saudi-Iranian Relations", in Jamal S. al Suwaidi (ed.), 'Iran and the Gulf: A Search for Stability', Abu Dhabi: TECSSR, 158-174.

11

Al-Qaeda and Franchise Terrorism

Jatin Kumar

Introduction

The threat of terrorism has never been as perilous as it is today. In the twenty-first century, Al-Qaeda has emerged as 'the first multinational terror outfit, which challenges the world with new types of threats' (Gunaratna, 2002: 1). Seventeen years after the World Trade Centre attacks that received sympathy and support from almost the whole international community, Al-Qaeda remains as a popular brand name of terrorism. Even after fighting more than a decade long war against Al-Qaeda in Af-Pak region, international community still faces a grave threat from Al-Qaeda and its franchise. But the threat at present is of course different from those seventeen years ago. In the twenty-first century, Al-Qaeda has emerged as first multinational terror outfit, which confronts the world with new types of threats. It has moved terrorism beyond the status of a technique of protest and resistance. Al-Qaeda turned it 'into a global instrument with which to compete with and challenge Western influence in the Muslim world' (Gunaratna, 2002: 1).

Al-Qaeda which emerged from Maktab al-Khidamat (Afghan Services Bureau), was founded in 1984 by Abdullah Azzam, Osama bin Laden and Ayman al-Zawahiri to raise funds and recruit foreign mujahidin for war against the Soviets in Afghanistan. Maktab al-Khidamat became the forerunner to Al-Qaeda and was instrumental in creating the fundraising and recruitment network that benefited Al-Qaeda during the 1990s (Shahzad, 2011). The purpose of this organization was to bring all those people together who had accumulated rich professional experience of guerrilla warfare during the war in Afghanistan. After the assassination of Azzam, the organization was succeeded by Bin Laden, one of his leading disciples. Osama bin Laden transformed the organization into Al-Qaeda in 1988.

Once MAK's was disposed, its resources were diverted by Al- Qaeda away from Afghanistan into regional conflicts where Islamist guerrillas were involved, principally in Kashmir and Chechnya, but also in Mindanao, Tajikistan, Uzbekistan, Somalia, Malaysia, Indonesia, Georgia, Nagorno-Karabakh, Azerbaijan, Yemen, Algeria and Egypt. In most of these countries, the governing regimes were openly hostile to Islamist movements, often repressing them ferociously.

Al-Qaeda established ideological, political, financial and military control over several Islamist terrorist groups, to get involved in regional violent conflicts successfully where Muslims were affected. 'Although Afghanistan was Al-Qaeda's principal military training base, it also trained recruits in Sudan, Yemen, Chechnya, Tajikistan, Somalia, and the Philippines. For instance, when Al-Qaeda trainees had difficulties entering landlocked Afghanistan through Pakistan after the East Africa embassy bombings in August 1998, Osama phoned Hashim Salamat, the leader of the MILF, in mid-February 1999, asking him to set up new training camps in the Philippines' (Gunaratna, 2002: 5).

To function at a global level, Al-Qaeda created a worldwide strategic framework of Islamist military and political organisations. From the early 1990s onwards, Osama invited representatives of Islamist terrorist groups and Islamic political movements to join Al-Qaeda's *shuramajlis*, or consultative council. Al-Qaeda also established relationships with thirty Islamist terrorist groups, inspiring and assisting them, both directly and indirectly, to attack targets at home and abroad. According to Syad Saleem Shahzad (2011), "Al-Qaeda would not have had the same impact if it had not been preceded by al-Zawahiri and the Egyptian camp's ideology and pattern of struggle. In fact, al-Zawahiri was the one who actually made Al-Qaeda into an organization the world knows today" (Shahzad, 2011). The principle objective of Al-Qaeda was to establish governing regimes throughout the world that functions according to the Sharia law, initially, in Saudi Arabia, Pakistan, Egypt and Indonesia and then in other parts of the world.

To prepare the powerful Islamist forefront, Al-Qaeda stresses on the physical as well as the psychological aspects of warfare training. If talking about the training, average Al-Qaeda fighters are well trained and 'better prepared for their mission than any other Islamist guerrilla or terrorist organisation'. For example, of the twenty 9/11 hijackers, it is remarkable that none one of them flinched, not one had second thoughts; all went willingly to their deaths, even the very young (Gunaratna, 2002: 5). At present, Al-Qaeda is no longer a centralized organization but a loose ideology that associates itself with any terror group who is interested in joining hands against the West by using its brand name.

Though American military operations have diminished its influence and capacities but threat perception from Al-Qaeda has not changed. The silent spread of Al-Qaeda's ideological virus has emerged as a vital danger for international peace and stability. The United States led the global war which played an important role in transforming the bureaucratic structure of Al-Qaeda. It initiated a quick decentralization process in the organization that paved the way for the emergence of franchise around the globe. It was an impact of this decentralization process which made Al-Qaeda a loose terror outfit with franchise groups in Iraq, Afghanistan, Syria, Somalia, North Africa and Libya (Quince, 2014).

What is Franchise Terrorism?

The term 'franchise terrorism' denotes those decentralised terror outfits that follows characteristics of Al-Qaeda's ideology to launch a war against the US and its allies, as well as the local inhabitants. In the language of business world, franchise means, an authority granted by an organization or company to an individual or a group of people, allowing them to carry out specific commercial activities, in its name (Oxford, 2016). In the context of Al-Qaeda, the word is used to define all those groups which use name Al-Qaeda but operate independently (See Table 11.1).

A substantial amount of literature has been written on franchise terrorism, but the topic still needs to receive more public attention. The concept of franchise terrorism is defined by Christina Hellmich in her book *Al-Qaeda: From Global Network to Local Franchise*, Syad Saleem Shahzad in his book *Inside Al-Qaeda and Taliban*, Abdel Bari Atwan in his book *The Secret History of Al-Qaeda and After bin Laden: Al-Qaeda, The Next Generation* and Barak Medelsohn in his book, *the Al-Qaeda Franchise: The Expansion of Al-Qaeda and Its Consequences.* Al-Qaeda has utilized the strategy of franchise terrorism to create a two-tier structure within the organization.

This two-tier structure includes Al-Qaeda Central and branches of franchise (Mendelsohn, 2016). Al-Qaeda central sets ideological orientation and political goals and the strategy to realize those. By gradually spreading its franchises, Al-Qaeda has maintained to be in headlines at times when its operational capabilities are very weak. Since 2003, the group has set up franchises all through the Muslim world, starting from Saudi Arabia to Iraq (2004), Algeria (2006), Yemen (2009), Somalia (2010), Syria (2012) and in the Indian sub-continent (2014).

These franchise groups adopted the characteristics of Al-Qaeda's philosophy but operate completely independently and receive financial and logistical assistance from the central organisation. Available literature on the group and its affiliates shows that most of these franchise groups flourish in areas where the governing bodies are comparatively weak and are tribal in the nature. Yemen, Somalia, Mali, Iraq, Afghanistan, Pakistan, Algeria, and northern Nigeria have been strategic hotspots for the spread of the outfit (Ronfeldt, 2008).

What makes these franchise groups more dangerous is

that, Al-Qaeda is unable to control many of these groups. Some of the Al-Qaeda's documents, which were released after the raid in Abbottabad and available with the US State Department's website, assert that the organization's leadership was internally divided over how to deal with its franchise groups and frustrated at its inability to control some local fighters. Former Director of National Intelligence, James Clapper has elucidated that 'in terms of threat to the homeland (US allies), Al-Qaeda franchises may pose as much of a danger as the Islamic State' (Francis, 2015).

At present, Al-Qaeda has approximately seventeen franchisee groups around the globe and has support of more than twenty terror groups (see Tables 11.1 and 11.2). They are actively functional in West Asia, Africa, South Asia, and Southeast Asia. It gives them global reach and capability to compensate for the setback. These groups have also proved themselves competent enough to adapt to rapidly changing technologies to mobilize maximum numbers of jihadists. In terms of co-operation among these groups, outsourcing of jihadists is a common practice to achieve their regional objectives.

According to the U.S. State Department, Abu Zubaydah, a senior Al-Qaeda member, was seized at a Lashkar-e-Taiba's (affiliate of Al-Qaeda) safe house in Faisalabad in Pakistan in 2002, which highlights that a number of Lashkar-e-Taiba members were assisting the movement of Al-Qaeda members in Pakistan (Bajoria, 2010). The incidents of terror strikes around the world show that, Al-Qaeda was not behind the Islamic State in the race of deadly terror strikes. Al-Qaeda and its franchises attacked Ivory Coast in 2016 and France (Charliei Hebdo) in 2015.

Some of the Powerful Franchise Groups of Al-Qaeda

1. Al-Qaeda in the Arabian Peninsula: Al-Qaeda in the Arabian Peninsula (AQAP) was created in January 2009 through a union of Saudi and Yemeni branches of Al-Qaeda. According to security experts, Yemen-based Al-Qaeda is the most lethal franchise, carrying out a domestic insurgency while maintaining its sights on Western targets.

Table 11.1: Al-Qaeda Supporters: A List of Terror Outfits

S. No.	Terror Outfit
1.	Nusra Front
2.	The Islamic State *(Separated in 2014)*
3.	Boko Haram
4.	Ansar al Sharia - Benghazi
5.	Ansar al Sharia - Tunisia
6.	AnsarBayt al Maqdis
7.	Tehrik-i-Taliban Pakistan
8.	Islamic Movement of Uzbekistan
9.	East Turkestan Islamic Movement
10.	Lashkar-e-Taiba
11.	Jaish-e-Mohammed
12.	Jemaah Islamiyah
13.	Abu Sayyaf
14.	Caucasus Emirate
15.	Egyptian Islamic Jihad
16.	Lashkar-e-Jhangvi
17.	The Haqqani Network
18.	JamatudDava

Sources: Syad Saleem Sehzad, 2011; U.S. State Department, 2014; Humud, 2016.

According to the US, AQAP's threats have disrupted operations in dozens of U.S. diplomatic facilities in the Middle East, Africa, and South Asia, and it has inspired or directed attacks in the United States and Europe. AQAP chief Nasir al-Wuhayshi is Al-Qaeda's No. 2 and has so far remained loyal to the terror network's leader, Ayman al-Zawahiri (CFR.org, 2015).

AQAP has taken responsibility for several attacks in the region since 2006. These have included the failed August 2009 assassination attempt on Saudi Prince Mohammed bin Nayef, an attack on the U.S. embassy in Sana'a in 2008, attacks on Italian and British embassies, suicide bombings targeting

Belgian tourists in January 2008 and the Korean tourists in March 2009, and the bombing of a Japanese oil tanker in April 2008.

Table 11.2: Al-Qaeda's Franchise Groups around the Globe

S. No.	Franchise Groups	Year of Establishment
1.	Al-Qaeda Central	1988
2.	Al-Qaeda in Iraq (*Tanzim Qaidat al-Jihad fi Bilad al-Rafidayn*)	2004-2013
3.	Al-Qaeda in the Islamic Maghreb	(2007- Present)
4.	Al-Qaeda Kurdish Battalions (Iran-Iraq Border)	(2007- Present)
5.	Al-Qaeda in Sinai Peninsula	(2011- Present)
6.	Khorasan Group	(2012- Present)
7.	Al-Qaeda in the Indian Sub-continent	(2014- Present)
8.	Jund al-Aqsa	(2014- Present)
9.	Al-Mourabitoun	(2013-2015, Joined AQIM in December 2015)
10.	Al-Qaeda in the Levant	(2012- Present)
11.	Al-Qaeda in Somalia	(2010- Present)
12.	Al-Qaeda in the Arabian Peninsula	(2009- Present)
13.	Al-Qaeda in Palestine	(2008- Present)
14.	Al-Qaeda in Bosnia and Herzegovina	(1992- Present)
15	Al-Qaeda in Yemen and the Horn of Africa	
16.	Al-Qaeda in Europe (Responsible for Madrid Attacks)	(----------)
17.	Al-Qaeda in the Malay Archipelago also known as Tanzim Qaedat al-Jihad	(----------)

Sources: U.S. State Department, 2014; Humud, 2016.

In May 2012, a suicide bomber killed more than ninety Yemeni soldiers rehearsing for a military parade in Sana'a. A

December 2013 attack on the defence ministry and military hospital left more than fifty people dead, and elicited a rare apology from AQAP for the killing of unarmed health workers (CFR.org, 2015; Smith-Spark, 2015). AQAP also claimed responsibility of the bloody shooting at the Charlie Hebbdo magazine's Paris offices, AQAP commander Nasr Ibn Ali al-Ansi took full responsibility for the attack (Smith-Spark, 2015).

2. Al-Qaeda in the Islamic Maghreb: Al-Qaeda in the Islamic Maghreb (AQIM) is another formal franchise group of Al-Qaeda based in North Africa. The group is dedicated to destroy regional governments and implementing Sharia (Islamic law) in areas where it operates, primarily in Algeria, Mali, Mauritania, Libya, Tunisia, and Niger. In December 2015, AQIM joined its former offshoot, al-Mourabitoun, to launch attacks throughout the Sahel region. The groups carried out a series of deadly terrorist attacks, including the November 2015 attacks in Mali, the January 2016 attacks in Burkina Faso, and the March 2016 attacks in Côte d'Ivoire. AQIM traces its sources to the Armed Islamic Group (GIA), an Islamist movement founded in Algeria in the early 1990s. GIA leader Hassan Hattab split from the GIA over ideological differences, and he later founded the Salafist Group for Preaching and Combat (GSPC). In September 2006, GSPC merged with Al-Qaeda, formally rebranding itself as AQIM months later. In Mali, AQIM is known for its de facto war with the French government beginning in 2013, as well as its extensive history of kidnapping and extortion.

3. Al-Shabaab: Al-Shabaab was the militant wing of the Somali Council of Islamic Courts that took over most of southern Somalia in the second half of 2006. Despite the group's defeat by Somali and Ethiopian forces in 2007, Al-Shabaab has continued its violent terror activities in southern and central Somalia. The group has exerted temporary and, at times, sustained control over strategic locations in those areas by recruiting, sometimes forcibly, regional sub-clans and their militias, using guerrilla warfare. "Since 2011, however, pressure from AMISOM and Ethiopian forces has largely degraded Al-Shabaab's control, especially in Mogadishu but also in other key regions of the country, and conflict among senior leaders has exacerbated fractures within the group. In 2013, Al-Shabaab rivalries culminated in a major purge of opponents of now-deceased group leader Ahmed Abdi Aw-Mohamed" (National Counter Terrorism Centre, 2016).

4. Abu Sayyaf: Abu Sayyaf is the name of the most feared and violent of all Philippine terrorist organizations. The terror group primarily operates on the southernmost island of Mindanao, in the Sulu island chain (Atkinson, 2012). According to the National Consortium for the Study of Terrorism and Responses to Terrorism (START), the group is linked to Al-Qaeda and receives sufficient support from Al-Qaeda (AFP, 2011; START, 2012). The group is allied with Jemaah Islamiyah, the Southeast Asian terrorist network and terror franchise of Al-Qaeda and implicated in numerous bombings in Indonesia.

However, according to START, the extent of the ASG's co-operation with al-Qaeda is thought to have diminished following the post-9/11 crackdown on the latter. Still, ASG members have trained in Al-Qaeda camps in Afghanistan and some continue to receive operational guidance from Al-Qaeda. According to START's Global Terrorism Database, between January 2009 and December 2010, the group was suspected of being responsible for 38 attacks resulting in 49 fatalities and injuring 124 people. The attacks occurred in the following cities: Indanan, Isabella, Jolo, Lantawan, Lamitan, Maimbung, Maluso, Panguataran, Patikul, Sumisip, Taburan, Talipao and Zamboanga.

5. Al-Qaeda in Indian Sub-continent: Al-Qaeda in Indian Sub-continent (AQC) is the most recent AQ's regional franchise. It was established in 2012 to operate across South Asia, with its centre of gravity and leadership based in Pakistan. Even though AQIS' proclaimed vision is of fighting a war for South Asia, since its formation, it has largely failed to live up to its ambitions, unable to carry out a terrorist spectacular and managing only a handful of relatively minor attacks across South Asia (Reed, 2015).

Threats to India

India is always seen as a soft target by terror outfits and it has aching history of terror attacks. In the last few years, the country has registered major terror strikes on military camps such as Pathankot, Pampore attack, Baramulla, Uri and Handwara. Most of these attacks were launched by Jaish-e-Mohammad, Lashkar-e-Taiba and United Jihad Council. As far as Al-Qaeda and its franchise groups are concerned, till now, they have not posed any serious direct threat to India. Though, it has been trying hard to expand its influence in India since 1996, when Osama Bin Laden talked about oppression of Muslims in India, particularly, Jammu and Kashmir and Assam (South Asia Terror Portal, 2015). In last few years, Al-Qaeda has been making efforts to become a dominant terror outfit in India. At least, Al-Qaeda's video and pamphlets are saying it. A pamphlet titled "why there is no storm in your ocean" (Ibid.), urged Indian Muslims to join AQIS.

Though, Al-Qaeda's activities are minimal in India and its Indian sub-continent franchise is not that powerful to pose any major threat, but its affiliated groups, such as Lashkar-e-Taiba and Jaish-e-Mohammad, may pose a real time danger. These groups are operational in India and outsourcing of jihadists among these groups is a common practice. The Mumbai attacks of 2008, also known as 26/11 is a living example of this danger, when a group of Lashkar terrorists attacked the economic capital of India Mumbai. In this attack, Indian Mujahidin played an important role in arranging logistical support for Lashkar-e-Taiba (U.S. State Department, 2011). The terror threat in India is certainly confined to Pakistan supported terror outfits, which are getting operational and logistical support from Pakistan. Though, in last few years

Islamic State has emerged as a vital danger for national security but till now Indian security agencies have somehow been successful in dealing with this threat. However, for the time being, India is out of the emerging danger from Al-Qaeda.

Conclusion

The case study of Al-Qaeda and its franchise groups shows that Al-Qaeda is re-emerging as a powerful terror outfit. Its rising influence in the West Asian region is a wakeup call for the international community. A decade long fight against terrorism has made it clear that military option will not solve this problem alone. There is a need to find other ways as well to deal with this danger. The rapidly rising terror violence around the world highlights that the international community is lacking the strategy to deal with terrorism. Last but not the least, there is an urgent need to develop a collective framework to deal with this monster politically, militarily and diplomatically.

References

AFP (2011, 28 July), "Abu Sayyaf Kill Seven Philippine Soldiers", *AFP*, available at: `https://www.afp.com/en/news/15/german-sailor-abducted-another-killed-philippines-military.

Atkinson, Garrett (2012), "Abu Sayyaf: The Father of the Swordsman: A Review of the Rise of Islamic Insurgency in the Southern Philippines", available at: https://www.americansecurityproject.org/wp-content/uploads/2012/03/Abu-Sayyaf-The-Father-of-the-Swordsman.pdf.

Bajoria, Jayshree (2010), "Lashkar-e-Taiba (Army of the Pure) (aka Lashkar e-Tayyiba, Lashkar e-Toiba; Lashkar-i-Taiba)", Council on Foreign Relation, available at: http://www.cfr.org/pakistan/lashkar-e-taiba-army-pure-aka-lashkar-e-tayyiba-lashkar-e-toiba-lashkar--taiba/p17882#p4.

Banlaoi, Rommel C. (2008), "Al-Harakatul Al Islamiyyah: Essays on the Abu Sayyaf Group", Philippine Institute for Political

Violence and Terrorism Research, available at: http://pipvtr.com/pipvtr/files/Book_AHAI_Essays_on_ASG_Book_Banlaoi_2008.pdf.

Bergen, Peter (2008), "Al-Qaeda, the Organization: A Five-Year Forecast", *The Annals of the American Academy of Political and Social Science*, Vol. 618, 14-30.

Bucci, Steven (2012), "Seven Terrorist Groups Affiliated with Al-Qaeda", *The Daily Signal,* available at: http://dailysignal.com/2012/05/07/seven-terrorist-groups-affiliated-with-al-qaeda.

Counter Terrorism Guide (2016), "The Secret History of Al-Qaeda and after Bin Laden: Al-Qaeda, The Next Generation", available at: https://www.nctc.gov/site/groups/al_shabaab.html.

Francis, David (2015), "Al-Qaeda's Blueprint for How to Start a Home-grown Terror Franchise", *Foreign Policy,* available at: http://foreignpolicy.com/2015/05/20/al-qaedas-blueprint-for-how-to-start-a-homegrown-terror-franchise.

Gunaratna, Rohan (2002), "Inside Al-Qaeda Global Network of Terror", New York: Columbia University Press.

Hubbard, Ben (2014, January 1), "The Franchising of Al-Qaeda", *New York Times,* available at: http://www.nytimes.com/2014/01/26/sunday-review/the-franchising-of-al-qaeda.html?_r=0.

Immigration and Refugee Board of Canada (2012), "Philippines: The Abu Sayyaf Group (ASG), Including Areas of Operation and Activities since 2009", available at: https://www.justice.gov/sites/default/files/eoir/legacy/2013/11/07/PHL104015.E.pdf.

Leney-Hall, Katya (2008), "The Evolution of Franchise Terrorism: Al-Qaeda", Hellenic Foundation for European and Foreign Policy, available at: https://www.files.ethz.ch/isn/94072/evolution_of_franchise_terrorism_al-qaeda.pdf.

Mendelsohn, Barak (2016), "The Al-Qaeda Franchise: The Expansion of Al-Qaeda and Its Consequences", New York: Oxford.

Office of the Director of National Intelligence (2014), "Terror Franchise: The Unstoppable Assassin Techs Vital Role for its Success", available at:

https://www.dni.gov/files/documents/ubl/english/Terror%20Franchise.pdf.

Quince, Annabelle (2014), "The Franchise Terrorism of Al-Qaeda after Osama bin Laden", available at: http://www.abc.net.au/radionational/programs/reavision/5375448.

Reed, Alastair (2016), "Al-Qaeda in the Indian Subcontinent: A New Frontline in the Global Jihadist Movement?", The International Centre for Counter-Terrorism, The Hague, available at: https://www.icct.nl/wp-content/uploads/2016/05/ICCT-Reed-Al-Qaeda-in-the-Indian-Subcontinent-May2016-1.pdf.

Rollins, John (2011), "Al-Qaeda and Affiliates: Historical Perspective, Global Presence, and Implications for U.S. Policy", available at: https://www.fas.org/sgp/crs/terror/R41070.pdf.

Ronfeldt, David (2010), "Al-Qaeda and its Affiliates: A Global Tribe Waging Segmental Warfare", available at: http://www.cfr.org/pakistan/lashkar-e-taiba-army-pure-aka-lashkar-e-tayyiba-lashkar-e-toiba-lashkar--taiba/p17882#p4.

Shahzad, Syed Saleem (2012), "Inside Al-Qaeda and the Taliban beyond Bin Laden and 9/11", St. Martin's: Palgrave Macmillan.

Shay, Christopher (2009), "A Brief History of Abu Sayyaf", *TIME*, available at: http://content.time.com/time/world/article/0,8599,1927124,00.ht.

Smith-Spark, Laura (2015), "What is Al-Qaeda in the Arabian Peninsula?", available at: http://edition.cnn.com/2015/01/14/middleeast/yemen-al-qaeda-arabian-peninsula.

South Asia Terror Portal (2015), "Why is There No Storm in Your Ocean? A Message For the Muslims of India", available at: http://www.satp.org/satporgtp/countries/India/document/papers/Wts.pdf.

Vogt, Heidi (2016), "African Terror Franchise Now Has Competition from Islamic State", *Wall Street Journal,* available at: http://smallwarsjournal.com/blog/african-terror-franchise-now-has-competition-from-islamic-state.

12

Israel's Continuing Zionist Project: The Main Obstacle to Palestinian Statehood

Bansidhar Pradhan

A century has passed since the issuance of the (in) famous Belfour Declaration and seventy years have gone by since the Palestinians experienced their *al-Nakba* (catastrophic). Still, the Palestine question, which embodies the legitimate demands of Palestinians for self-determination and independent statehood, remains unresolved. Why? There are many reasons. These include the continuation of the Zionist project which seeks to colonize the post-1948 Palestine through settler colonies; the methodical marginalization of the Palestinian leadership and its options through the politics of procrastination, fragmentation and stalemate; partisan role of the US, the apathy of the Arab countries, bordering on abdication; and the unwillingness or ineffectiveness of the international community to decisively intervene.

The main reason, however, this article argues, is the continuing Zionist Project by Israel. While underlining the dual character of the Israeli state, this article argues that as long as the Zionist Project remains embedded into the state of Israel, specially so when it is under the control of a broad coalition of extreme right wing forces, the Israeli public posture about peace with Palestinians and the occasional reference to a two-state solution remain a hallow rhetoric serving as a smokescreen for the implementation of the project. Indeed, the ultimate objective of the Zionist Project—the so-called *Eretz* Israel—cuts at the very roots of Palestinian self-determination and statehood.

Israel's Post-1967 Political-Security Discourse

It is well-known that the state of Israel was created on the basis of Zionism. What is not so well-known, much less recognized, is that Israel continues to remain committed to the Zionist ideology even after nearly seventy years of its establishment. Zionism's foundational myth, "for people without a land to a land without people", remains the Israeli state's guiding policy, in one form or the other, towards the Occupied Palestinian Territory (OPT). This becomes evident from the Israeli policy towards the West Bank, East Jerusalem and the Gaza Strip since the occupation of these territories by Israel in the 1967 war.

The policy of land grabbing and settlement expansion, both vertical and horizontal, mainly aims at once again, changing the demographic balance beyond the Green Line, particularly in West Bank and East Jerusalem where Palestinians constitute an overwhelming majority. The objective is to create conditions which would leave the Palestinians with no option but to flee their homes and desert their cultivable land out of existential fears or they would be forced to leave at an appropriate time through "appropriate methods". This reminds one of the Zionist strategies adopted during the creation of the state of Israel. Let us put the whole debate in the context of the Israeli political security discourse with regard to the West Bank, East Jerusalem and Gaza Strip which form the non-negotiable territorial core of a future Palestinian state.

In the post-1967 period, two distinct schools of thought have evolved with regard to the occupied Palestinian territories, which broadly move along party lines: the Sociological School and the Territorial School. The whole debate revolves around the feasibility and implications of annexing the occupied territories. Because, as Tanya Reinhart argues, the "leaders of the 1948 generation—Yigal Alon Moshe Dayan, Yitzhak Rabin Sharon and Peres—were raised on the myth of the 'redemption of land'. The myth, which every Israeli of that generation grew up with, was that the land that once belonged to the Jewish people should be 'redeemed' and saved, namely taken back from its alien residence" (Reinhart, 2003). This myth needs to be seen in the context that land is the fundamental basis of the Israeli-Palestinian conflict. Further, successive generations of political leaders, military establishment and historians have portrayed the 1948 Arab-Israeli conflict as a liberation war.

The idea of "liberation" constituted the core of the official Zionist narrative about the establishment of the state of Israel till it was challenged by a group of new historians in the 1990s as part of the post-Zionist movement (Pappe, 2014). One can very well see the close links between the idea of liberation, the land grabbing psyche of the Israeli politico-military establishment and the concept/myth of *Eretz* Israel (Greater Israel). This remains deeply ingrained in the Israeli state and society for most parts of its existence. The dissenting voices are too short lived and the counter narratives have become increasingly insignificant and marginalized.

Take, for instance, the statements of Ariel Sharon after he came to power in 2001. He sought to justify a new wave of repressive measures against the Palestinians in the Israeli occupied territories by terming it "the second half of 1948". He stated in April 2001, "The war of Independence has not ended. [1] But annexing the West Bank and densely populated Gaza Strip would mean granting Israeli citizenship to around four million Palestinians living in these territories. In that case, Israel would lose its exclusive Jewish character. Additionally, in due course of time the Jews would be reduced to a minority given the high rate of population growth among the Palestinians".

This is what has been referred to as the "demographic problem" in Israeli political discourse. Over the years, as stated earlier, two basic approaches have evolved which broadly move along party lines. The first is the Alon Plan of the Labour Party which proposes to annex 30 to 40 percent of the territories to Israel and placing the rest on which actually the Palestinians reside under "either Jordanian rule" or "some form of self-rule". The proponents of this plan believe that it "is impossible to repeat the 1948 'solution' of mass expulsion, either for moral considerations or because world public opinion would never allow it to happen again". [2] This is known otherwise as the sociological school of thought in Israel. As opposed to this is the Territorial school which has been dominating the military circle and forms part of the world view of the Likud Party and other far-right forces in the Israeli political spectrum. This school believes that "given Israel's military superiority Palestinian resistance could be eventually broken". First Ariel Sharon and then Benjamin Netanyahu, as we will see later, adhered to this logic and sought to implement it ruthlessly with their own tactical shifts and changing narratives about the so-called peace process.

The ideas of the sociological school were given a trial under the Oslo Accords, concluded between Israel and the PLO in September 1993. The West Bank was divided into three distinct areas, "A", "B" and "C", under graded Israeli control of Palestinian land. Area "C" which constituted nearly 60 percent of the West Bank and covered mostly empty land, for instance, remained under absolute Israeli control. [3] The Oslo euphoria died down very soon; the Hebron massacre of early 1994 and Prime Minister Yitzhak Rabin's assassination in late 1995 were clear indications of the weak foundation of the peace deal in Israel. It also signalled the resurgence of the extreme right-wing forces in Israeli political and security establishments.

In fact, the Oslo Accords, specially the way Israel implemented it, sharpened differences not only between Israelis and Palestinians abut also within themselves. Many would argue that had Rabin been alive, things could have been different. History, however, does not unfold on the basis of assumptions but on the basis of objective realities on the ground. As it happened, the failure of the Camp David-II talks, Ariel Sharon's provocative and controversial visit to Haram al-Sharif/Temple Mount in September 2000 and the subsequent outbreak of the second *intifada* sounded the death knell of the peace process. While the al-Aqsa *intifada*, as the second *intifada* is known, marked the culmination of Palestinian frustration and anger over real Israeli intentions with regard to their nationalist goals, the militant nature of the *intifada* totally securitized the political discourse in Israel vis-à-vis the Palestinians. Thus, began the vicious cycle putting the Palestinians at the receiving end.

During the Sharon era, which began in the immediate aftermath of the second *intifada*, and subsequent years, one witnessed the predominance of the security narrative in Israeli political discourse. It needs to be remembered that in the post-2000 period, the ruling establishment in Israel was led by Likud and its variants and allies, with brief Labour interregnum. The security narrative which was so forcefully peddled by both Ariel Sharon and Benjamin Netanyahu, as Prime Ministers at different times, and so uncritically parroted by the Western media, shook the very foundation of the Oslo process. Because the main thrust of this narrative was, and has been, that the Palestinians pose a threat to the very existence of the state of Israel and its Jewish identity.

Such a narrative strengthened the arguments advanced by the Territorial School and facilitated the pursuance of the Zionist project methodically. Netanyahu never believed in Oslo while Sharon declared it dead just few years after he came to power (Reinhart, 2003). But tactically, both maintained their public posture of seeking a negotiated peace with Palestinians even while colonizing West Bank and East Jerusalem step-by-step. The case of the Gaza Strip was little different, the handling of which also reflected Sharon's master tactical manoeuvre with regard to the Gaza withdrawal in August 2005.

Gaza Strip in Israeli Strategy

The densely populated narrow strip along the Mediterranean coast, constituting just little more than two percent of Palestine and with two million population, has had a strange place in Israeli strategy vis-à-vis the Palestinians. Before the Zionist colonization of Palestine, Gaza was "always connected administratively and politically to rest of Palestine". It was an important entry point for the outside world to Palestine through land and sea (Chomsky and Pappe, 2010). The creation of Israel created a wedge between Gaza and the West Bank. From its occupation in 1967 till the 1993 Oslo Accords, Israel sought to "construct the strip as an enclave" the future status of which became a matter of debate in the country. While the peace camp thought it would be "either autonomous or part of Egypt", the nationalists wanted to make it part of Greater Israel. Israel greatly succeeded in almost legitimizing Gaza "as a separate geopolitical entity" through the Oslo Agreement (Reinhart, 2003).

Thus, one can argue that in the Zionist scheme of things, the Gaza Strip did not constitute a non-negotiable ideological position/attachment like the West Bank and East Jerusalem. In other words, it was open for being used as a tactical bargain with the Palestinians, sometimes to project it as a peace overture, sometimes to divert the world attention, and still at other times to divide the Palestinians and pit one faction against the other. Sharon used it a peace overture in August 2005 out of internal and external compulsions. The basic objective was to strengthen the Israeli stranglehold over the West Bank, even while posing as a great champion of peace and compromise by taking such "painful" decisions. Few months before the actual withdrawal, Sharon made a statement, before an annual academic conference in Herzliya where he stated that Israel had no desire to rule over the Palestinians. This was interpreted by many as Sharon's endorsement of an independent Palestinian state.

But what he spoke at Herzliya was only half the truth; the other half lay in the following sentence: "It is clear that in a permanent peace accord we will not be in Gaza. [4] What about the West Bank? Sharon did not speak anything about the Israeli occupations of the West Bank and he never did so in the subsequent months till he left office on health grounds. In similar vein, Sharon's Sharm el-Sheikh statement on Palestinian independence was quite vogue. "Israel intends to honour", he stated, "Palestinians right to live in independence and dignity". [5] But where?

The real Israeli intentions came to the fore within few months after the so-called withdrawal, which was so much touted by the Western media. Because, as Idith Zertal and Akiva Eldar point out, the Israeli military control over the devastated strip did not cease "for even a single day" and the "price of the occupation" was paid by the Gazans "every day" (Chomsky and Pappe, 2010). Since January 2006, Israel has been inflicting collective punishment on the Gazans by using various methods in violation of the international law. Two key methods stand out: carrying out continual military attack, with varying intensively and duration, against the Strip; and imposing the most inhuman and crippling blockade by maintaining full control over Gaza's air strip, land border and sea frontiers. During the period from 2006 to 2014, Israel launched three major military operations against the Gaza Strip. These were: "Operation Cast Lead" during December 2008- January 2009, "Operation Pillar of Defence" in November 2012 and "Operation Protective Edge" in July-August 2014. While the first was launched by Prime Minister Ehud Olmert, Sharon's successor, the other two were carried out under the directions of Prime Minister Benjamin Netanyahu.

A closer scrutiny of these operations indicates some trends that reflect a clear pattern of Israeli state behaviour as well as the attitude of politicians at the helm at the given time. First, all these attacks were carried out with prior preparation and a perfect sense of timing. The 2008-09 operation had been planned methodically for more than six months (Chomsky and Pappe, 2010) and coincided with a transition in the American administration. Similarly, the 2012 operation took place during the month of US Presidential election. The last operation was launched in the immediate aftermath of a crucial unity agreement between Fatah and Hamas. In the first two cases, the aim was to take advantage of the vulnerability of both the Democrats and Republicans in the US as far as criticizing the Israeli action is concerned.

In the last case, the objective was to divert the attention from Palestinian unity to Israel's security. Second, invariably every operation was preceded by Israeli provocation of Hamas. One could see a very familiar pattern here: first the Israeli forces would provoke Hamas as to retaliate and then the Hamas retaliation would be used as a pretext to justify a massive military onslaught on the Gaza Strip. The Western Press would sensationalize the Hamas retaliation to justify the Israeli attack on "security grounds" while totally ignoring the initial Israeli provocative acts against the Hamas. Third, all these operations caused hugely disproportionate human casualties on the Palestinian side that too on an overwhelming majority of innocent civilians that included children, women, handicapped and elderly people.

They also resulted in massive infrastructural destruction involving hospitals, schools, residential buildings, power stations, factories, even UN-run facilities, etc. [6] Fourth, sophisticated US military technology and weapons were used during the operations prompting scholars to comment that a new term (as the terms "aggression" and "terrorisms" were inadequate) was required to explain "the sadistic and cowardly torture of people caged with no possibility to escape, while they are being pointed to dust" (Chomsky and Pappe, 2010). In other words, the operations served the interests of the Military-Industrial-complex (MIS) in the US very well. A similar case can be made for the Israeli arms industry because Jewish-Israeli scientists "coordinate with the army to use the territory as a convenient testing ground for advanced, experimental technologies".

After the experiment in Gaza, "corporate Israel later repackages those technologies for global export". [7] Fifth, the operations were aimed at deepening the fragmentation within the Palestinian politics and society, further sabotaging the genuine democratic Palestinian political process, and delegitimizing the peace process. It needs to be recalled that the Gazans became victims of continual and systemic Israeli brutality after the Hamas victory in the January 2006 Palestinian Legislative Council (PLC) elections which were free, fair and open in accordance with established democratic norms and practices.

The champions of democracy and human rights which included not only Israel but its Western patrons, most notably the US, did not have any moral compunction in punishing the Palestinians in Gaza, by subjecting them to most inhuman blockade, for exercising their free democratic choice. Gaza is under blockade, as Ben White argues, because there are severe restriction on what enters Gaza, on the exit of goods, on the free movement of people, routine attacks on Palestinian fisherman and farmers and the long closure of the Rafah border (White, 2016).

The blockade of Gaza almost since 2006, which is a textbook case of collective punishment, has converted the strip into world's largest open prison depriving its residents of basic necessities of life like food, water, electricity, minimum healthcare, education, employment, etc. By this, the Israel-US combine has a devious scheme in operation. This acts like a double-edged weapon. Since Hamas has a strong popular base in Gaza, both Israel and the US seek to isolate and weaken it by punishing the Gazans. A constant focus on Hamas as the main source of trouble for the Palestinians would not only weaken the Islamist organization but also correspondingly strengthen its rival Fatah which then can be coerced or coaxed to be more plaint and accept a peace deal on Israeli terms.

From another angle, by carrying out periodic attacks against the Gaza, Israel seeks to perpetuate a security narrative before the international community by portraying Hamas as a mortal threat to the very existence of Israel and thereby finds an alibi to not merely delegitimize the peace process but also legitimize its lethal attacks against the Gazans in the name of "security" and "self-defence". Therefore, finally, by constantly keeping the regional and international limelight on the Hamas "threat" from Gaza, Israel has greatly succeeded in diverting the world attention from its creeping annexation of the West Bank and East Jerusalem, which is at the heart of the Zionist Project.

West Bank and East Jerusalem

In the Zionist scheme of things, the issue of the West Bank and East Jerusalem has huge significance from ideological standpoint so much so that the Likudniks and other right-wing forces in Israel prefer to address these territories by their Biblical names, Judea and Samaria. Further, Menachem Begin, the late Likud Prime Minister who was instrumental in ending the long held Labour dominance in Israeli politics and thereby heralding a new era in 1977 by winning the elections, challenged the very nomenclature which these territories had acquired in international parlance after the 1967 war during which Israel had occupied huge portions of Arab and Palestinian territories. Within passage of the UN Security Council Resolution 242 in November 1967, these territories were categorized as occupied territories from which Israel was required to withdraw.

For Begin, the West Bank and East Jerusalem were "liberated territories"; liberated from "alien control" for the Jewish people to be integrated to Israel to form the Biblical *Eretz* Israel. Begin's decision to withdraw from the Sinai Peninsula and have peace with Egypt was a masterly strategic move to neutralize the most powerful country in the Arab-Israeli hostility equation so to concentrate all of Israel's resources and power in the West Bank and East Jerusalem. Begin was an ardent advocate of increasing settlements in these Palestinian territories. Hence, the Zionist colonization of the territories west of the River Jordan began quite early on. In that sense, Sharon was right when he stated that, "1948 was the first phase" of the whole project; Sharon was implementing merely his mentor's ideas. These were probably the early harbinger of neo-Zionism which basically involved the Zionist colonization of the West Bank and East Jerusalem and came to the fore more prominently in the aftermath of the *Al Aqsaintifada.*

The act of colonization involves two parallel things. First, it involves a concrete process of occupying a country/territory and "subjugating" its people by controlling their politics, economy, society and culture. Second, this "concrete process of control" is "backed up" and supported/justified by an ideology of "hegemony" and "cultural supremacy" (Hiddleston, 2012). The concept of *Eretz* Israel exclusively meant for the Jewish people in God's "Promised Land" still forms the ideological basis of the Zionist Project. That "Promised Land" consists of the modern state of Israel plus the West Bank and East Jerusalem.

Therefore, the Arab Palestinians living in these territories are not only aliens but also culturally inferior and anti-modern who need to be removed to make way for the Jews who are the "rightful owners" of the land. Linked to this narrative of ownership is the process of demonization of Palestinians by portraying the Palestinians as "terrorists" who are out to destroy the state of Israel. This ideology is being promoted and strengthened through a combination of skilful propaganda, myth perpetuation, control of the media, use of huge financial resources, constant lobbying in the Western capitals, mostly Washington DC and London, and effective use of military methods against the Palestinians. Within Israel, the ideology is promoted through a subtle way which shows the linkage between power and knowledge production.

In fact, 2000 onwards has witnessed not only the near disappearance of the post-Zionist viewpoint but also its replacement with a "new, consensual interpretation" of Zionism which was represented by the main parties: Likud, Kadima and Labour. This trend "competed with an even harshly version of Zionism" which Ilan Pappe calls neo-Zionism" (Pappe, 2014). The essence of all this is to deny the

Palestinians their Palestine identity, forceful assertion of the Jewish-Zionist identity of the Land of Israel and an uncompromising attitude towards occupation (Ibid). As regards the concrete process, the Zionist project is being implemented at three levels: systematic, persistent and brutal oppression of the Palestinians living in the West Bank and East Jerusalem by controlling every aspect of their life, denial of the Palestinian refugees' right to return, and methodical marginalization and discrimination of the Arab Palestinian citizens within Israel itself. This article will focus on the first level of implementation as the other two need an entirely separate discussion.

Israel's continuing Zionist project in the West Bank is being implemented through various methods. These include land grabbing; settlement building and expansion; construction of the apartheid wall; monopolizing Palestine's water resources; controlling the movement of Palestinians with a vast and complicated network of checkpoints, gates and barriers; policy of demolition, detention and deportation; carrying out pre-dawn raids and arrests of Palestinians including children; confiscation of Palestinian private property; policy of ethnic cleaning; etc.

Of all the above, the most important impediment on the way to independent Palestinian statehood is the Israeli policy of land grabbing and settlement construction. Israel's settlement policy is based on pure ethno-religious chauvinism championed by the settler movement and supported by brute state power and the huge financial resources of the Zionists through the Jewish National Fund. Ever since 1967, successive governments in Israel have supported the settlement policy in one way or the other, thanks to the growing strength and influence of the settler movement over the years across the Israeli political spectrum.

Since there is a strong ideological affinity between the Israeli right-wing political forces and the settler movement, the latter has been more powerful in influencing Israel's settlement policy when the country is governed by a right-wing party or a coalition dominated by right-wing parties. As a result, the "expansionist vision of the right-wing settlers" became Israel's state policy (Falk, 2014). This has been more so ironically though, after the Oslo process. Because the right-wing forces never accepted Oslo which, according to them, cut at the very roots of their "Greater Israel" vision. Prime Minister Yitzhak Rabin's assassination in November 1995 by a right-wing extremist, Yigal Amir, should be seen from this perspective.

The building of new settlements for Jews and the expansion of the old ones are done in a very creeping manner. The process follows a familiar pattern. Palestinian land in the West Bank, which has not been formally annexed by Israel and which forms the core territory of a future Palestinian state under international legality and morality, is grabbed by the Israeli state in two ways. First, if the land is not privately owned, then it is declared as abandoned and occupied for military use and then it is seized for public use making it a "state land" to facilitate settlements. Second, in the event, a piece of land is owned by a Palestinian then the Israeli state expropriates it by extending Israeli law to the occupied West Bank. This applies to those cases whose owners are not known. In case the land owners are known, they will be compensated. Invariably, the settlements develop as illegal outposts and then get legalized through cabinet decisions and related legislative measures from time to time.

But the fact remains that the Israel state remains involved at every stage—from planning to construction and development to providing special benefits for the settlers which many Israeli citizens are not entitled. Most of the settlements are built in area 'C', which is under full Israeli control, and are situated in prime strategic locations. Invariably, settlements are built just nearby an Arab village by expropriating the land belonging to the Palestinian *fellahin* of that village. Apart from the loss of prime farm land, the Arab Palestinian villagers constantly suffer from aggressive settlement vigilantism perpetrated by the nearby Jewish settlement. These include periodic physical attacks, acts of desecration, stealing or burning of crops during the harvest seasons, etc. All these are done with the full knowledge, protection and even encouragement of Israeli security forces. [8]

The contrast is striking: while Palestinian homes are demolished almost every day on one pretext or the other, illegal Jewish settlements are allowed to flourish with full state patronage. These settlements violate international law and norms as established by both the Fourth Geneva Convention of 1949 and the UN. For instance, the latest UN Security Council Resolution (2334) of December 2016 demanded that Israel cease all settlement construction in the occupied territories. It needs to be remembered that this resolution was supported by all the UNSC members including the US. Thus, during the last five decades, Israel has built around 200-250 settlements in the West Bank, including Jerusalem with a settler population of more than 6,00,000. [9] According to sources, there is a huge difference between average growths of settler population in comparison to Israeli population in a ratio of 5.3 percent to 1.8 percent. [10] In fact, there is resentment among some sections within Israel against the huge resources allocated for building, promoting and sustaining the settlements in the occupied territories. [11]

Another broader/overarching aspect of Israel's continuing Zionist project is the apartheid framework which it has put in place in the occupied West Bank and East Jerusalem over the years. Ben White's book convincingly argues how Israel functions like an apartheid state in its policy towards both the Palestinians in Israel and Palestinians in the occupied territories. UN General Assembly Resolution 3068, (November 30, 1973) defines apartheid as "inhuman acts committed for the purpose of establishing and maintaining domination by one racial group of persons over any other social group of persons and systematically oppressing them" (White, 2014). According to White, Israeli apartheid operates at two levels: within the Jewish state against the Palestinian citizens and inside the OPT against the Palestinian residents. Israel pursues its ruthless racist policy inside the OPT through a "matrix of control" which not only regulates the daily lives of Palestinians but also imposes collective punishment on them with alarming frequency.

These include as has already been mentioned, establishing Jewish settlements in strategic locations, settler only roads, numerous checkpoints, closures, the separation wall, pre-dawn raids, detention and torture, home demolitions, land confiscation, etc. White highlights three main categories of "inhuman acts". The first category impinges on the "right to life and liberty". The second relates to "measures designed to divide the population along racial lines by the creation of separate reserves and ghettos". The final category concerns "measures calculated to prevent a racial group from participation in the political, social, economic and cultural life of the country". [12] On the whole, it is a "story of land theft, colonization and ethnic separation" (Ibid.).

The clearest evidence of the continuing Zionist project by Israel is to be seen in its policy towards Jerusalem since the 1967 war. East Jerusalem which includes the old city, holds huge significance for both Jews and Muslims due to historical, religious, cultural, political and national reasons (Maoz, 2014). For both the people, the old city forms part of their collective memory, which is partly constructed based on belief and partly recorded based on facts. Hence, there is a continuing concern for the city by both the communities, inevitably leading to contentious claims. At the heart of the dispute is a structure in the old city which is known to Jews as Temple Mount and as Al-Haram Al-Sharif (Noble or Sacred Sanctuary) to the Muslims.

The structure is deeply revered by both the communities and, therefore, it has become a highly emotive and sensitive issue since the beginning of the British mandate in Palestine in 1920. As it stands, the structure contains the al-Aqsa Mosque, the Golden Dome (or Dome on the Rock) and the adjacent

Wailing Wall (al-Buraq). Jews pray near the Wailing Wall while Muslims pray in the al-Aqsa mosque. The Wailing Wall is also known as the Western Wall. Non-Muslims are allowed to visit the compound where the al-Aqsa mosque is located but are strictly prohibited entry inside the mosque or pray there. As regards the Jews, they can visit the site that houses the mosque but are not allowed to pray there. The fundamental point to be underlined in this context is the Jewish belief that the al-Aqsa Mosque today stands at the very site where once a Jewish temple stood in ancient times, hence the Jews refer and revere the site as Temple Mount. The fact, however, remains that archaeological findings do not suggest any link between the Western Wall of the Al-Aqsa Mosque compound and the ancient Jewish Temple. This is the finding of none other than the Israeli archaeologist, Meir Ben-Dov. Meir also asserted that the Wailing Wall "has no sacred significance" in the Jewish faith. [13]

It is interesting to note that the UNESCO voted on a resolution, on October 13, 2016, denying any connection between the Al-Aqsa Mosque and the Western Wall in occupied East Jerusalem. Because of this strong-held belief, for centuries religious Jews in the Diaspora prayed in the direction of Jerusalem and longed to return to the city symbolized by the toast "next year in Jerusalem". Generations of Jews were socialized in this process; the spirit and symbol of Jerusalem formed a significant aspect of Jewish socio-cultural and religious tradition through the ages. So much so that the predominantly secular Zionist movement, which took shape in the late 19th century, had to accommodate this overwhelming priestly trend to gain the wider support of the world Jewry for its nationhood project.

For the Muslims, on the other hand, it is a lived-in reality since the seventh century. Al-Aqsa mosque is considered to be the third holiest shrine. The Al-Haram Al-Sharif compound and East Jerusalem on the whole remained under Arab-Muslim political sovereignty from the seventh century CE till the

Allied occupation of it during the First World War, except the brief Crusades' rule. It needs to be underlined here that the military campaign by Crusades to "liberate" Jerusalem was guided more by political then theological reasons, even though Jerusalem is considered to be equally holy by the followers of Christianity because of the presence of the Church of Holy Sepulcher. Further, there is hardly any evidence to suggest that the Jews and Christians were persecuted for their faith by Muslim rulers before and after the Crusades; there was a near perfect communal harmony and amity among the followers of three monotheistic religions in Jerusalem, particularly between Jews and Muslims.

The struggle for control over East Jerusalem and the Al-Aqsa compound began with the impositions British made over the predominantly Arab-Muslim Palestine as part of the post-First World War settlement. The Zionist Programme of land acquisition had already vitiated the inter-communal relations in Palestine by then. Anti-Zionists, even anti-Jews, sentiments were emerging gradually (Maoz, 2014). This needs to be viewed in the context of the changing power equation in Palestine due to the inherently partisan mandatory provisions which put the Zionists/Jews in an advantageous position vis-à-vis the Arab Palestinians in their relationship with the mandatory power, Britain. [14] It was during this period that the whole issue assumed definite political and nationalist dimensions.

The Grand Mufti of Jerusalem, Haj Amin al-Husayni, for instance, sought to mobilize and strengthen his pan-Islamic and Pan-Arab movement against the Zionists and Jews on the basis of the Temple Mount/Al-Haram Al-Sharif issue. The Grand Mufti demanded that the British mandatory authority ban Jewish prayer at the Western Wall as it formed part of the Al-Aqsa Mosque (Maoz, 2014). The degree of polarization between the Muslims and Jews can be gauged from the fact even during the Ottoman rule, Jews were allowed to pray at the Western Wall, though not on the Temple Mount. Some scholars have argued that the issue remained at the forefront of the 1929 riots, which began at the Western Wall, as well as the 1936-1939 Arab rebellion against the British and the Jews (Ibid).

While it was true that the Al-Haram Al-Sharif issue was used as an instrument of mobilization, it cannot be denied that the objective conditions for such mobilization was created by the extreme Zionist programme of making Palestine a Jewish state that had been forewarned by the King-Crane Commission findings. It was also true that the "mainstream" of the Zionist movement was more accommodative on the Temple Mount issue by not aspiring to "rebuild the Jewish temple" and confining its goal to the "control" of the Western Wall as a "historical national symbol", while many Jewish radical leaders sought not only to "control" the Wall but also to "rebuild the Ancient Temple" (Ibid).

The Zionist movement, as is well-known, was primarily concerned about a state rather than places of religious significance. As a result, during the 1948 Arab-Israeli war, the Temple Mount and East Jerusalem were not the focus of the Zionists. But the Arab side was more concerned about the protection of the Haram al-Sharif from Israeli control. Ultimately, West Jerusalem came under Israeli control and was declared as Israel's Capital. Jordan retained the control over the West Bank, including East Jerusalem. Thus, both the sides violated the UN Partition Resolution 181 with regard to the status of Jerusalem which was to be under a special international regime. In the coming two decades, East Jerusalem in general and the holy places in particular became rarely a point of contention or major controversy. While Israel made efforts to consolidate itself in a new hostile environment, Jordan governed the holy places in a relatively fair manner.

The 1967 Six-Day War came as a major turning point for all the parties involved in the conflict. Israel's somewhat unexpected decisive victory over the Arab states created new dynamics in the state and society; it has to redefine its identity in view of its occupation of Arab, specially Palestinian, territories, including East Jerusalem. The Arab states could never recover from their crushing defeat and, therefore, had to adopt methods of war and peace towards Israel to regain their lost territories. Egypt, under Anwar el-Sadat, represented and led that distinct trend. Ironically, the very defeat of the Arab states led to the emergence of radical, independent Palestinian nationalism asserting its right to self-determination and statehood. Since the radical PLO, under the leadership of Yasser Arafat, called for the full liberation of Palestine, it approached the issue of Jerusalem from a purely "spiritual", rather secular, point of view which did not display any emotional, religious or particularistic attitude. Nor did it stake any exclusive claim to the holy city on the basis of some belief or past myth. In fact, the revised Palestinian National Charter did not mention the name of Jerusalem, recognizing its importance to all three monotheistic religions. Article 16 simply stated:

"The liberation of Palestine, from the spiritual point of view, provides the holy land with an atmosphere of security and peace whereby all the religions sanctities will be protected and religious freedom guaranteed. All people will be allowed to visit their holy places with no discrimination to colour, language and creed or race. For this reason, the people of Palestine look forward to the support of all the spiritual forces in the world". [15]

As has already been stated, the PLO gradually moderated its stand and opted for a compromise formula widely known as the two-state solution. This meant there will be two states in mandatory Palestine, Israel and Palestine existing side by side along the pre-1967 war border. Therefore, the basic premise under which the PLO opted for a peaceful, negotiated solution of the conflict was that Israel would withdraw from the Palestinian territories it occupied during the 1967 war to facilitate the establishment of an independent Palestinian state in the West Bank, including East Jerusalem, and Gaza Strip. In other words and from the Palestinian viewpoint, East

Jerusalem, including the Haram al-Sharif, would be under the jurisdiction of a future Palestinian state.

Gradually, East Jerusalem was projected as the capital of a future state. In that sense, East Jerusalem assumed huge political, national and religious importance in the context of the Palestinian struggle for statehood. Further, this has been also the position of the Arab-Islamic world and the international community at large. Therefore, the PLO recognized Israel's right to exist, renounced terrorism, accepted UNSC Resolution 242 and joined both the Madrid and Oslo processes with great hope and understanding. This was despite the opposition from the radical and Islamist forces within the Palestinian community.

On the Israeli side, the occupation of East Jerusalem revived the old debate over Temple Mount in the political, military and religious establishments. Opinion remained deeply divided across the spectrum having a bearing on Israeli state policy. Some considered the capture of the old city as a moment of liberation for Temple Mount after 2000 years of alien rule. This section advocated not only taking full control of the Temple Mount by asserting Israeli sovereignty over the structure but also called for the "reconstruction of the Jewish temple" after destroying the Haram Mosques. The other trend sought to avoid such an extreme step and instead favoured full sovereignty over entire East Jerusalem while allowing the Jordanian authority to be the custodian of the Haram al-Sharif compound. Jews could visit the Temple Mount but they could not pray there (Maoz, 2014). The latter trend was reflected in Israel's overall declared state policy.

But what is more important is that the former got embedded into Israeli society and expanded its constituency steadily, thanks to the encouragement of political leaders, especially from the right wing dispensation, by certain actions and policies from time to time. Therefore, over the years the extremist trend has become more predominant and its advocates have exercised considerable influence in policy making. The following brief discussion will make this clear.

The first-step Israelis took, in the immediate aftermath of the 1967 victory was to annex East Jerusalem on June 27 which was against the international law. Further, the Jerusalem municipality border was redrawn which annexed to the city around 70 square kilometres from the West Bank that included East Jerusalem and 28 Palestinian villages. [16] Ever since, Israel has embarked on a policy of what is generally called "Judaization" of East Jerusalem. The process of Judaization operates at two levels, simultaneously. At one level, there has been a constant, aggressive psychological war, through a well-organized and well-funded propaganda machinery, to justify Jewish exclusive claim on and control over East Jerusalem and its holy places.

Few examples would illustrate this point. In March 2017, a panel of judges decided to award the Israel prize for Lifetime Achievement to David Be'eri who pioneered the cause of Judaizing East Jerusalem through his so-called non-governmental organizations Elad. The basic objective of this organization is to create a Jewish majority in Arab neighbourhoods of Jerusalem by using the Biblical myth as its basis of campaign. The panel members stated that Be'eri was given the award for his "Contribution to the state in single-handedly establishing a national enterprise—the city of David...He initiated, founded, led and still leads this blessed activity that has turned the city of David into a national and international heritage, education and tourism site of the first order. The city of David is the historic kernel from which Jerusalem grew—the heart of the Jewish people and the focal point of the Book of Book (the Bible)" (Eldar, 2017).

Commenting on how Be'eri's project had been successful in implanting the mythical aura of the city of David in Israeli psyche, Archaeologist Yonathan Mizrachi stated, "Those who tour the site within an Elad guide are treated to an emotional, even spiritual experience, where religious texts and traditions shed light on the antiquities, creating a 3D time tunnel that seals itself into the consciousness of every Israeli" (Ibid.). It needs to be mentioned that going by historical and archaeological evidence, the city of David is a small settlement or nothing more than a mound of antiquities", near the Western Wall, whose origin and importance are "unclear", though some believe that the site was the "original core" of Jerusalem. In that sense, Be'eri's Elad is "an organization with a declared ideological agenda" which "presents history of the city of David in a biased manner" (Ibid).

The aggressive and systematic state-funded campaign to "rebuild" the Jewish Temple by destroying the Al-Aqsa Mosque is also part of this psychological war. Over the years, Jewish extremist organizations, with the avowed aim of "rebuilding" the Temple, have proliferated in Israel. What is more worrisome is that the Israeli government itself is supporting this "rebuilding" project in one way or another. For instance, in 2017, the government funded a Smartphone app exhibition titled "The Western Wall Experience". This app allows visitors to see an imagined landscape where the existing Al-Aqsa Mosque and the Dome of the Rock disappeared and are replaced by the Jewish Temple. This provides an opportunity for the tourists to "pose for a souvenir photograph" with the imagined Temple. The Zionist group Aish Hatorh, founded by Rabbi Steven Berg, also sponsors this app programme. [17]

Such programmes embolden the efforts of extremist groups, such as the Temple Movement, which is again funded by the government and which has already prepared the master plan to build the Jewish Temple in the Haram al-Sharif compound by destroying the Al-Aqsa Mosque. All this perpetuate the "myth of the existence" of a Jewish Temple at the site where the Al-Aqsa Mosque stands today, "despite archaeological evidence to the contrary". It needs to be remembered that the excavation works under the Noble Sanctuary to look for the evidence of a mythical non-existent Temple are basically aimed at severely weakening the foundation of the Haram al-Sharif compound.

A related aspect of this aggressive psychological war has

been the demand by extremist Jewish groups to pray at the Temple Mount. In pursuance of this objective, growing number of Jews visit the compound, especially during Jewish festivals and holidays with open support from Jewish extremist groups and even senior government officials. [18] More importantly, hundreds of settlers frequently and forcibly enter the Al-Aqsa compound, in coordination with Israeli security forces, and perform rituals and take pledge to destroy the Mosque, forcing the Muslim worshipers to remain outside. [19] Settlers and Israeli forces often desecrate the mosque to the extent of entering the Al-Qabali Mosque with boots and setting hire to it. Israel also imposes severe restrictions, from time to time, on Jerusalemites to pray inside the Al-Aqsa Mosque (Al-Dajani, 2015).

Such activities have claimed the Palestinians and have increased their apprehensions regarding Israel's plan to change the status quo at the Haram al-Sharif by taking full control over the compound. This has resulted in violent clashes between Jews and Palestinians as well as between the Palestinians and Israeli security forces from time to time. Two instances from the recent past can be cited to prove this point. First, the Jerusalem *intifada* (2015), as it came to be known as later, began with clashes between Israeli forces and the young Palestinians at the Al-Aqsa compound.

The main reason behind the clashes was the apprehension by Palestinians of the Israeli plan to take over the compound. Violence continued for weeks resulting in the killing of 39 Palestinian and eight Israelis. Hundreds of Palestinians were also wounded during clashes with the security forces. The violence continued for weeks during which one witnessed a strange, new trend among the Palestinian youth who sought to vent their anger and frustration against Israelis by indulging in a stabbing spite. Few Israelis, both civilians and security forces, were stabbed to death by ordinary young Palestinians with no connection/affiliation to any militant organizations. This sent shock waves across the Israel and created a "sense of panic" among Israeli citizens as well as security forces. The situation became so alarming that Palestinians demanded UN-sanctioned international "protection force" to be deployed in East Jerusalem to control violence around the Al-Aqsa Mosque. This was obviously rejected by Israel (Ibid).

Secondly on July 14, 2017, two Israeli policemen were killed when Arab gunmen fired at them from the Al-Aqsa Mosque. Israel responded by installing metal detectors at the "gates of 37 acre walled compound". This unprecedented security measure resulted in "bloodiest clashes" between Palestinians and Israeli security forces in Jerusalem and West Bank. Palestinians viewed the installation of metal detectors as Israeli "assertion" of "further control" over the Muslim holy site whose protection and security is the sole responsibility of Jordan. Israeli authorities argued that the July 14 shooting at the two Israeli Policemen was possible because the Palestinian attackers had been able to "smuggle" guns into the holy site. Therefore, Israel argued, the new security measures were necessary to "prevent" such attacks in the future. [20]

The situation became sensitive and surcharged escalating tension between the Israelis and Palestinians once again. Outraged by the metal detectors and cameras that would monitor their entry into the holy site, the Palestinians "refused to enter the compound in protest" and instead decided to offer their prayers on the streets outside Haram al-Shrif. Israelis reacted with a sense of arrogance and obstinacy by stating "They [metal detector] will remain. The murderers will never tell us how to search the murderers. If they [Palestinians] do not want to enter the mosque, then let them not enter the mosque". [21] Similarly, the father of a young Palestinian, who "stabbed to death" three members of an Israeli family, believed that the reason behind his son's violent behaviour was the killing of Palestinians by Israeli forces and his desire to "protect the 'honour' of the Jerusalem holy site". [22]

At another level, Israel has been pursuing a policy of de-Arabization through concrete measures to change the demography of East Jerusalem. These include revocation of residency rights, forced displacement of Palestinians, demolition of Palestinian homes, expropriation of Palestinian land, imposition of more taxes on the Palestinians Jerusalemites, devious means to divide Palestinians within Jerusalem, building of Jewish settlement inside as well as around East Jerusalem, severely restricting the issue of building permits to Palestinians, making extremely low investment in the development of Palestinian neighbourhoods in comparison to the investment in Jewish neighbourhoods, encouraging wealthy Jewish settlement organizations to dupe/allure gullible Palestinian residents by offering millions of dollars to sell their homes and properties, so on and so forth.

The basic objective of all these measures is to control "the largest possible area of land with least amount of Palestinian residents. This is one of the "most important foundations on which the Zionist policy towards Jerusalem is built" (Al-Dajani, 2015). The following statistics would speak for itself. To begin with, as has already been pointed out, Israel annexed 70 square kilometres from the West Bank to make it a part of the Jerusalem municipality, or one can call Greater Jerusalem, in the immediate aftermath of the 1967 war.

A third of this annexed territory was appropriated by the Israeli government to establish 12 Israeli neighbourhoods in the midst of Arab inhabitants. The basic objective behind setting up these Jewish neighbourhoods is to "isolate" East Jerusalem from the West Bank and "prevent" it from becoming the future capital of an independent Palestinian state whenever that becomes a possibility. As of 2017, around 210,000 Israelis live in these neighbourhoods. As regards Palestinians, around 316,000 live in the Palestinian neighbourhoods of East Jerusalem. [23] Another indicator which clearly shows how Israel seeks to increase the Jewish population in East Jerusalem is the ratio of government-funded construction of housing units to Jewish and Palestinian neighbourhoods; it stands at 99 percent to just one percent.

As of 2017, around 55,335 housing units were constructed in

Jewish neighbourhood as opposed to just 600 housing units in Palestinian neighbourhoods (Ibid). The "belt strategy" is yet another indicator of Israel's well-thought out policy of isolating East Jerusalem from the larger West Bank and fragmenting it from within. This is probably a typical method adopted by settler colonialism whereby the settler occupiers not only seek to encroach the natives' land and affect their daily lives but also create points of friction between the settlers and natives by positing them close to each other and yet separate them by various mechanisms of segregation and discrimination. The "belt strategy" revolves around constructing large settlements around the city and settlements within the city and then connect these two with roads; this obviously encroaches and divides the Palestinian areas to the advantage of Jewish settlers. Further, this creates the conditions for clashes and tension between the two communities on a daily basis. [24]

Further, some supposedly private organizations are also engaged in increasing the number of Jewish settlers in East Jerusalem through various means. The settlement organizations try to "bribe" and allure the Palestinians residents by offering them millions of dollars to "sell their properties and homes" and also ensure them to facilitate European and American citizenship in return. Take the case of Sillwan, a Palestinian neighbourhood in East Jerusalem, which was populated by Jews by Elad or the city of David Foundation of David Be'eri. In fact, the whole project of Be'eri is to turn Sillwan into the "city of David" to ensure a Jewish majority in a Palestinian village.

Ateret Cohanim is yet another group which is competing with Elad to "aggressively" move into Palestinian neighbourhoods with the sole objective of tipping the demographic balance. What is more worrying than the mere numbers is that these organizations are systematically working to move in "ideological settlers" to change the religious footprint of East Jerusalem. They are not merely building new settlements and housing units but also establishing Jewish seminaries and synagogues in Palestinian areas. These are done with the full backing of the government as "part of the pattern of transferring the area around the old city into some sort of pseudo-biblical theme park and putting exclusionary religion on the ascendance in the area" (Hatuqa and Carlstrom, 2014).

Along with the process of setting Jews from different parts of the world in East Jerusalem runs the policy of denying residency rights to the native Palestinians of the city. Since 1967, the residency rights of around 14,000 Palestinians have not been restored. These included those who went to study abroad. The justification Israel provides to revoke their residency rights is that "the centre of their lives had moved elsewhere for seven years or more". How draconian and prejudiced this policy is evident from the fact that while Israel grants the right to settle in Jerusalem to those Jews from Russia, the US, New Zealand and other places who were not born in Jerusalem nor did they stay in the city ever simply on the ground that their "grandmothers were Jewish", at the same time it denies these very rights to Palestinians who were born in the city and whose ancestors lived there. This glaring contrast was brought to light during a ruling on March 14, 2017 by three Supreme Court justices of Israel on an appeal by Akhram Adbalhak, a Palestinian born in East Jerusalem and who immigrated to the US with his parents.

In the ruling, the court "defined the status of such Palestinians as 'resident-native' who are entitled to "permanent residency upon their return" (Eldar, 2017). In this context, it needs to be mentioned that most of the West Bank and Gaza Palestinians cannot enter the city as a matter of right to offer prayer or to visit the magnificent old Jerusalem market or even to meet family and friends. As a result, a whole generation of young Palestinians is being deprived of their right to identify themselves with a city having such cultural and religious importance in their national history. Further, to keep the Palestinians divided, the residents of East Jerusalem have been given a separate identity card which is quite different from the ones given to the Palestinians living in other parts of the West Bank (Pradhan, 2012).

The most ruthless and visible Israeli policy to de-Arabize East Jerusalem and create space for more Jews is reflected in the frequent demolition of Palestinian houses and the displacement of the residents. According to the Land Research Centre (LRC), a Palestinian source, since 1967, Israel has demolished around 5,000 houses in Jerusalem. According to the same report, 380,000 Jerusalemite Palestinians need 2,000 new housing units every year and 50 percent of them live in unlicensed houses. In 2017 alone, Israel demolished 116 Jerusalemite facilities rendering approximately 241 residents homeless.

Between 2000 and 2017, Israel demolished 1,706 homes displacing 9,422 Palestinians which included 5,443 children. While the Israeli occupation authorities demolish Palestinian houses almost indiscriminately, they are very restrictive in issuing building permits to Palestinians. Take for instance, as per the UN data, Israel granted only 1.5 percent of all the Palestinian requests for building permits between 2010 and 2014. As a result, in 2017, more than 20,000 housing units have been constructed in East Jerusalem without permits. The LRC pointed out that the Jerusalem municipality has prescribed such tough conditions and complex procedures as to make Palestinian construction in Jerusalem just impossible. [25]

This goes on to prove that ever since East Jerusalem was annexed and brought under the jurisdiction of Jerusalem municipality, the Arab-Palestinian residents have suffered immensely due to Israel's discriminatory policies and arbitrary measures. For instance, in the 2013 Jerusalem municipality budget, investment in the Jewish neighbourhoods constituted 87 percent (3.9 billion NIS) as compared to just 13 percent (591 million NIS) for Palestinian neighbourhoods. Similarly, since 1967, the Israeli government has constructed around 55,335 housing units in Jewish neighbourhoods compared to a meagre 600 housing units in Palestinian neighbourhoods, with the ratio standing at 99:1 percent. [26]

In fact, according to a report by B'tselem, the Israeli NGO, just 15 percent of the "land area" in East Jerusalem is earmarked for "residential use" by Palestinians, even though Palestinians constitute 40 percent of the city's population". The LRC also reported that the total area allotted for urban development is only 12 percent of Palestinian land and out of this just 7 percent is earmarked for residential buildings. [27] Moreover, the Jerusalem municipality is constantly planning to change the very Arab and Palestinian character of East Jerusalem by "erasing the city's landmarks" (Al-Dajani, 2015).

The above designs/plans to Judaize and de-Arabise East Jerusalem is crucially linked to a key strategic objective of Israel after the 1967 war: to shape up a "united, undivided" or the "Greater Jerusalem" that would be exclusively Jewish in nature. That would be the crowning achievement of the Zionist Project, it succeeded. That, in turn, may sound the death-knell of the Palestinian statehood project from cultural and historical standpoints, as among the Palestinian and across the Arab-Islamic world, East Jerusalem was to be the capital of a Palestinian state.

The Israeli decision and persistence on making Jerusalem as the "united undivided and eternal" capital of the Jewish state violated international law and the broad consensus of the international community on East Jerusalem being an occupied territory and Jerusalem as a disputed territory whose future status should be decided through negotiations between the two parties. For instance, the Knesset law of 1980 was declared "null and void" by the UNSC Resolution 478 in the same year. The broad international consensus is reflected in the fact that no country has established its embassy in Jerusalem; most of the embassies are located in Tel Aviv which is the official capital of Israel. The US case is different. In response to the Knesset law on Jerusalem and probably due to years of consistent Zionist lobbing in the US, the US Congress passed the Jerusalem Embassy Act in 1995. This Congressional Act called for the US to move its embassy to Jerusalem and thereby recognize it as Israel's capital.

That was a huge diplomatic gain for Israel from the viewpoint of its Zionist project and seriously undermined the Palestinian hope and claim for East Jerusalem. The fallout of the Embassy Act could not be visualized in the immediate term because of a specific clause that allowed the American president to defer the shifting of the US embassy to Jerusalem for six months at a time. Bill Clinton, George W. Bush and Barack Obama used this clause every six months during their respective tenure. Such a tactical ambiguity served two purposes. Firstly, it reaffirmed US blanket support to Israel's continuing expansionist design in the occupied Palestinian territory. Secondly, it also somehow provided the American presidents a scope to maintain the facade of an honest peace broker or mediator in the vexed Israeli-Palestinian conflict.

As a result, the Palestinians, the PA leadership precisely, continued to rely on the US to achieve its peace deal with Israel in the post-Oslo phase, notwithstanding the US partisan role in the subsequent peace talks, even if the talks were quite few and futile. That also explained the cordial relationship between the PA and the US, especially after Arafat's death, in all these years even without any concrete achievement for the Palestinians in terms of their independent statehood goals.

However, President Donald Trump's December 2017 decision to recognize Jerusalem as the capital of Israel and also to move the US embassy there marked a new phase in the Israeli-Palestinian conflict and the US role. By all counts, Trump's decision came as a reckless move fraught with unpredictable consequences. First, at the broader level, it came at a time when everybody was expecting a significant American initiative not only to revive the almost dead talks but also to clinch a final agreement between Israelis and the Palestinians; President Trump talked profusely about his "deal of the century" after coming to power. [28] Second, the exceptionally unilateral decision by the US violated international humanitarian law which "rests on the central proposition" that the character and status of an occupied territory cannot be "altered" without the consent of the occupied people. [29] Trump's decision also marked rapture in the international consensus on the status of Jerusalem. This became evident from the response of the international community; there was near universal condemnation of Trump's unilateralism.

There was a huge diplomatic and political backlash against the US in the wider Arab-Islamic world. Trump's decision was received with angry Friday protests in West Bank, Gaza, Egypt, Lebanon, Syria, Yemen, Turkey, Jordan, Pakistan, Indonesia, Malaysia, etc. While the Arab League wanted the US to change its decision, some leaders like Ismail Haniya of Hamas and President Recep Tayyip Erdogan of Turkey warned of dire consequences in the coming years. [30] The reaction of the European allies was no less damaging. The discussions in the emergency UN Security Council session that was convened to deliberate upon Trump's Jerusalem decision, gave enough indications of that. The US stood completely isolated as all other 14 members of the Council openly denounced Trump's decree. The EU also expressed its total displeasure. The essence of the criticism was that the unilateral decision by the US "subverted" the prospect of the two-state solution which had been the central framework of the UN approach to resolve the Israeli-Palestine conflict for decades.

In fact, the joint statement issued by the representatives of Britain, France, Sweden, Germany and Italy, after the Council debate, criticized the change in US policy on the ground that it was "not in line with Security Council resolutions and was unhelpful in terms of prospects for peace in the region" (Gladstone, 2017). The strong denunciation of the US move and its international isolation was further reflected in the UN General Assembly when on December 21, 2017, the world body in an overwhelming majority vote 128-8 (with 35 abstentions) not only condemned Trump's Jerusalem decision but also demanded the US to rescind its dangerous policy. [31] Thus, Trump's Jerusalem decision was both "provocative and disruptive".

Third, the only country which supported Trump's decision and welcomed it as "historic" and "courageous" was naturally Israel. From the Israeli viewpoint, it was indeed so. Trump's Jerusalem declaration came as the second most decisive statement by a dominant Western power in support of the Zionist project, the first being the infamous Balfour declaration. The similarities between the two declarations, in terms of the content, the total disregard to ground realities by the issuing authority, the implications and even the irony, are quite uncanny. It also reaffirmed the continuing strong alliance between the dominant power of the day in international politics and the Zionists, specially the ability of the latter to influence the decision-making process of the former.

The statements issued by Israeli leaders, including the President and Prime Minister, in early 2018 clearly suggest that there is an undeclared understanding/agreement between the US and Israel with regard to the future of the rest of occupied West Bank, as the status of East Jerusalem has already been unilaterally decided. In the second week of February 2018, there were reports that Prime Minister Netanyahu had discussed with the US regarding the "possibility of Israel annexing" Jewish settlements in the West Bank (Heller, 2018). This was followed by yet another startling statement by the President Reuven Rivlin at the Israeli Institute for Democracy in the third week of March 2018. Rivlin called for "imposing Israeli Sovereignty over Judea and Samaria", Israel's preferred term for the occupied West Bank. [32]

These cannot be dismissed as un-substantive statements or baseless speculations, given the sequence of developments and most importantly, the close personal rapport between Jared Kushner, President Trump's close adviser and the key strategist entrusted with preparing a so-called grand Israeli-Palestinian Peace Plan, and Prime Minister Netanyahu.

Finally, and most importantly, for the Palestinians, it came as a rude shock. Trump's Jerusalem decision can be regarded as third major defeat in the Palestinian struggle for statehood in the Post-UN Partition plan era, the other two being the 1948 *al Nakbah* and the 1967 *al Naksha*. The only difference was that it was a diplomatic defeat unlike the earlier two in the battlefield. Naturally, the Trump-Abbas meeting raised a lot of hopes in the region regarding the possibility of final settlement. However, President Trump's "deal of the century" turned out to be the "slap of the century" for the Palestinians. With this, the disconnection between the US and Palestinians became complete whose consequences are hard to predict.

Conclusion

From the above, it is obvious that the fundamental objective of Zionism cuts at the very roots of the Palestinian nationalist aspirations. The Zionist ideology is racist and supremacist in nature which strongly believes that the native Arab Palestinians are not only culturally inferior but also do not have the right to be in the so-called "promised land". Indeed, for the Zionist, the Palestinians are outside occupiers". The acceptance of the UN partition plan and the establishment of Israel in parts of mandatory Palestine was a tactical move by ardent Zionists to get legitimacy from the international community.

Till the decisive 1967 war, the Israeli state concealed its Zionist ambitions as it was engaged to ensure its existence in a hostile neighbourhood. It should be left to historical speculation only to understand as to what would have been the Israeli state behaviour had there be no 1967 war or decisive Arab defeat in that war. With significant Arab territories under its occupation, the Israeli state became more confident and assertive in dealing with the Arab-Islamic world. Therefore, in the post-1967 phase, the Israel state resumed its Zionist project in the occupied Palestinian territories. Correspondingly, one also witnessed the emergence of an independent, militant Palestinian National Movement against Israel during this phase.

The Israeli state response to this new phase of Palestinian nationalism was purely aggressive and ruthless, starting from the annexation of East Jerusalem, building settlements in the West Bank and Gaza Strip and waging a war against the Palestinian movement. It was a sort of zero-sum game in which Israel succeeded, thanks to the blanket US support and the gradual abandonment of the Palestine cause by the Arab world in terms of real commitment through a combination of peaceful coexistence and clandestine rapprochement with and even support to Israel. Such a formidable co-relation of forces compelled the Palestinian movement to compromise and work towards coexistence with Israel in mandatory Palestine, the two-state solution.

The Palestinian recognition of Israel's right to exist within the framework of a two-state solution—Israel and Palestine existing side by side in the same piece of land—challenged the hidden intentions of Israel's continuing Zionist project in the post-1967 phase. The façade of the Peace Process with the US as the so-called honest broker became the best instrument to circumvent the Palestinian nationalist goals even while pursuing the Zionist Project in West Bank, including East Jerusalem.

At the other end, the recognition of Israel by the PLO deeply divided the Palestinian community and this was used by Israel to its best advantage by pitting Hamas against Fatah since 2006. All these years, under the smokescreen of peace process, Israel systematically pursued a policy of creating facts on the ground—building settlements and grabbing Palestinian land—so as to make the idea of an independent and viable Palestinian state in the West Bank and Gaza redundant. The lack of effective international intervention merely served and facilitated the Israeli design. Trump's Jerusalem decision completed the full circle.

This does not mean that the Palestinians will meekly surrender to the US-Israeli designs. But which direction the Palestinians national movement will take and which way the Palestine question will be championed by the wider international community are hard to predict. But the growing strength and appeal of the BDS movement and the Great March of Return on Israeli-Gaza border, which continued for six long weeks beginning with the Land Day Protest and ending/coinciding with the *al-Nakba* and shifting of US embassy to Jerusalem resulting in the death of nearly 100 Palestinians, may provide some indications for the future. Mere statements of condemnation by the international community and occasional UN resolutions against Israel have not stopped the Zionist Project. The only option before the UN, it appears, is to initiate and lead a sanction regime against Israel along the lines of the movement against the erstwhile apartheid regime in South Africa.

Endnotes

1. Cited in Reinhart, p. 106.
2. See Ibid., pp. 191-92.
3. Under the Oslo provisions, area A, accounting for 22 percent, remained under the total jurisdiction of the Palestinian Authority. Area B, which covers 18 percent of the West Bank, remained under Israel and PA joint control. Area C remained under the exclusive jurisdiction of the Israeli Government. It needs to mention that even in area A, Israel can exercise power on security matters. Many Palestinians believe that area B is a misnomer and almost non-existed; it is either A or C.
4. See, "PM Ariel Sharon's address at the Herzliya Conference", December 16, 2004, Israeli Ministry of Foreign Affairs, Government of Israel, Tel Aviv, www.mfa.gov.il.
5. *The Hindu*, February 9, 2005, p. 1.
6. During Operation Cast Lead, 1,399 Palestinians were killed as against just 4 Israelis (one soldier). The number of Palestinians killed during Operation Pillar of Defence stood at 167 as against 6 Israelis (two soldiers). However, during Operation Protective Edge, the Palestinian casualty figure was the highest so far, 2,202. The number of Israelis killed during the last military offence against Gazans was 68 out of which 62 were soldiers. Source: B' Tselem.
7. Ahmed Moor, "How it Started in Gaza: PM Netanyahu Had to Seek a Way Out of Isolation", available at: https://www.aljazeera.com/indepth/opinion/2014/07/how-it-

started-gaza.20147/2920/62-60625.html.

8. These are based on the impressions of the author's field visit to different parts of the West Bank in 2012. For details, see Bansidhar Pradhan, "Palestine under Occupation: Some Reflections", *Mainstream*, New Delhi, Vol. L, No. 26, June 16, 2012, pp. 11-18.
9. These are approximate figures. Different sources provide different figures, available at:
http://peacenow.org.il/en;
https://www.timesofisrael.com/billions-spent-on-settlements-since-israel-captured-westbank.
10. Israel Central Bureau of Statistics, cited in UNGA A/HRC/22/63.
11. Settlements are encouraged by providing huge financial incentives by way of subsidies and preferential treatment on many aspects. For instance, the average settler gets 3 times more in public subsidies then an Israeli citizen living in Israel. Estimates suggest that the cost of settlement since June 1967 is US$ 20 billion, available at:
https://www.timesofisrael.com/billions-spent-on-settlements-since-israel-captured-westbank.
12. Ibid. p. 4.
13. See "Israeli Archaeologist Denies Jewish Ties to Al-Aqsa Mosque", October 13, 2016, www.middleeastmonitor.com.
14. Specifically, Articles 2, 4 and 6 put the Jews in an advantageous position vis-à-vis the Arabs.
15. See "The Palestinian National Charter (Revised)", *Arab World Weekly*, No. 23, March 22, 1969, pp. i-v.
16. See East Jerusalem, 2017, PEACE NOW, available at:
http://www.peacenow.org.il/en.
17. "Israel-Funded App Destroys Al-Aqsa Mosque. Builds Temple in Its Place", available at: www.palestinechronicle.com/israel-funded-app-destroys-aqsa-mosque-builds-temple-in-its-place.
18. "Israelis Kill 3 Palestinian Attackers", Associated Press, *The Hindu*, October 18, 2015, p. 16.
19. "Israel-Funded App Destroys Al-Aqsa Mosque. Builds Temple in Its Place", available at: www.palestinechronicle.com/israel-funded-app-destroys-aqsa-mosque-builds-temple-in-its-place.
20. "West Bank Tense as Crisis Escalates", AP and Reuters, *The Hindu on Sunday,* July 23, 2017, p. 4; "Netanyahu Faces

Pressure over Jerusalem Violence", AFP and Reuters, *The Hindu*, July 24, 2017, p. 12.

21. This statement was made by the Israeli Minister for Regional Development, Tzachi Hamegbi to Army Radio, AFP and Reuters, "Netanyahu Faces Pressure over Jerusalem Violence", *The Hindu*, July 24, 2017, p. 12.
22. "West Bank Tense as ...", *The Hindu on Sunday*, July 23, 2017.
23. "East Jerusalem, 2017", PEACE NOW.
24. Hussam Al-Dajani, "The Motives Behind the Jerusalem Intifada".
25. The LRC figures and data are cited in "Israel Demolished 5,000 Homes in Jerusalem since 1967", available at: www.palestinechronical.com, March 15, 2018, Blog News.
26. "East Jerusalem, 2017", PEACE NOW.
27. Cited in "Israel Demolished 5,000 Homes in Jerusalem since 1967".
28. This word gained currency after President Donald Trump assured office and the meeting he had with both the sides at the White House. Even though the details are not yet known, the usage underlined Trump's determination to resolve the Israeli Palestinian conflict one way or the other. The indications of that deal probably emerged after the controversial decision on moving the US embassy to Jerusalem in December 2017. To get a perspective on this, see Akiva Eldar, "Why Trump-Arabs Meeting Has Rattled Netanyahu", available at: http://www.al-monitor.com/pulse/originals/2017/05/Israel-palestini..., May 4, 2017; Ben Caspit, "Why Netanyahu Won't Attend this Year's AIPAC Conference", available at: http://www.al-monitor.com/pulse/originals/2017/05/Israel-us-palest.
29. C.J. Polychroniou, "The Middle East is Heating Up Again: An Interview with Richard Falk", March 28, 2018.
30. For anti-American protests across the Arab-Islamic World, see *The Hindu*, December 18, 2017, p. 12; December 9, 2017, p. 12; December 11, 2017, p. 12. Haniya called for a new *intifada*. He stated: "we think this is an unaccountable gamble and an adventure that will not have a ceiling. The decision will be the beginning of a time of horrific transformations across the region". Another Hamas leader, Ismail Radwan warned, "This decision will open the gates of hell on US interests in the

region". Manuel Hassassian, the Palestinian representative to Britain, told the BBC radio: "He (Trump) is declaring war against 1.5 billion Muslims (and) hundreds of millions of Christians that are not going to accept the holy shrines under the hegemony of Israel".

31. See, UNGA Resolution of December 21, 2017.
32. See, "Palestinians Reject Israeli President's Call to Impose Sovereignty over West Bank", available at: www.palestinechronicle.com, March 13, 2018.

References

Al-Dajani, Hussam, (2015), "The Motives behind the Jerusalem Intifada", available at: https://www.middleeastmonitor.com/20151104-the-motives-behind-the-jerusalem-intifada.

Chomsky, Noam and Ilan Pappe (2010), "Gaza in Crisis: Reflections on Israel's War against the Palestinians", Haymarket Books: Chicago, Illinois.

Eldar, Akiva (2017), "What Does it Mean to be a Jerusalemite", available at: http://agora-dialogue.com/2017/03/23/what-does-it-mean-to-be-a-jerusalemite.

Falk, Richard (2014), "Palestine's Future: What are the Options?" *Al-jazeera*, June 21.

Gladstone, Rick (2017), "US Faces Blunt Criticisms in United Nations over Jerusalem Decree", *The Indian Express*, December 10.

Hatuqa, Dalia and Gregg Carlstrom (2014), "Jerusalem Simmering over 'Judaisation' Plan: An Influence of Ideological Settlers into East Jerusalem Threatens to Put an End to the Two State Solutions", *Al-Jazeera,* October 13.

Heller, Jeffrey (2018), "Israel in Talk with US to Annex Settlements", *The Indian Express*, February 13.

Hiddleston, James (2012), "Understanding Post Colonialism", Rawat Publications: New Delhi.

Maoz, Moshe (2014), "The Role of the Temple Mount/Al-Haram Al-Sharif in the Deterioration of Muslilm-Jewish Relations", *Approaching Religion*, Vol. 4, No. 2, December, 60-70.

Moor, Ahmed, (2014), "How it Started in Gaza: PM Netanyahu Had to Seek a Way Out of Isolation", available at:

https://www.aljazeera.com/indepth/opinion/2014/07/how-it-started-gaza.20147/2920/62-60625.html.

Pappe, Ilan (2014), "The Idea of Israel", Verso: London, New York.

Polychroniou, C.J. (2018), "The Middle East is Heating Up Again: An Interview with Richard Falk", contact@ifamericansknew.org, March 28.

Pradhan, Bansidhar (2012), "Palestine under Occupation: Some Reflections", *Mainstream*, New Delhi, Vol. L, No. 26, June 16, 11-18.

Reinhart, Tanya (2003), "Israel/Palestine: How to End the War of 1948", Left Word: New Delhi, 188-89.

White, Ben (2014), "Israeli Apartheid: A Beginner's Guide", London: Pluto Press.

White, Ben (2016), "Five Reasons Why Gaza is Still Under Blockade", June 29, available at: www.middleeastmonitor.com.

13

Hamas-Fatah Contradictions and Their Impact on Palestinian Movements

K.M. Sajad Ibrahim

The current impasse of the Palestinian movement was outcome of the contradictory approach of the two main Palestinian movements, Al-Fatah and Hamas. Both the movements have been employing different lines of thinking and strategies which adversely affected the Palestinians' dream for statehood. In the eyes of many, reconciliation between Fatah and Hamas is a prerequisite for advancing peace between Israelis and Palestinians. The idea is that Palestinians cannot negotiate with Israel in any serious way when divided between the West Bank under the rule of the Fatah-dominated Palestinian Authority (PA) and the Gaza Strip under the rule of Hamas. In fact, PA officials in the West Bank can make neither demands nor concessions when it comes to the Gaza Strip, which they do not control. But the same cannot be said for the West Bank, where the PA is firmly in control. There, in the West Bank, there is much that could be done that would improve the daily lives of Palestinians and Israelis both. The difference between Hamas and Al-Fatah provided all the opportunity to undermine the prospects of an independent state of Palestine.

Hamas and Fatah Relations since Oslo

The Palestinian movements for an independent state witnessed radical shift since the end of the Cold War in 1990. The birth of Hamas in 1989 out of the dissatisfaction of Palestinian Liberation Organisation (PLO)-led movement was a positive factor for the Palestinians to expect an independent state. The Oslo accord signed on September 13, 1993 between Israel and the PLO leader Yasser Arafat under the US brokered peace agreement was viewed as a landmark in the Palestinian struggle for independence movement. However, the extremist wings of the Palestinians like Hamas, Islamic Jihad etc. rejected the accord since it could not address the basic issues of the Palestinians like the status of refugees and the land which were occupied by Israel during the 1967 war and before. In the life of the Palestinians and over their history, many settlements meant to be temporary in nature, nevertheless became permanent and long-term.

Since the establishment of the Palestinian Authority (PA) in 1994, Palestinian Hamas had refused to recognize, let alone participate in the formal institutions of Palestinian government. On both ideological and pragmatic grounds, the Islamists found it counterproductive to take part in the formal political process, which they considered illegitimate. Instead, they opted for playing a role outside the formal structures of governance, using violence and street mobilization to advance their aims (Beinin and Hajjar, 2014).

Two fundamental needs have shaped Palestinian politics since the establishment of the PA in 1994: ending the Israeli occupation that began in 1967, and building a sovereign state based on the principles of good governance. Four events shaped, and in turn were shaped by Palestinian domestic outcomes during those years: the Oslo peace process, which began in 1993; the second intifada, which began in September 2000; the passing of Yassir Arafat in November 2004; and the Israeli disengagement from Gaza in September 2005 (Shikak, 2007).

For Palestinians, Oslo promised the gradual end of occupation and the launching of a state-building process. However, owing to Oslo's open-ended nature, its postponement of the resolution of the most important dimensions of the conflict, the ultimate emphasis it placed on short-term security requirements, and the PLO's own authoritarian legacy, the Oslo process failed to deliver either of these two vital needs. Some Palestinian groups continued to perpetuate violence against Israelis, and Israel consolidated its occupation by doubling the size of its settlement enterprise within seven years after the launching of the Oslo process. Gradually, the Palestinian public came to perceive the PA, created by the Oslo process, as authoritarian and corrupt. The Palestinians realised that the collapse of the Camp David permanent status talks in the fall of 2000 which also ended the expectations for the realisation of the Oslo accord (Shikak, 2007).

The death of Yasser Arafat in November 2004 shifted this perspective. Under Arafat, Hamas was convinced that the Fatah-dominated system would always remain authoritarian and that Islamists would never be able to influence public policy through the ballot. With the demise of Arafat, however, Hamas expected the political system to open up and Fatah, the dominant political player, to weaken. Fatah's twin failures in peace-making and state-building had already more than doubled Hamas' strength among Palestinians between 2000 and 2005. Throughout 2003 and 2004, polls conducted by PSR showed Islamists becoming the most popular political faction, with Fatah coming in second. Capitalizing on this increased public support and relying on existing support for armed resistance to Israeli occupation, Hamas sought to translate that popularity into parliamentary seats without having to give up its armed capacity. It, therefore, agreed to take part in the Palestinian legislative elections scheduled for July 2005 and later rescheduled for January 2006 (Shikaki, 2015).

The opening up of the political system after Arafat's death allowed the integration of Hamas into the political process and facilitated the holding of local elections beginning in December 2004, followed by presidential elections in January 2005. In March 2005, a nationalist-Islamist agreement brokered by Egypt and known as the Cairo Declaration was reached. In return, the nationalists agreed to hold parliamentary elections, in which Hamas would take part, adopting a new electoral system; and inviting Hamas to join the PLO, which led to a cease-fire (Bhasin, 2013).

With Arafat out of the picture, the new nationalist leadership under the newly elected president, Mahmud Abbas, sought to gain approval from all groups in the hope of avoiding infighting while trying to put in place a tentative cease-fire with the Israelis. Moreover, with Arafat out of the picture and the political system now open to its involvement, Hamas capitalized on the opportunity to translate its popularity in the Palestinian street into formal political power by agreeing to participate in local and national elections and to be integrated, under certain conditions into the PLO. Capitalizing on the perceived corruption and the lack of law and order, Hamas sought to control the political system from within by replacing Fatah as the ruling party. Widespread public belief that Israeli disengagement from Gaza had constituted a victory for violence served Hamas's interests well, as the public gave it credit for forcing the Israelis out of Gaza "under fire" (PSR, 2016).

The rise of Hamas throughout 2005, coupled with Fatah's failure to deal with its fragmentation and with PA's corruption, dealt a severe blow to Abbas's efforts to take advantage of the cease-fire in order to formulate a national security policy and to effectively engage Israel and the U.S. Neither Israel nor the U.S. was interested in serious engagement with a leader who had failed to take charge of the PA. One reason for Fatah's inability to attract voters was its failure to put its own house in order. The fragmentation that characterized Fatah during the last several years—and was responsible for its loss, in the last elections, of some 16 seats in the electoral districts, where a "winner takes all" system was used—remains a major impediment for its return to power (House of Commons Library, 2007).

Hamas's victory added to Fatah's divisions, with most of the "young guard" supporting the acceptance of Hamas's victory and calling for a coalition with it. These "inclusionists" are led by Marwan Barghouti, who initiated the Prisoners' Document, later modified and renamed the National Conciliation Document. They publicly sought to forge a broad coalition with Hamas: a coalition that, they believed, would build stronger and less corrupt state institutions while presenting the Israelis with a credible negotiating partner—one that would be more effective in stopping the violence as Israel ended its occupation of more Palestinian territory and allowed the establishment of a sovereign Palestinian state (Shikak, 2007).

Once a Fatah-Hamas coalition is created, four possible options for organizing Palestinian-Israeli relations will become possible. Two of these options—an extended cease-fire and a negotiated Israeli disengagement from most of the West Bank—will immediately open up, and will not require a strategic shift on the part of either member of the new Palestinian coalition or a significant change in Israel's position. The other two options—a Palestinian state in the West Bank and the Gaza Strip with no "end of conflict" and a permanent peace with an "end of conflict"—will each require both a strategic shift on the part of Hamas and a significant change on Israel's part (Rynhold and Waxman, 2008).

When Hamas was formed at the outbreak of the first intifada in 1989, it did not recognize PLO as "the sole legitimate representative of the Palestinian People", a status the PLO had enjoyed at the Arab League and at the UN General Assembly since 1974. Hamas spokesmen asserted that, because the PLO leadership had not been elected by the Palestinian people, the organization did not have a mandate to monopolize the political representation of the Palestinians. In its founding charter, Hamas presented the PLO's values as incompatible with its own:

"Due to the circumstances that surrounded the formation of the organization [the PLO] and the ideological confusion that prevails in the Arab world as a result of the ideological invasion that has befallen the Arab world since the defeat of the Crusades and that has been intensified by orientalism, the [Christian] mission and imperialism, the organization has adopted the idea of a secular state, and this is how we view it. But secular thought is entirely contradictory to religious thought...[W]e cannot use secular thought for the current and future Islamic nature of Palestine. The Islamic nature of Palestine is part of our religion, and everyone who neglects his religion is bound to lose (Charter of Hamas, 2017).

Reconciliation Attempts

The Hamas/Fatah agreement announced in Cairo in May 2011 proposed to end the split between the two groups, setting up a unity government (Cairo Hamas–Fatah Agreement, 2011). The agreement foresees new parliamentary elections in 2012. There were many reconciliation agreements between them since Mecca deal in 2007. Some of the prominent deals were Cairo (2011), Doha (2012) and Gaza (2014). Unfortunately, none of the deals were fruitful for reconciling their differences. Most important differences were regarding the formation of the national governments in West Bank and Gaza, the resumption of Palestinian Legislative Council activities, elections, and general freedoms, which envisaged the release of Fatah and Hamas prisoners held by the opposite party, the return of Fatah-affiliated public employees—including security personnel—to Gaza, and the free travel of officials between the West Bank and Gaza.

However, the greatest stumbling blocks remain Hamas's continued embrace of armed resistance against Israel and its rejection of a negotiated two-state resolution to the Israeli-Palestinian conflict. Some Hamas leaders have declared publicly that they do not oppose Abbas per se in his capacity as the PLO chairman, negotiating with Israel, but they remain steadfast in their opposition to any comprehensive peace agreement and refusal to recognize Israel. While Hamas enjoys popular support of Palestinians in the occupied territories and in refugee camps in other countries, Al-Fatah is recognised as the most accepted representatives of the Palestinians by the majority of the world countries, especially the US and Western countries.

As such, only Al-Fatah received international aid, and Hamas was unable to find funds due to its policy of non-recognition of the state of Israel. Despite this, Hamas was able to maintain its popularity on accounts of its charity services to the Palestinians. At the same time, Fatah remained corrupt as it was the only agency that receives funds internationally. Moreover, Fatah feared that a unified movement would be advantageous for Hamas. This might be reason for the Fatah's unwillingness to accommodate Hamas in the PLO, despite the latter not making any pre-conditions. Anyway, the statehood would be a distant dream for the Palestinians so long as there is no unified action from Hamas and Fatah. There were many complexities involved in the relations between Hamas and Fatah for a joint Palestinian movement.

The main outcome of the Cairo talks held on March 11, 2009 was the establishment of the following five dialogue committees:

1. Government Committee, charged with forming a temporary transitional government until the end of the PLC's mandate, preparing a draft program, and resolving civil and administrative issues resulting from the Gaza-West Bank division (e.g., re-opening of organizations and societies, development projects, reunifying the PA).
2. Elections Committee, to work on a new date for the next legislative and presidential elections, create a system to monitor them, review the election laws according to national interest, and re-establish the Central Elections Committee.
3. PLO Restructuring Committee, responsible for preparing the reform of the PLO in accordance with the Cairo Agreement of 2005 and with regard to including Hamas and the Islamic Jihad, as well as preparing for the eventual election of a new Palestinian National Council.

4. Security Forces Reform Committee, tasked with developing plans for future security arrangements, discussing the reorganization of the Palestinian security apparatuses, and administering, running and overseeing security agencies as well as appointing their leaders.
5. Reconciliation Committee, to follow up on all the reconciliation issues (prisoners, closed institutions, freedom of movement and political expression), stop all actions having a negative impact on achieving political unity, and create an 'Honour Charter' to prevent the use of arms and violence (PASSIA, 2013).

In April 2011, after a few other fruitless meetings, representatives of both sides finally announced an Egypt-mediated agreement to form a joint transitional government of technocrats and a joint security committee to decide on future security arrangements. They also agreed to hold elections in 2012 and to prepare for Hamas' accession to the PLO. That agreement was formally signed by Abbas and Mashaal on May 4, 2011 at a ceremony in Cairo. While the Cairo Agreement was welcomed as a hopeful step towards unity, it failed to achieve anything, mainly stumbling over the question of who would assume the position of prime minister, with Hamas rejecting the incumbent Salam Fayyad. Talks continued nevertheless and Abbas and Mashaal signed the Doha Agreement in the Qatari capital in February 2012, placing President Abbas at the head of an interim government charged with organizing elections later in the year.

On May 20, 2012, Azzam Al-Ahmad (Fatah) and Musa Abu Marzouq (Hamas) signed yet another document (also known as the Cairo Agreement), meant essentially to implement the earlier Doha Agreement, particularly the registering of new voters in Gaza and the formation of an interim government, both to start later that month. However, neither agreement accomplished goals nor the local elections, which took place in October 2012, were boycotted by Hamas and did not involve Gaza residents.

Following Israel's "Operation Pillar of Defence" launched

on November 14, 2012 following the assassination of second-in-command of Hamas' military wing, Ahmad Al-Jaabari (and ending with a US-Egyptian mediated ceasefire on November 21), and the Palestinian diplomatic victory at the UN upgrading Palestine's status to 'non-member observer state' on November 29, 2012, calls for a unified Palestinian front increased and both Hamas and Fatah took several steps to reconcile their differences. This involved a decline in their media clashes, a release of their respective detainees in the West Bank and Gaza, the first ever visit of Arab Foreign Ministers to Gaza (including the PA Foreign Minister on November 19, 2012), and, for the first time since 2007, Hamas being allowed to mark its 25th anniversary in the West Bank on December 4, 2012 and Fatah its 48th anniversary in Gaza on January 5, 2013 (Benton, 2013). All the above led to renewed reconciliation talks in Cairo in January 2013, with both sides agreeing to form a technocratic unity government within three months to pave the way for elections.

Reconciliation steps during 2014-17

Fatah-Hamas reconciliation agreement announced in the Gaza Strip on April 23, 2014 was another long line of attempts to bridge the intra-Palestinian divide. The timing of the agreement amid U.S.-brokered peace talks, as well as both parties' internal weaknesses, points to more serious intent than past efforts. However, the deal fails to address the most sensitive issues separating the two sides and likely can be explained by the political boost it offers to both leaderships. The only certainty is that the reconciliation deal severely complicates efforts to extend Israeli-Palestinian peace negotiations past their April 29 deadline. Discussions would continue about "general freedoms", a term used in the Doha declaration to include the release of Fatah and Hamas prisoners held by the opposite party, the return of Fatah-affiliated public employees—including security personnel—to Gaza, and the free travel of officials between the West Bank and Gaza. The first test of the deal is reported to be a visit to Gaza by PA president Mahmoud Abbas.

Since Hamas and Fatah signed a "national reconciliation" agreement in 2014, the two were no nearer to bridging their differences or tackling the mounting challenges Palestinians faced. Fatah was convinced Hamas, which fought a war with Israel in Gaza nine months ago, was trying to carve out an Islamist fiefdom in the 360 square kilometres of the Gaza Strip. Hamas goads Fatah about its unwillingness to hold elections out of fear it will lose and Hamas will end up in full control.

Such deep internal divisions were in part the reason why Israel repeats that it has no Palestinian partner to deal with, making a return to peace negotiations near impossible. "Hamas does not want the division to end", said senior Fatah official Amin Maqboul, adding that Hamas, whose leader lives in self-imposed exile in Qatar, has its own plan for Gaza. "We know that Hamas has never been in favour of a Palestinian state", he said, (Reuters, 2015) suggesting that rather than forging unity with the West Bank and East Jerusalem, the group is determined to create an Islamist "emirate" on the Mediterranean. For its part, Hamas says Palestinian President Mahmoud Abbas shows no real inclination towards reconciliation, sending envoys to Gaza rather than coming himself from the West Bank. His large home in Gaza, not far from the sea, has been turned into an office for cabinet ministers and a venue for angry rallies.

Major Issues Left Unaddressed

For all the planned moves toward closer Fatah-Hamas ties, even the announced text of this latest agreement does not seek to resolve the most sensitive issues separating the two sides. Indeed, the agreement stipulates that the reconciliation committee's work will be ongoing indicating that the deal reached is a "framework" for moving forward and not, as currently constituted, the end of the process (Yaari and Zilber, 2014). For instance, confusion still exists about whether the national unity government will be headed by Mahmoud Abbas (acting as both president and prime minister), whether Hamas members will be included in the cabinet, or whether a technocratic government made up of independents will be formed. In addition, the agreement does not mention whether Gaza will remain under exclusive Hamas control or whether the PA will be brought back to govern the breakaway territory, specifically the border crossings with Israel and Egypt.

Moreover, the agreement did not address the vast duplication of government functions now prevailing in the West Bank and Gaza, including the possibility of uniting the disparate security forces. Public employees present another challenge. At present, 70,000 Fatah public employees in Gaza still receive salaries from the PA, but their actual positions have long been filled by Hamas-affiliated personnel. In December 2015 and January 2016, Hamas and Fatah secretly held Qatar-brokered talks in Doha to try and complement the 2014 agreement. Talks were renewed on February 7-8. In this round of negotiations, Egypt was not involved. Hamas issued a brief statement on February 8, saying both parties reached a practical vision of a solution to be discussed and implemented. However, the impasse continues as both sides were not ready to compromise in their basic lines.

Hamas-al Fatah reconciliation agreement in October 2017 at Cairo was viewed with lot of expectations. The agreement envisaged that legislative, presidential and national council elections should be conducted within one year of its signing. The deal also expected to realise both Hamas and Fatah to form an interim government before elections (Al Jazeera, 2017). The most recent meeting held in November 2017 in Cairo agreed to conduct general elections by the end of 2018 (Reuters, 2017). However, these talks could not bring neither cordial relations between these factions or any mechanism to sort out their differences.

Conclusions

Since its unexpected electoral victory in 2006, Hamas has

undergone fundamental transformation in its attempt to reconcile its erstwhile Islamist ideology with the need to meet practical political requirements and project itself in a different light to the outside world so as to challenge hostile political realities and international isolation. It has, for instance, repeatedly demonstrated a willingness to halt all forms of violent resistance and to get involved in mainstream Palestinian politics abiding by the rules of international law, if also respected by Fatah and Israel.

At the same time, Hamas has, unlike Fatah, maintained its credibility as a coherent movement committed to the Palestinian cause by continuing to confront the Israeli occupationand refusing to recognize Israel as a precondition for talks. So far, successive Israeli governments have rebuffed Hamas' attempts to reach a truce and there are no signs for genuine Israeli reciprocity with regard to peace talks with any Palestinian party, including Fatah. This, in turn, plays into the hands of Hamas, as it gives Fatah a no negotiation partner and makes Abbas look completely mistaken. Along with Hamas' efforts in the area of social welfare and a reputation for honesty and discipline, in contrast to the numerous Fatah officials accused of corruption, this has significantly contributed to its popularity. Fatah, on the other hand, still enjoys international backing and is considered the contact for international political and funding partners, many of whom fear that a unity government would induce them to support Hamas also. Indeed, while Fatah may not be moderate, it is at least not Islamist.

International support for Fatah/the PA is very much linked to its recognition of Israel and its principle acceptance to pursue peace negotiations—the refusal of both has in turn made Hamas very popular among Palestinians. Some voices even claim that the US and Israel, fearing the legitimization of Hamas, have signalled to the Fatah leadership that they are not keen to have the reconciliation process succeed. On the national level, the situation is aggravated by the fact that there is no end in sight to the physical separation of Gaza and the West Bank and that both sides mistrust each other with regard to the envisioned future elections.

Hamas argues that first a new unity government should be formed to lead the electoral process, while Fatah wants elections first. Both sides favour elections which will allow them to re-establish their respective constituencies in the West Bank and Gaza Strip. However, Hamas fears that even if it wins future elections it will be denied any role in the West Bank by both Israel and Fatah, and that if it loses, its legitimacy for the control of Gaza would fade as well. Similarly, although Fatah believes that Hamas will never give up Gaza, it wants elections to maintain its power in the West Bank, re-establish its constituency in Gaza, and garner support for its declared position in favour of peace negotiations with Israel.

However, Fatah has a serious crisis of succession which may eventually weaken its ability to lead the PA. Besides, it is in dire need to deliver domestically and with regard to the "peace process", where the chances for progress are very less because of the rising right-wing approach of Israel, the apparent satisfaction of the main players with the status quo, and an Arab world too busy with its own problems. Nonetheless, despite the dim prospects of negotiating with the Netanyahu government, Abbas agreed to US Secretary of State John Kerry's efforts to resume direct peace talks in the hope to improve the economic situation in the West Bank through increased donor aid to the PA. Hamas is also at a critical juncture. Considering the recent changes in the political landscape of West Asia, its leverage vis-à-vis Fatah appears to have weakened.

Indeed, Hamas may feel even more under pressure to progress on rapprochement as it is increasingly losing support from its traditional allies, most notably Syria and Hezbollah, after leaving its base in Damascus in 2011 and subsequently, Iran, which stopped most of its financial support, and Egypt, after the ousting of Muslim Brotherhood President Morsi by the Military in early July 2013. These developments along with the destruction of the tunnels between Sinai and Gaza and the limited opening of the Rafah border crossing, pose a threat to the movement's continued rule in Gaza.

In addition, new groups, such as the so-called 'Tamarud Aza' ('Gaza Resistance'– a reference to the Egyptian Tamarud movement, which was behind the demonstrations that led to Morsi's ouster) may pose growing challenges to Hamas. At the bottom line, however, and despite some recent progress on reconciliation, it is rather unlikely that Fatah and Hamas will unify of their own accord any time soon as neither side has anything to offer the other that is greater than the power each currently holds.

References

Al Jazeera (2017), "Hamas, Fatah Sign Reconciliation Agreement in Cairo", October 13, available at: https://www.aljazeera.com/news/2017/10/hamas-fatah-sign-reconciliation-agreement-cairo-171012115017367.html.

Beinin, Joel and Lisa Hajjar (2014), "Palestine, Israel and the Arab-Israeli Conflict: A Primer", Middle East Research and Information Project, available at: https://www.merip.org/sites/default/files/Primer_on_Palestine-Israel(MERIP_February2014) final.pdf.

Benton, Sarah (2013), "Step by Step Fatah and Hamas Make Space for Each Other", Jews for Justice for Palestinians, available at: http://jfjfp.com/step-by-step-fatah-and-hamas-step-carefully-in-each-others-steps.

Bhasin, Tavishi (2013), "Hamas as a Political Party: Democratization in the Palestinian Territories", *Journal of Terrorism and Political Violence*, Vol. 25, Issue 1, 75-93.

Cairo Hamas-Fatah Agreement (2011), The Israeli-Palestinian Conflict: An Interactive Database, available at: https://ecf.org.il/issues/issue/1167.

"Charter of Hamas", (2017), *Contemporary Review of Middle East*, November 1, 4(4), 393-418.

Ehud Yaari and Neri Zilber (2014), "The Hamas-Fatah Reconciliation Agreement: Too Early to Judge", Policy Watch

2243, The Washington Institute, available at: https://www.washingtoninstitute.org/policy-analysis/view/the-hamas-fatah-reconciliation-agreement-too-early-to-judge.

House of Commons Library (2007), "Hamas and the Seizure of Gaza", Research Paper 07/60, July 6, available at: http://www.refworld.org/pdfid/494783582.pdf.

Johannsen, Margret et al. (n.d.), "The Reconciliation of Hamas and Fatah", Policy Brief, No. 3, December 11, available at: http://library.fes.de/pdf-files/iez/09217.pdf.

Jonathan Rynhold and Dov Waxman (2008), "Ideological Change and Israel's Disengagement from Gaza", *Political Science Quarterly*, Vol. 123, No. 1, Spring, 11-37.

Passia (2013), "Fatah and Hamas and the Issue of Reconciliation", December, available at: http://passia.org/media/filer_public/ca/b4/cab4e657-4a4a-42c7-927c-716fbf69efc0/fateh-hamas-webv.pdf.

PSR (2016), "Palestinian Public Opinion Poll No. (19), Palestinian Centre for Policy and Survey Research, March 16-18, available at: http://www.pcpsr.org/en/node/236.

Reuters, (2015), "Hamas-Fatah Face-off Leaves Hard Road Ahead for Palestinians", May 6, 2015, available at: https://af.reuters.com/article/worldNews/idAFKBN0NR0ZD20150506.

Reuters (2017), "Palestinian Factions Agree to Hold General Elections by end-2018", November 23, available at: https://www.reuters.com/article/us-palestinians-talks/palestinian-factions-agree-to-hold-general-election-by-end-2018.

Shikak, Khalil (2007), "With Hamas in Power: Impact of Palestinian Domestic Developments on Options for the Peace Process", Crown Centre for Middle East Studies, Brandeis University, available at: https://www.brandeis.edu/crown/publications/wp/WP1.pdf.

Shikaki, Khalil (2015), "Can Hamas Moderate? Insights from Palestinian Politics during 2005-2010", Middle East Brief, Crown Centre for Middle East Studies, available at: https://www.brandeis.edu/crown/publications/meb/MEB88.pdf.

Tartir, Alaa (2012), "Fatah and Hamas: An Elusive Reconciliation", Open Democracy, available at: http://eprints.lse.ac.uk/51804.

Index

Index